Low-Salt
cookbook
second edition

Also by the American Heart Association

*The New American Heart Association Cookbook,
6th Edition*

*American Heart Association Low-Fat, Low-Cholesterol Cookbook,
Second Edition*

American Heart Association Low-Calorie Cookbook

American Heart Association Quick & Easy Cookbook

American Heart Association Meals in Minutes Cookbook

American Heart Association Low-Fat & Luscious Desserts

American Heart Association Kids' Cookbook

*American Heart Association To Your Health! A Guide to
Heart-Smart Living*

American Heart Association 6 Weeks to Get Out the Fat

American Heart Association Fitting In Fitness

American Heart Association 365 Ways to Get Out the Fat

American Heart
Association®
Fighting Heart Disease and Stroke

Low-Salt

cookbook second edition

a complete guide to reducing sodium and fat in your diet

BALLANTINE BOOKS • NEW YORK

A Ballantine Book
Published by the Random House Publishing Group
Copyright © 1990, 2001 by the American Heart Association

Your contribution to the American Heart Association supports research that helps many publications like this possible. For more information, call 1-800-AHA-USA1 (1-800-242-8721) or contact us online at www.americanheart.org.

This edition published by arrangement with Clarkson Potter/Publishers, a division of Random House, Inc. Originally published in hardcover by Clarkson Potter/Publishers in 2001. An earlier edition of this work was published in 1990.

www.ballantinebooks.com

ISBN 0-345-46183-5

Manufactured in the United States of America

First Ballantine Books Edition: November 2003

OPM   10   9   8   7   6   5   4   3   2   1

Front cover: Risotto with Shrimp and Vegetables (pages 92–93)
Cover photograph by Susan Goldman

Contents

Preface

Cutting down on salt, or sodium, in your diet is a good idea for a lot of reasons. Maybe your doctor recommended that you reduce your sodium intake to control high blood pressure or congestive heart failure. Maybe you just decided on your own that you'd like to cut down on salt.

You may have put off making the change if your idea of low-sodium cooking is that it would be about as tasty and appealing as cardboard on a plate. Well, you're in for a wonderful surprise! Regardless of your reason, if you're trying to cut the salt, this second edition of the *American Heart Association Low-Salt Cookbook* is *your* cookbook!

Much has changed on the food front since 1990, when the first edition of this cookbook was published. For instance, convenience foods, low-sodium foods, and other ingredients that simply didn't exist or weren't widely available a decade ago are easy to find now, so we've incorporated lots of them into the existing recipes. We've also reduced the total fat and saturated fat in many of them. In addition, this updated cookbook contains more than 50 brand-new recipes. With their emphasis on fresh ingredients, herbs, and spices, both the old and the new recipes pack flavor into each dish. You'll be so impressed by these taste sensations, you'll never miss the salt. Finally, the revision includes fiber in the nutrient analysis of every recipe.

Most of us know from experience that change—any change—is hard. Changing longtime eating habits is no exception, so take it slowly, one step at a time. With this book to help you make gradual changes, you can devise a low-salt eating plan that lets you eat healthfully without feeling deprived. In a few months, you'll wonder why you didn't start eating this way years ago.

Acknowledgments

The credit for originally recognizing the need for a low-sodium, low-saturated fat, low-cholesterol cookbook—and for the hard work and dedication that goes into developing such a book—goes to a group of American Heart Association volunteers in the Cleveland area.

The teamwork and expertise of those volunteers resulted in the publication in 1978 of *Cooking Without Your Salt Shaker*. The task force members and significant contributors were Sharon Reichman, R.D., chairperson; Charlene Krejci, R.D.; Karen Wilcoxon Izso, R.D.; Grace Petot, R.D.; Sally Gleason, R.D.; Tab Forgac, R.D.; Rosemary Manni, R.D.; Auretha Pettigrew, R.D.; Robert Post, M.D.; Mary Ann Weber, R.D.; and the Cleveland Dietetic Association, Diet Therapy Section.

That cookbook was available only through the American Heart Association, but its popularity convinced us to offer it to a wider audience. At the same time, changes in science and trends in food preparation prompted us to update and expand the book significantly in the *American Heart Association Low-Salt Cookbook*, published in 1990.

Now we've done it again. In this new edition of the *American Heart Association Low-Salt Cookbook*, our recipe developers have added exciting recipes to give you more variety. They have also updated many of the recipes from the first edition, using new ingredients and more convenience foods.

Thanks to all those who worked on this second edition—this is a real upgrade to low-salt cooking!

American Heart Association Science Consultant:
Terry Bazzarre, Ph.D.

American Heart Association Consumer Publications Director:
Jane Anneken Ruehl

American Heart Association Science Editor:
Ann Melugin Williams

American Heart Association Senior Editor:
Janice Roth Moss

American Heart Association Editor:
Jacqueline Fornerod Haigney

American Heart Association Assistant Editor:
Roberta Westcott Sullivan

American Heart Association Senior Marketing Manager:
Bharati Gaitonde

Recipe Developers: Carol Ritchie
                Nancy S. Hughes
                Ruth Mossok Johnston
                Frank Criscuolo
                Sarah Fritschner
                Christy Rost

Nutrient Analyst: Tammi Hancock, R.D.

Introduction

Congratulations!

You're about to learn a new and exciting way to cook—less salt, more flavor.

They Said It Couldn't Be Done

We often hear the claim that food cooked without added salt is boring, flat, and tasteless. The recipes in this book will prove that's wrong.

With low-salt cooking, you'll learn to use your imagination. You'll try spices and herb combinations you may never have heard of before. You'll create new taste sensations with exotic spices and oils, with wines and liqueurs. Since one of the greatest challenges in cutting down on salt is the high amount of sodium found in many commercial products, including condiments, you'll even learn to make your own low-sodium versions of mustard, horseradish, chili sauce, pickles, and other foods that can spice up your meals. Because food manufacturers realize that not everyone needs or wants high-sodium products, they've added many lower-sodium food products since the first edition of this cookbook was published. We've used reduced-sodium, low-sodium, and no-salt-added ingredients in many of these recipes.

The most important thing to remember is that cooking without added salt can be as easy or as elaborate as you wish—and it can always be deliciously flavorful.

What You Can Do About
Heart Disease and Stroke

Through years of research, much of it supported by the American Heart Association, science has learned about many of the possible causes of heart attack and stroke—and what can be done to try to prevent them.

We know that the most effective ways to help prevent these and other cardiovascular diseases are

- Controlling high blood pressure
- Being physically active
- Achieving and maintaining a healthy weight
- Controlling diabetes
- Having a desirable blood cholesterol level
- Avoiding tobacco

As a result, more and more Americans have begun to take charge of their own health. Millions are watching what they eat—counting calories, cutting down on saturated fat and cholesterol in their diet, and helping to control their high blood pressure by reducing the salt in their diet. Millions are walking, running, and working out at health centers. Millions more have stopped smoking. All these lifestyle changes work together to promote health and prevent disease.

Eating with Your Heart in Mind

The recipes in this cookbook can help you make changes toward a more healthful lifestyle. Low in salt, they are also low in saturated fat and cholesterol. Watching your fat intake does more than just help your heart. It helps your waistline, too, if you also limit calories. All these changes can help lower your risk of heart and blood vessel disease.

Depending on whether you feel adventurous (Buffalo Baked in Pumpkin, page 154) or in need of comfort food (Meat Loaf, page 136), you'll find a choice of sure-to-please recipes in this cookbook. When you savor the exotic taste of our Mango-Havarti Crepes (page 12) or a light, flavor-filled bite of Mediterranean Fish Fillets (page 71), you'll realize that help-your-heart cooking is creative and delicious.

So go ahead and take the salt shaker off the table. Then pick up this cookbook. Consider it the beginning of a great culinary adventure.

If you have questions, ask your doctor or call your local American Heart Association or 800-AHA-USA1 (800-242-8721). Also, check our website at www.americanheart.org. We're here to help.

Bon appétit!

How to Use These Recipes

When planning menus, remember to read the analysis accompanying each recipe to help you keep track of your sodium, saturated fat, cholesterol, and calorie intake. Also listed are total fat, monounsaturated fat, polyunsaturated fat, protein, carbohydrate, fiber, calcium, and potassium values. All values are rounded to whole numbers.

Note that the values for saturated, monounsaturated, and polyunsaturated fat may not add up precisely to the total fat value in the recipe. That's because rounding affects the total and also because the total fat includes not only fatty acids but also other fatty substances and glycerol. Fatty acids are the chemical form that saturated, monounsaturated, and polyunsaturated fats have in foods. Each type of fat consists of several different fatty acids.

Each analysis is based on a single serving. The analyses do not include optional ingredients. They also do not include ingredients suggested as accompaniments unless this is noted in the analysis.

In addition to listing the number of servings, we've indicated the size of the serving in ounces, cups, or tablespoons.

Most calories in alcohol evaporate when heated, and this reduction is reflected in the calculations. When a marinade is used in a recipe, some of the liquid is discarded. This is also accounted for in our calculations.

Ingredients

All the recipes were analyzed using mostly unsalted or low-sodium ingredients, such as no-salt-added tomato sauce and light soy sauce. In a few instances where we used "regular" ingredients, such as "acceptable margarine," you may wish to use the low-salt version.

If a recipe calls for acceptable margarine, we used corn oil stick margarine in the analysis. For these recipes, choose any margarine that lists liquid vegetable oil as its first ingredient. Some recipes, especially baked goods, need acceptable stick margarine or light stick margarine for texture. Many other recipes can be made with light tub margarine, which is lower in fat (and higher in water) than the others. We used the lowest-fat margarine possible in each recipe.

For "acceptable vegetable oil," we used canola oil in the analysis. Acceptable vegetable oils include monounsaturated oils, such as canola and olive, and polyunsaturated oils, such as corn and safflower. (For more information on fats and oils, see pages 309–311.)

Special Diet Instructions

If your doctor or dietitian has given you a low-sodium diet instruction sheet, check it against the ingredients in our recipes. If there is a difference—for example, your instructions tell you to use only unsalted bread but our recipe calls for regular bread, follow your sheet. Such substitutions will result in slightly different values from those listed in our nutrient analysis for that particular recipe.

Finally, although specific ingredients are listed for each recipe, feel free to experiment or substitute when necessary—as long as your ingredient substitutions don't add sodium or fat. For instance, interchanging herbs, spices, vinegars, and vegetables offers variety without substantially changing the nutritional value of the dish. Above all, remember the cardinal rule of adventurous cooking and eating: Have fun!

American Heart
Association®

Fighting Heart Disease and Stroke

Low-Salt

cookbook
second edition

Recipes

Appetizers & Snacks

potato-skin nachos

lettuce wraps with chicken and vegetables

smoked turkey spread

red bell pepper crostini

mango-havarti crepes

mushrooms stuffed with sherried chicken

hot and smoky chipotle-garlic dip

black bean dip

party mix

mango chips

sparkling apple punch

Potato-Skin Nachos

Serves 4 • 1 cup per serving

Using potatoes instead of high-salt tortilla chips lets you enjoy this south-of-the-border favorite without the guilt.

> 1   pound whole finger potatoes or small red potatoes, cut into wedges
>   Olive oil spray
> 1   teaspoon Chili Powder (page 225) or commercial no-salt-added chili powder

Bean Topping

> 1   teaspoon olive oil
> 1   small onion, chopped (about ½ cup)
> 2   medium cloves garlic, minced, or 1 teaspoon bottled minced garlic
> 1   cup canned no-salt-added fat-free refried beans or 1 cup pureed canned no-salt-added pinto beans, rinsed and drained
> 1   teaspoon Chili Powder (page 225) or commercial no-salt-added chili powder
> 1   teaspoon very low sodium beef bouillon granules
> ⅛   teaspoon pepper

Tomato Salsa

> 2   medium Italian plum tomatoes, chopped (about 1 cup)
> ½   cup chopped bell pepper, any color
> ¼   cup chopped red onion
> 1   tablespoon snipped fresh cilantro or parsley
> 1   tablespoon chopped fresh jalapeño (optional)

> ½   cup fat-free shredded Cheddar cheese
> 2   tablespoons sliced black olives, drained
> 2   tablespoons nonfat or light sour cream

Preheat oven to 375° F.

Put potatoes on a nonstick baking sheet; lightly spray potatoes with olive oil spray. Sprinkle potatoes evenly with 1 teaspoon Chili Powder.

Bake for 30 minutes, or until potatoes are tender when pierced with a fork.

Meanwhile, for bean topping, heat a medium skillet over medium heat. Add oil and swirl to coat bottom. Cook onion and garlic for 3 to 4 minutes, or until onion is translucent, stirring occasionally.

Add remaining topping ingredients and cook for 1 minute, or until mixture is warmed through, stirring occasionally. Spread mixture in a large, shallow serving bowl and let cool for 5 to 10 minutes.

For salsa, in a medium bowl, combine all ingredients.

Arrange potatoes on a serving plate. To let diners assemble their own nachos, sprinkle bean topping with cheese, olives, and a dollop of sour cream. Serve salsa on the side. Or layer ingredients directly on potatoes: bean topping, then salsa, olives, and cheese. Spoon sour cream into middle of the serving plate.

Calories 228	Total Fat 3 g	Fiber 9 g
Protein 13 g	Saturated 0 g	Sodium 174 mg
Carbohydrates 42 g	Polyunsaturated 1 g	Potassium 1165 mg
Cholesterol 2 mg	Monounsaturated 2 g	Calcium 291 mg

Lettuce Wraps with Chicken and Vegetables

Serves 16 • 1 lettuce wrap per serving

Who says a wrap has to be starchy? Try these crisp lettuce wraps topped with your choice of two sauces for a winning combination of flavor, texture, color, and aroma. We like dried mushrooms in this dish because of their interesting flavor and texture. Can't eat just one? Serve four wraps each as an entrée. Just remember to multiply the nutrient numbers by four.

    2   **heads iceberg lettuce**
    1   **tablespoon rice vinegar**
    2   **teaspoons light soy sauce**
   ½   **teaspoon sugar**

Sauce 1

   ¼   **cup Chicken Broth (page 23) or commercial low-sodium broth**
   ¼   **cup rice vinegar**
    2   **green onions (green and white parts), thinly sliced**
    1   **tablespoon light soy sauce**
    1   **teaspoon sugar**
   ¼   **teaspoon toasted sesame oil**
   ⅛   **to ¼ teaspoon crushed red pepper flakes**

Sauce 2

   ⅓   **cup pineapple juice**
    2   **green onions (green and white parts), thinly sliced**
    2   **tablespoons rice vinegar**
    1   **tablespoon light soy sauce**
   ¼   **teaspoon toasted sesame oil**
   ⅛   **to ¼ teaspoon crushed red pepper flakes**

Filling

    6   **shiitake mushrooms (dried preferred)**
       Boiling water for soaking dried mushrooms
    1   **medium zucchini**
    1   **medium carrot**
   ½   **medium red bell pepper**
   ½   **cup whole water chestnuts, rinsed and drained**

½ cup canned bamboo shoots, rinsed and drained

2 green onions (green and white parts)

4 boneless, skinless chicken breast halves (about 4 ounces each), all visible fat removed, or 1 pound lean ground chicken or turkey breast, skin removed before grinding poultry

⅛ teaspoon white pepper

⅛ teaspoon ground ginger

2 teaspoons acceptable vegetable oil, divided use

2 medium cloves garlic, minced, or 1 teaspoon bottled minced garlic

2 tablespoons chopped unsalted peanuts

Cut each head of lettuce in half vertically (through core). Remove core with a knife. Carefully peel off four outside layers from each half.

In a small bowl, stir together rice vinegar, soy sauce, and sugar. Set aside.

Combine all ingredients for either Sauce 1 or Sauce 2 in a small bowl.

If using dried mushrooms, put them in a small bowl and pour enough boiling water over them to cover by 1 inch. Let soak for 15 minutes; pour off water, then squeeze excess water from mushrooms. Coarsely chop mushrooms. Set aside.

Meanwhile, dice zucchini, carrot, and bell pepper, keeping them separate.

Coarsely chop water chestnuts and bamboo shoots. Thinly slice green onions.

If using chicken breasts, rinse and pat dry with paper towels. Finely cut chicken into ¼- to ½-inch pieces. Put chicken pieces or ground chicken or turkey in a medium bowl; sprinkle with pepper and ginger.

Heat a large nonstick skillet over medium-high heat. Add 1 teaspoon oil and swirl to coat bottom. Cook chicken pieces for 3 to 4 minutes, or until lightly browned and no longer pink in the center, stirring occasionally (allow 4 to 5 minutes for ground chicken or turkey). Transfer to a medium bowl.

Add remaining 1 teaspoon oil to skillet and swirl to coat bottom. Cook garlic, carrot, and bell pepper for 1 minute, stirring occasionally.

Add zucchini (and fresh mushrooms); cook for 2 minutes, stirring occasionally.

Add dried mushrooms, water chestnuts, bamboo shoots, green onions, and rice vinegar mixture; cook for 1 minute, or until heated throughout, stirring occasionally.

Add chicken to vegetable mixture.

To serve, spoon mixture into a decorative bowl; sprinkle with peanuts. Place bowl in center of a platter. Arrange lettuce leaves around the bowl. Let each diner spoon about ¼ cup poultry mixture into a lettuce wrap, then top with about ½ tablespoon Sauce 1 or Sauce 2. Gently roll lettuce to enclose filling.

Cook's Tip on Lettuce Wraps: Use kitchen scissors to trim the edges to make the lettuce wraps manageable, if necessary. Don't worry if the lettuce tears somewhat; you can still use the leaves as wraps if they are large enough to hold the filling.

Cook's Tip: Cover lettuce leaves with plastic wrap or store in an airtight plastic bag and refrigerate for up to two days. Cover and refrigerate sauce for up to two days. Filling can be refrigerated for up to four days. At serving time, put filling in a microwave-safe bowl, cover, and heat on 100 percent power (high) for 1 to 2 minutes.

LETTUCE WRAPS WITH CHICKEN AND VEGETABLES WITH SAUCE 1

Calories 67	Total Fat 2 g	Fiber 1 g
Protein 8 g	Saturated 0 g	Sodium 66 mg
Carbohydrates 5 g	Polyunsaturated 1 g	Potassium 247 mg
Cholesterol 16 mg	Monounsaturated 1 g	Calcium 18 mg

LETTUCE WRAPS WITH CHICKEN AND VEGETABLES WITH SAUCE 2

Calories 68	Total Fat 2 g	Fiber 1 g
Protein 8 g	Saturated 0 g	Sodium 66 mg
Carbohydrates 5 g	Polyunsaturated 1 g	Potassium 253 mg
Cholesterol 16 mg	Monounsaturated 1 g	Calcium 19 mg

Smoked Turkey Spread

Serves 15 • about 2 tablespoons per serving

A delicious, light spread that's a stand-in for chopped liver. Serve this party hit on low-sodium crackers or as a topping for cucumber slices, celery sticks, or bell pepper wedges.

1½	tablespoons light stick margarine
¾	cup chopped sweet onion (Vidalia preferred)
5	ounces low-sodium, low-fat turkey (deli type), thinly sliced
1½	cups fat-free or low-fat cottage cheese
2	tablespoons tarragon vinegar
1½	teaspoons dried tarragon, crumbled
½	teaspoon no-salt-added liquid smoke
1	teaspoon very low sodium chicken bouillon granules or condensed low-sodium chicken soup base
	White pepper to taste

Heat a large skillet over medium-high heat. Add margarine and swirl to coat bottom. Cook onion for 2 to 3 minutes, or until translucent, stirring occasionally.

In a food processor or blender, process onion with remaining ingredients until smooth. Transfer mixture to a glass serving bowl or dish; cover with plastic wrap and chill for 4 hours, or until firm.

Calories 39	Total Fat 1 g	Fiber 0 g
Protein 6 g	Saturated 0 g	Sodium 88 mg
Carbohydrates 2 g	Polyunsaturated 0 g	Potassium 93 mg
Cholesterol 5 mg	Monounsaturated 0 g	Calcium 16 mg

Red Bell Pepper Crostini

Serves 8 • 2 crostini per serving

This appetizer is for the roasted bell pepper lover in us all. Arrange these triangular "little toasts" in a pinwheel fashion for a spectacular presentation.

> Olive oil spray
> 2 medium red bell peppers
> 2 tablespoons cider vinegar
> 2 ounces low-fat or fat-free cream cheese
> 1 tablespoon chopped fresh basil or 1 teaspoon dried, crumbled
> 1 tablespoon fat-free milk
> 1 medium clove garlic, minced, or ½ teaspoon bottled minced garlic
> ¼ teaspoon red hot-pepper sauce
> ⅛ teaspoon salt
> 16 slices low-sodium melba toast
> 3 tablespoons chopped fresh basil or parsley

Preheat broiler. Spray a broiling pan and rack with olive oil spray. Put bell peppers on rack.

Broil bell peppers 3 to 4 inches from heat until almost completely black, turning peppers to char evenly. Transfer peppers to an airtight plastic bag and seal, or put peppers in a large bowl and cover with plastic wrap. Let peppers cool for 20 to 30 minutes.

Slice peppers in half and remove stems, seeds, and veins. Gently peel skin off peppers, using your fingers or rubbing between paper towels, or scrape skin off with a knife (see Cook's Tip on Roasted Bell Peppers). Discard skin and chop peppers. Put peppers in a small bowl; stir in vinegar.

In a small mixing bowl, combine cream cheese, 1 tablespoon basil, milk, garlic, hot-pepper sauce, and salt. Using an electric mixer, beat on medium until smooth.

At serving time, spoon ½ teaspoon cream cheese mixture on each toast slice, top with roasted peppers, and sprinkle with 3 tablespoons fresh basil.

Cook's Tip on Roasted Bell Peppers: Some cooks like to rinse roasted peppers after peeling them. This removes some of the bits of charred skin that cling to the peppers. Other cooks say that rinsing the peppers washes away some of the flavor. So it's up to you—whichever way you prefer. Instead of broiling bell peppers yourself, purchase a jar of roasted bell peppers at the grocery store. Be sure to get those that are packed in water, not in oil, and that have the least sodium. Rinse and drain them before slicing. You can substitute 1/2 cup bottled roasted peppers for 2 medium fresh bell peppers. In this recipe, omit the vinegar and salt in the ingredients list.

Cook's Tip: You can prepare this appetizer up to 24 hours in advance and assemble it at serving time. Refrigerate the cream cheese mixture and the roasted bell peppers in separate airtight containers. Store the toasts in an airtight container at room temperature.

Calories 68	Total Fat 2 g	Fiber 1 g
Protein 2 g	Saturated 1 g	Sodium 69 mg
Carbohydrates 10 g	Polyunsaturated 0 g	Potassium 96 mg
Cholesterol 5 mg	Monounsaturated 1 g	Calcium 23 mg

Mango-Havarti Crepes

Serves 5 • 2 crepes per serving

A potential show-stopper at your next party, these exotic crepes are full of surprises. The blend of flavors is delightful.

1	teaspoon olive oil (light preferred)
1	medium yellow onion, thinly sliced (about 1 cup)
1	tablespoon sugar
3	to 4 teaspoons minced seeded fresh jalapeño
1	recipe Crepes (page 278)
6	ounces reduced-fat Havarti cheese, diced
3/4	cup snipped fresh cilantro, stems removed
2	medium mangoes, each cut into about 20 slices
3/4	cup nonfat or light sour cream
3/4	cup Roasted Tomato Chipotle Salsa (page 215) or commercial fat-free variety with lowest sodium available

Heat a medium skillet over medium-high heat. Add oil and swirl to coat bottom. Cook onion for 2 to 3 minutes, or until just translucent, stirring occasionally.

Stir in sugar and cook for 5 to 7 minutes, or until onion is golden brown.

Stir in jalapeño; let cool slightly, 1 to 2 minutes.

Arrange crepes on a flat surface. Place some cheese, cilantro, 2 mango slices, and some onion mixture on half of each crepe; fold crepe over filling.

In a large nonstick skillet, brown crepes on both sides over medium-high heat until golden, 3 to 4 minutes total. Transfer crepes to a serving plate and cover with aluminum foil to keep warm. Serve with sour cream and salsa.

Cook's Tip: You can prepare the fillings ahead and store them in the refrigerator for up to 24 hours.

Cook's Tip on Peeling Mangoes: Each mango has a very large seed, which is somewhat difficult to work around, and mangoes are slippery when you start peeling them. So it's much easier to work with quarters than to peel the whole mango at once. Simply cut a mango lengthwise into quarters, cutting each quarter away from the seed. Peel each quarter and then slice the pulp on a cutting board.

Cook's Tip on Handling Onions: To keep from crying when you peel an onion, chill it for a few hours before cutting. First slice off the stem end (top) and peel down the outer onion skin, leaving root end (bottom) intact. Slice or chop the onion, cutting into the root end last. That's where you find the heaviest concentration of sulfur compounds, the stuff that makes you cry.

Calories 222	Total Fat 6 g	Fiber 2 g
Protein 10 g	Saturated 2 g	Sodium 176 mg
Carbohydrates 32 g	Polyunsaturated —	Potassium —
Cholesterol 8 mg	Monounsaturated —	Calcium 161 mg

Mushrooms Stuffed with Sherried Chicken

Serves 4 • 4 mushrooms per serving

This popular appetizer will immediately break the ice at your party.

16	medium fresh mushrooms
	Vegetable oil spray
1	small onion, chopped (about ½ cup)
½	cup diced cooked chicken breast without skin, cooked without salt or added fat
1	slice bread, torn into small pieces
2	tablespoons dry sherry
¼	teaspoon dried marjoram, crumbled
⅛	teaspoon pepper
⅛	teaspoon dried oregano, crumbled
2	teaspoons light tub margarine, melted

Preheat broiler.

Remove and finely chop mushroom stems. Put mushroom caps, round side up, on a baking sheet.

Heat a medium nonstick skillet over medium-high heat. Remove skillet from heat and spray with vegetable oil spray (being careful not to spray near a gas flame). Cook mushroom stems and onion for 2 to 3 minutes, or just until tender, stirring occasionally.

Stir in remaining ingredients except margarine.

Brush mushroom caps with half the margarine.

Broil for 2 minutes. Turn mushrooms over and fill with chicken mixture. Brush with remaining margarine. Broil for 3 minutes, or until mushrooms are tender and lightly browned on top.

Cook's Tip on Fresh Mushrooms: You can refrigerate unwashed mushrooms for up to three days. Close them loosely in a brown bag or cover with a barely damp paper towel in the original container with the plastic wrap removed or on a plate.

Calories 83	Total Fat 2 g	Fiber 1 g
Protein 9 g	Saturated 0 g	Sodium 66 mg
Carbohydrates 8 g	Polyunsaturated 1 g	Potassium 324 mg
Cholesterol 15 mg	Monounsaturated 1 g	Calcium 16 mg

Hot and Smoky Chipotle-Garlic Dip

Serves 8 • 2 tablespoons per serving

*Serve this spicy mixture on cucumber rounds or baked tortillas
(see Cook's Tip on Baked Tortillas, pages 16–17). Or thin it with 2 to 3
tablespoons of fat-free milk and use it as a dip for vegetables. It's
especially good with carrots, celery, cauliflower, cherry tomatoes,
broccoli, and yellow summer squash.*

⅔	cup nonfat or light sour cream
3	tablespoons low-fat or fat-free, cholesterol-free mayonnaise dressing
2	tablespoons fresh lemon juice
1	chipotle pepper, canned in adobo sauce
1	medium clove garlic, minced, or 1 teaspoon bottled minced garlic
⅛	teaspoon salt
	Fresh cilantro sprigs (optional)

In a food processor or blender, process all ingredients except cilantro
until smooth. Transfer to a serving bowl and garnish with cilantro.

Cook's Tip on Chipotle Peppers: These smoked, dried jalapeños provide a unique, smoky heat. You can find cans of these flavorful chiles, frequently in
adobo sauce, in major supermarkets in the international or ethnic section. (Adobo
sauce, also known as adobo paste, is a rather spicy mixture of chiles, vinegar, garlic,
and herbs.) Chipotles are also sold dried in packages. To rehydrate the packaged type,
place in hot water for 20 minutes, then drain and use as directed above. You can use the
soaking water to spice up soup or beans.

Calories 36	Total Fat 0 g	Fiber 0 g
Protein 1 g	Saturated 0 g	Sodium 129 mg
Carbohydrates 6 g	Polyunsaturated 0 g	Potassium 53 mg
Cholesterol 2 mg	Monounsaturated 0 g	Calcium 28 mg

Black Bean Dip

Serves 20 • about 2 tablespoons per serving

Spread this smooth, spicy dip on crispy baked tortilla chips or use as a dip for your favorite raw vegetables.

2	teaspoons acceptable vegetable oil
¾	cup chopped onion
4	oil-packed sun-dried tomatoes, drained and coarsely chopped
2	large cloves garlic, chopped, or 1½ teaspoons bottled minced garlic
2	15-ounce cans no-salt-added black beans, rinsed and drained
2	tablespoons lime juice
2	tablespoons water
1½	teaspoons sugar
1	tablespoon snipped fresh cilantro or 1 teaspoon dried, crumbled
1	teaspoon ground coriander
1	teaspoon ground cumin
¼	teaspoon cayenne, or to taste
¼	cup sliced green onions (green part only)
¼	cup nonfat or light sour cream

Heat a large nonstick skillet over medium heat. Add oil and swirl to coat bottom. Cook onion, tomatoes, and garlic for 3 to 5 minutes, or until onion is translucent, stirring constantly. Set aside to cool slightly.

In a food processor or blender, process beans, lime juice, water, sugar, cilantro, coriander, cumin, cayenne, and onion mixture until smooth. Transfer dip to a serving bowl and refrigerate, covered, for at least 3 hours. To serve, top with green onions and decorative dollops of sour cream.

Variation

For a zippy flavor addition, stir in some Roasted Tomato Chipotle Salsa (page 215) or commercial fat-free variety with lowest sodium available.

Cook's Tip on Baked Tortillas: For a different presentation—and a low-fat, low-sodium accompaniment for dips and soups—cut shapes from corn tortillas with 2-inch cookie cutters. Put the cutouts on a nonstick baking sheet. Preheat the oven to 400° F, and place the rack on the lowest level. Bake for 6 to 8 minutes, or until lightly golden brown.

Calories 50	Total Fat 1 g	Fiber 2 g
Protein 3 g	Saturated 0 g	Sodium 5 mg
Carbohydrates 9 g	Polyunsaturated 0 g	Potassium 185 mg
Cholesterol 0 mg	Monounsaturated 0 g	Calcium 21 mg

Party Mix

Serves 12 • ¼ cup per serving

This crunchy bowlful is great to serve instead of high-fat potato chips.

1¼	cups corn cereal squares
¾	cup bite-size shredded wheat cereal squares
½	cup thin unsalted pretzel sticks
2	low-sodium bagel chips, broken into ½-inch pieces (about ½ cup)
¼	cup unsalted peanuts
1½	tablespoons very low sodium or low-sodium Worcestershire sauce
1	tablespoon Hot Mustard (page 216) or commercial honey mustard
2	teaspoons toasted sesame oil .
½	teaspoon garlic powder
½	teaspoon ground cumin
⅛	teaspoon cayenne
¼	teaspoon salt
	Vegetable oil spray

Preheat oven to 400° F.

In a large bowl, stir together cereal squares, pretzels, bagel chips, and peanuts.

In a small bowl, stir together remaining ingredients except salt and vegetable oil spray. Stir into cereal mixture. Spread in a single layer in a jelly-roll pan. Bake for 2 minutes, stir, and bake for 2 more minutes. Remove from oven.

Lightly spray mixture with vegetable oil spray. Sprinkle evenly with salt. Let cool on a cooling rack for 10 minutes (mixture will become crisp).

Calories 65	Total Fat 3 g	Fiber 1 g
Protein 2 g	Saturated 0 g	Sodium 90 mg
Carbohydrates 9 g	Polyunsaturated 1 g	Potassium 49 mg
Cholesterol 0 mg	Monounsaturated 1 g	Calcium 5 mg

Mango Chips

Serves 8 • ¼ cup per serving

Mango chips make a great garnish. Use them on cakes, ice cream, sorbet, and cream pies, or eat them as a light snack.

Simple Syrup
2	cups water
1⅓	cups sugar
½	cup light corn syrup

2	medium mangoes

For simple syrup, in a medium saucepan, bring all ingredients to a boil over medium heat (no need to stir). Let mixture boil for a few seconds; remove from heat and let cool. Skim top if mixture appears foamy.

Preheat oven to 200° F. Cover two baking sheets and two cooling racks with cooking parchment.

Using a very sharp knife, slice each mango lengthwise into quarters around the seed. Cut each quarter away from seed. Peel back skin; cut each quarter into about 16 very thin slices (think potato chips!). Dip each slice into cool simple syrup; lay on baking sheets.

Bake mango slices for 2 hours; turn each slice over and bake for additional 1 hour, or until chips are crisp. Watch carefully so mango doesn't brown. Transfer slices to cooling racks. Store in airtight containers, separating layers with cooking parchment or wax paper. Chips should keep for up to two months.

Cook's Tip on Simple Syrup: Refrigerate leftover simple syrup in an airtight container. It will keep almost indefinitely.

Cook's Tip on Light Corn Syrup: Light corn syrup is light only in color, not in calories or sugar.

Calories 441	Total Fat 0 g	Fiber 2 g
Protein 1 g	Saturated 0 g	Sodium 56 mg
Carbohydrates 116 g	Polyunsaturated 0 g	Potassium 164 mg
Cholesterol 0 mg	Monounsaturated 0 g	Calcium 15 mg

Sparkling Apple Punch

Serves 8 • 6 ounces per serving

*Your guests won't guess that this delightful punch with its
sophisticated flavor is so simple to make.*

        12-ounce can frozen apple juice, thawed
    36 fluid ounces lime-flavored sparkling spring water, chilled
        Ice or ice ring (optional)

Pour apple juice into punch bowl. Stir in sparkling water. Add ice or
ice ring.

Cook's Tip: An easy way to measure the sparkling water is to fill the apple juice
can three times.

Calories 88	Total Fat 0 g	Fiber 0 g
Protein 0 g	Saturated 0 g	Sodium 15 mg
Carbohydrates 22 g	Polyunsaturated 0 g	Potassium 236 mg
Cholesterol 0 mg	Monounsaturated 0 g	Calcium 12 mg

Soups

beef broth
chicken broth
vegetable broth
gazpacho
creamy carrot soup
onion soup with cheesy pita crisps
yellow pepper and celery root soup
baked potato soup
tomato basil pesto soup
soup to go
minestrone
black bean soup
lentil soup with lemon
curried split pea soup
new england fish chowder with thyme
turkey vegetable soup
vegetable beef soup

Beef Broth

Serves 12 • ¾ cup per serving

Beef broth is good on its own and is useful for adding flavor to many other dishes. Roasting the bones adds both flavor and color to the broth. Keep some in the freezer so you'll have it handy whenever you need it (see Cook's Tip on Broth, page 23).

4	pounds beef or veal bones (preferably shank or knuckle bones)
3	quarts water
1	medium onion, coarsely chopped (about ¾ cup)
8*	sprigs of fresh parsley
1	teaspoon dried thyme, crumbled
5	or 6 peppercorns
2	whole cloves
1	bay leaf

Preheat oven to 400° F.

Put bones in a roasting pan and bake for 25 to 30 minutes, turning bones once. Pour off fat.

Transfer bones to a stockpot or Dutch oven. Add remaining ingredients. Bring to a boil over high heat. Reduce heat and simmer for 4 to 6 hours; don't boil. Skim fat from top and strain broth. Refrigerate for 1 to 2 hours, or until fat hardens on surface. To serve, remove and discard hardened fat; reheat soup.

Calories 8	Total Fat 0 g	Fiber 0 g
Protein 2 g	Saturated 0 g	Sodium 23 mg
Carbohydrates 0 g	Polyunsaturated 0 g	Potassium 75 mg
Cholesterol 0 mg	Monounsaturated 0 g	Calcium 8 mg

Chicken Broth

Serves 12 • ¾ cup per serving

With this big batch of broth, you'll have plenty to serve as an appetizer and to freeze for later use in a variety of recipes. Save the cooked chicken for Chicken Salad (page 58) or Chicken Enchiladas (page 114).

3	pounds skinless chicken, all visible fat removed
2	to 3 pounds chicken bones (optional)
3	quarts cold water
2	large carrots, chopped (about 2 cups)
2	medium ribs celery, sliced (about 1 cup)
1	medium onion, chopped (about ¾ cup)
5	or 6 whole peppercorns
1	bay leaf
1	teaspoon dried thyme, crumbled
¼	teaspoon pepper

In a stockpot or Dutch oven, combine all ingredients and bring to a boil over high heat. Reduce heat and simmer for 1 to 2 hours without bones or 3 to 4 hours with bones.

Skim froth off top, remove and reserve chicken for another use, and strain broth. Refrigerate broth for 1 to 2 hours, or until fat hardens on surface. To serve, remove and discard hardened fat; reheat soup.

Cook's Tip on Broth: Freeze leftover broth in ice cube trays for future use. Put 1 tablespoon of broth in each compartment of the tray, then freeze. Remove the broth cubes from the tray and store them in an airtight plastic freezer bag. Then the broth is ready to use—a tablespoon at a time whenever you need it. In some recipes, you can toss in the still-frozen cubes. Otherwise, just thaw them in the refrigerator for several hours or in the microwave.

Calories 8	Total Fat 0 g	Fiber 0 g
Protein 2 g	Saturated 0 g	Sodium 19 mg
Carbohydrates 0 g	Polyunsaturated 0 g	Potassium 75 mg
Cholesterol 0 mg	Monounsaturated 0 g	Calcium 4 mg

Vegetable Broth

Serves 13 • ¾ cup per serving

Use this tasty broth in place of beef or chicken broth. It adds a wonderful flavor change and is so easy to make.

    4   cups trimmings, such as carrots, celery, tomatoes, onions,
        spinach, and leeks
    6   cups water
    ⅛   to ¼ teaspoon pepper

In a stockpot or Dutch oven, combine all ingredients. Bring to a simmer over medium-high heat. Reduce heat to medium-low and cook, covered, for 1 hour. Strain and discard solids.

Calories 12	Total Fat 0 g	Fiber 0 g
Protein 2 g	Saturated 0 g	Sodium 35 mg
Carbohydrates 2 g	Polyunsaturated 0 g	Potassium 41 mg
Cholesterol 0 mg	Monounsaturated 0 g	Calcium 5 mg

Gazpacho

Serves 12 • ½ cup per serving

This no-cook soup will sustain you through the dog days of summer.

2   medium cucumbers
1   medium tomato
1   small green bell pepper
1   small zucchini
½   medium onion
3   or 4 green onions (green and white parts)
4   cups reduced-sodium mixed vegetable juice
¼   cup snipped fresh parsley or 1 tablespoon plus 1 teaspoon
      dried, crumbled
1   tablespoon fresh lemon juice (optional)
2   medium cloves garlic, minced, or 1 teaspoon bottled minced
      garlic
1   teaspoon very low sodium or low-sodium Worcestershire sauce
½   to 1 teaspoon pepper
1½   medium lemons, cut into wedges (optional)

Finely chop cucumbers, tomato, bell pepper, zucchini, onion, and green onions. Put in a large bowl.

Stir in remaining ingredients except lemons. Cover and refrigerate for at least 2 hours before serving.

Garnish each serving with a wedge of lemon on the side.

Calories 34	Total Fat 0 g	Fiber 1 g
Protein 1 g	Saturated 0 g	Sodium 158 mg
Carbohydrates 8 g	Polyunsaturated 0 g	Potassium 173 mg
Cholesterol 0 mg	Monounsaturated 0 g	Calcium 31 mg

Creamy Carrot Soup

Serves 5 • about 1 cup per serving

*Beautiful in color, this soup is creamy without using dairy products.
Serve it hot in the winter and chilled in the summer.*

    3   teaspoons olive oil (light preferred)
    2   cups thinly sliced sweet onions (Vidalia preferred) (2 large)
    3   cups ½-inch-thick sliced carrots (about 5 large)
    4   cups Chicken Broth (page 23) or commercial low-sodium broth
        Dash of cayenne
    2   teaspoons unsalted shelled pumpkin seeds or dry-roasted
        sunflower seeds (optional)
        Chopped green onions (green part only) (optional)   •

Heat a stockpot or Dutch oven over medium heat. Add oil and swirl
to coat bottom. Cook onions for 2 to 3 minutes, or until translucent,
stirring occasionally.

Add carrots and cook for 1 to 2 minutes, stirring occasionally.

Add broth. Increase heat to high and bring soup to a boil, 6 to 8 minutes. Reduce heat and simmer, uncovered, for 30 minutes, or until carrots are tender. Remove from heat.

Stir in cayenne.

Working in batches, process soup in a blender or food processor until
smooth. Ladle into soup bowls and sprinkle with pumpkin seeds and
green onions.

Cook's Tip on Light Olive Oil: Light olive oil is light in color and in flavor, not in fat or calories.

CREAMY CARROT SOUP—WITH PUMPKIN SEEDS

Calories 87	Total Fat 3 g	Fiber 3 g
Protein 3 g	Saturated 1 g	Sodium 47 mg
Carbohydrates 12 g	Polyunsaturated 1 g	Potassium 398 mg
Cholesterol 0 mg	Monounsaturated 2 g	Calcium 34 mg

CREAMY CARROT SOUP—WITHOUT PUMPKIN SEEDS

Calories 81	Total Fat 3 g	Fiber 3 g
Protein 3 g	Saturated 0 g	Sodium 47 mg
Carbohydrates 12 g	Polyunsaturated 0 g	Potassium 389 mg
Cholesterol 0 mg	Monounsaturated 2 g	Calcium 33 mg

Onion Soup with Cheesy Pita Crisps

Serves 4 • about 1 cup soup and 2 crisps per serving

Crisp pita wedges topped with melted cheese garnish a rich broth teeming with caramelized onions.

Soup

1	tablespoon light stick margarine
2	medium onions, sliced
1	teaspoon olive oil
1/8	teaspoon sugar
3	tablespoons all-purpose flour
4	cups Beef Broth (page 22) or commercial low-sodium broth
2	tablespoons dry vermouth or dry white wine (regular or nonalcoholic)
1/8	teaspoon pepper

Cheesy Pita Crisps

	6-inch whole-wheat pita bread
	Vegetable oil spray
1/8	teaspoon garlic powder
1/4	cup shredded low-fat Cheddar cheese
1	tablespoon plus 1 teaspoon shredded or grated Parmesan cheese

For soup, in a large saucepan, melt margarine over medium-high heat. Add onions and oil; cook for 2 to 3 minutes, or until onions are translucent, stirring occasionally.

Stir in sugar and cook, uncovered, for 7 to 10 minutes, or until onions are a deep, golden brown, stirring occasionally.

Preheat oven to 350° F.

Stir flour into onion mixture, combining thoroughly.

Stir in remaining soup ingredients; increase heat to high and bring to a boil. Reduce heat to medium-low and cook for 15 to 20 minutes, or until flavors have blended, stirring occasionally.

Meanwhile, cut pita bread into 4 wedges. Separate each wedge into top and bottom pieces (you will have 8 wedges total). Place wedges on a baking sheet and spray tops lightly with vegetable oil spray. Sprinkle each wedge with some garlic powder, Cheddar, and Parmesan. Bake for 8 to 10 minutes, or until cheese has melted.

To serve, ladle soup into bowls and float 2 pita crisps on each serving.

ONION SOUP WITH CHEESY PITA CRISPS

Calories 149	Total Fat 4 g	Fiber 2 g
Protein 7 g	Saturated 1 g	Sodium 213 mg
Carbohydrates 19 g	Polyunsaturated 1 g	Potassium 235 mg
Cholesterol 3 mg	Monounsaturated 2 g	Calcium 83 mg

CHEESY PITA CRISPS

Calories 62	Total Fat 2 g	Fiber 1 g
Protein 4 g	Saturated 1 g	Sodium 162 mg
Carbohydrates 9 g	Polyunsaturated 0 g	Potassium 33 mg
Cholesterol 3 mg	Monounsaturated 0 g	Calcium 60 mg

Yellow Pepper and Celery Root Soup

Serves 8 • about ¾ cup per serving

Rich and intensely flavored, this soup is equally delightful for brunch, lunch, or dinner and can be frozen for later use. Serve it cold in hot weather or hot when the weather is chilly.

	Olive oil spray
5	*medium yellow or red bell peppers*
2	*tablespoons olive oil (light preferred) (see Cook's Tip on Light Olive Oil, page 26)*
3	*leeks (white part only), thinly sliced (about 2 cups)*
2	*cups peeled and sliced celery root (celeriac) (about 8 ounces)*
3	*medium cloves garlic*
8	*cups Chicken Broth (page 23) or commercial low-sodium broth Cayenne to taste*

Preheat broiler. Spray a broiling pan and rack with olive oil spray.

Broil peppers 3 to 4 inches from heat on a broiling rack for 3 to 5 minutes, or until almost completely black, turning peppers to char evenly. Remove from broiler and seal in an airtight plastic bag or put in a large bowl and cover with plastic wrap. Let peppers cool for 20 to 30 minutes.

Slice peppers in half and remove stems, seeds, and veins. Gently peel skin off peppers, using your fingers or rubbing between paper towels, or scrape skin off with a knife. Discard skin and slice peppers (see Cook's Tip on Roasted Bell Peppers, pages 10–11).

In a stockpot or Dutch oven, heat olive oil over medium-high heat. Cook leeks for 5 to 6 minutes, or until transparent.

Add celery root and garlic; cook for 6 to 8 minutes, stirring occasionally.

Add roasted peppers and stir to mix thoroughly.

Add broth, reduce heat to medium, and bring to a boil, about 20 minutes. Reduce heat and simmer for 40 minutes, or until all vegetables are tender (no stirring needed). Remove from heat.

Working in batches, process soup in blender or food processor until smooth.

Stir in cayenne. Serve hot or cold.

Cook's Tip on Leeks: The white part of a leek has a mild onion-garlic flavor. The green leaves usually are a bit tough to chew, but they're also flavorful. Use them when making chicken, beef, or vegetable stock or a poaching liquid for fish. You can even blanch the leaves in boiling water for 1 minute, cut them into long, thin strips, and tie bunches of food, such as cooked asparagus or very thin carrot strips, for an unusual presentation.

Cook's Tip on Celery Root: Also called celeriac or celery knob, celery root is delicious but unattractive. It's an ugly, knobby, brown vegetable, available from September through May. When buying celery root, choose one that is relatively small and firm with a minimum of rootlets and knobs. Avoid those with soft spots, which is a signal of decay. Celery root should be refrigerated in a plastic bag, where it will keep for 7 to 10 days.

Calories 110	Total Fat 4 g	Fiber 2 g
Protein 4 g	Saturated 1 g	Sodium 73 mg
Carbohydrates 17 g	Polyunsaturated 1 g	Potassium 528 mg
Cholesterol 0 mg	Monounsaturated 3 g	Calcium 56 mg

Baked Potato Soup

Serves 4 • 1 cup per serving

Use leftover baked potatoes for this soup or bake some just for this recipe. We prefer golden potatoes because of their buttery flavor and color, but any baking potato will do.

Soup
1	pound golden or russet potatoes (about 3 medium) (about 2 cups when mashed)
1	teaspoon olive oil
¼	cup chopped onion
2	medium cloves garlic, minced, or 1 teaspoon bottled minced garlic
2	cups Chicken Broth (page 23) or commercial low-sodium broth
½	cup fat-free evaporated milk
2	tablespoons all-purpose flour
½	to 1 teaspoon Horseradish (page 217) or ½ to 1 teaspoon dried horseradish (optional)
¼	teaspoon pepper

Toppings
¼	cup shredded fat-free or reduced-fat Cheddar cheese
¼	cup sliced black olives, drained
¼	cup nonfat or light sour cream
1	tablespoon plus 1 teaspoon chopped fresh green onions (green part only) or dried chives
1	tablespoon plus 1 teaspoon bacon-flavor chips

Preheat oven to 350° F. Pierce potatoes several times with a fork and put on a baking sheet.

Bake potatoes for 1 hour, or until tender when pierced with a fork or knife.

Let potatoes cool for at least 10 minutes. Peel potatoes; put in a medium bowl and mash with a potato masher until slightly chunky. (You can also cut potatoes in half and scoop out flesh, then mash.)

Heat a medium saucepan over medium heat. Add oil and swirl to coat bottom. Cook onion and garlic for 3 to 4 minutes, or until onion is translucent, stirring occasionally.

Stir in broth and continue to cook, stirring occasionally.

While broth heats, whisk together evaporated milk and flour in a small bowl. Whisk into broth mixture.

Stir in potatoes, horseradish, and pepper. Cook, uncovered, over medium-high heat for 4 to 5 minutes, or until soup thickens, stirring occasionally. To serve, sprinkle each serving with some of the toppings.

Calories 187	Total Fat 3 g	Fiber 2 g
Protein 10 g	Saturated 0 g	Sodium 228 mg
Carbohydrates 31 g	Polyunsaturated 0 g	Potassium 596 mg
Cholesterol 3 mg	Monounsaturated 2 g	Calcium 250 mg

Tomato Basil Pesto Soup

Serves 7 • ⅔ cup per serving

*Roasted tomatoes give this soup a really concentrated flavor. Serve
with half a turkey sandwich for a lunch treat.*

	Vegetable oil spray
4	*large tomatoes (about 2 pounds)*
1	*tablespoon plus 1 teaspoon pine nuts*
1	*teaspoon olive oil*
1	*small onion, chopped (about ½ cup)*
1	*medium carrot, thinly sliced (about ¾ cup)*
2	*medium cloves garlic, minced, or 1 teaspoon bottled minced garlic*
2	*tablespoons water*
¼	*cup fresh basil leaves*
1	*cup Chicken Broth (page 23) or commercial low-sodium broth*
½	*to 1 teaspoon lemon juice*
¼	*to ½ teaspoon sugar*
¼	*teaspoon pepper*
2	*teaspoons shredded or grated Parmesan cheese*

Preheat oven to 400° F. Lightly spray a baking sheet with vegetable
oil spray.

Core tomatoes and cut in half horizontally. Squeeze juice and seeds
through a strainer, discarding seeds and reserving liquid. Cut tomato
halves in half, and place wedges with skin side down on a baking sheet.

Bake for 20 minutes, or until edges are slightly golden.

Meanwhile, put pine nuts on an ungreased baking sheet. Bake nuts in
same oven as tomatoes for 3 to 4 minutes, or until golden brown. Watch
carefully so they don't burn. Transfer nuts to a small plate. Set aside.

Peel tomatoes if desired.

Heat a medium nonaluminum saucepan over medium-high heat. Add
olive oil and swirl to coat bottom. Cook onion, carrot, and garlic, uncovered, for 3 to 4 minutes, or until tender crisp, stirring occasionally.

Add water; reduce heat to low and cook, covered, for 5 minutes, or
until carrots are tender.

In a food processor or blender, puree tomatoes and onion mixture together in batches until smooth, about 1 minute per batch. Before pureeing last batch, add basil. Return tomato mixture to saucepan.

Add reserved tomato juice and remaining ingredients except Parmesan. Bring to a simmer over medium-high heat; reduce heat to medium and cook, uncovered, for 8 to 10 minutes, or until mixture is warmed through.

For each serving, ladle ⅔ cup soup into a bowl. Sprinkle with Parmesan and pine nuts.

Calories 58	Total Fat 2 g	Fiber 2 g
Protein 2 g	Saturated 0 g	Sodium 31 mg
Carbohydrates 10 g	Polyunsaturated 1 g	Potassium 382 mg
Cholesterol 1 mg	Monounsaturated 1 g	Calcium 27 mg

Soup to Go

Serves 1 • 1 cup per serving

*Here's the low-sodium answer to how to have a quick cup of soup.
Keep this mixture on hand at work for a quick lunch, take it on a
camping trip—in fact, you can use it wherever boiling water is
available.*

Basic Chicken Soup to Go

1/4	cup instant brown rice or 2 tablespoons couscous, uncooked
1/4	cup no-salt-added dried vegetables, such as carrots, tomatoes, peas, and corn
1 1/2	teaspoons very low sodium chicken bouillon granules
1/2	teaspoon dried parsley, crumbled
1/2	teaspoon dried minced onion
1/8	teaspoon dried thyme, crumbled
1/8	teaspoon pepper

Basic Beef Soup to Go

1/4	cup instant brown rice or 2 tablespoons couscous, uncooked
1/4	cup no-salt-added dried vegetables, such as carrots, tomatoes, peas, and corn
1 1/2	teaspoons very low sodium beef bouillon granules
1	teaspoon dried shallots
1/2	teaspoon dried parsley, crumbled
1/8	teaspoon dried marjoram, crumbled
1/8	teaspoon pepper

1	cup boiling water

Combine all ingredients for chicken or beef soup mix in a small, air-tight plastic bag or covered plastic container.

To prepare soup, pour 1 cup boiling water over dry mixture and stir. Let stand for 1 to 2 minutes, or until rice is tender.

Cook's Tip: Experiment with different dried vegetable combinations and no-salt-added herb or seasoning combinations (1/4 to 1/2 teaspoon), such as those on pages 222–226. Keep a small bottle of toasted sesame oil handy and pour a few drops on the chicken soup for an Asian flavor (similar to that of egg drop soup).

Cook's Tip: If you begin with new jars of herbs and bouillon granules, these mixtures will keep in an airtight container for up to a year. Be sure to keep in a closed cabinet away from the light.

SOUP TO GO—BASIC CHICKEN

Calories 184	Total Fat 2 g	Fiber 3 g
Protein 5 g	Saturated 0 g	Sodium 45 mg
Carbohydrates 38 g	Polyunsaturated 1 g	Potassium 1192 mg
Cholesterol 0 mg	Monounsaturated 1 g	Calcium 40 mg

SOUP TO GO—BASIC BEEF

Calories 103	Total Fat 2 g	Fiber 3 g
Protein 5 g	Saturated 0 g	Sodium 53 mg
Carbohydrates 37 g	Polyunsaturated 1 g	Potassium 1143 mg
Cholesterol 0 mg	Monounsaturated 1 g	Calcium 39 mg

Minestrone

Serves 10 • 1 cup per serving

Enjoy a bowl of this nourishing soup for lunch, and you won't be troubled by midafternoon hunger pangs.

	Vegetable oil spray (olive oil spray preferred)
1½	teaspoons olive oil
½	cup chopped onion
½	cup thinly sliced carrots
½	cup diced celery
1	to 2 medium cloves garlic, minced, or ½ to 1 teaspoon bottled minced garlic
6	cups Chicken Broth (page 23) or commercial low-sodium broth
1	cup canned no-salt-added tomatoes
1	cup cooked macaroni (cooked without salt or oil)
1	cup canned no-salt-added white beans, rinsed and drained
½	teaspoon pepper
¼	cup shredded or grated Parmesan cheese

Heat a stockpot or Dutch oven over medium heat. Remove from heat and spray with vegetable oil spray (being careful not to spray near a gas flame). Add oil and swirl to coat bottom. Cook onion, carrots, celery, and garlic for 3 to 4 minutes, or until onion is translucent, stirring occasionally.

Stir in remaining ingredients except Parmesan. Simmer, covered, for 5 minutes, or until thoroughly heated. To serve, sprinkle Parmesan over each serving.

Calories 77	Total Fat 2 g	Fiber 2 g
Protein 5 g	Saturated 1 g	Sodium 72 mg
Carbohydrates 11 g	Polyunsaturated 0 g	Potassium 265 mg
Cholesterol 2 mg	Monounsaturated 1 g	Calcium 60 mg

Black Bean Soup

Serves 10 • about 1 cup per serving

Interesting and flavorful, this soup is perfect as a first course with baked tortilla strips or sesame seed crisps. It also pairs well with a deep green salad and warm bread for a simple, hearty meal.

2	tablespoons olive oil (light preferred) (see Cook's Tip on Light Olive Oil, page 26)
2½	cups chopped onion (3 to 4 medium)
1	cup diced celery (3 medium ribs)
5	large cloves garlic, chopped, or 3 teaspoons bottled minced garlic
3	15-ounce cans no-salt-added black beans
4	cups Chicken Broth (page 23) or commercial low-sodium broth
	28-ounce can no-salt-added stewed tomatoes, undrained
1	tablespoon ground cumin
1½	teaspoons dried cilantro, crumbled
⅛	to ¼ teaspoon cayenne
½	cup nonfat or light sour cream, beaten until smooth

Heat a stockpot or Dutch oven over medium-high heat. Add oil and swirl to coat bottom. Cook onion for 2 to 3 minutes, or until translucent, stirring occasionally. Reduce heat to medium.

Add celery and garlic; cook for 4 minutes, or until celery is transparent, stirring frequently.

Meanwhile, drain beans, reserving 1 cup liquid. Rinse beans. Add beans and reserved liquid to stockpot.

Stir in remaining ingredients except sour cream. Increase heat to high and bring soup to a boil, about 9 minutes. Reduce heat and simmer, covered, for 25 minutes (no stirring needed). Remove from heat.

Working in batches, puree soup in food processor or blender until smooth. To serve, garnish each serving with a dollop of sour cream.

Cook's Tip: If the liquid drained from the beans doesn't measure 1 cup, add enough water to make up the difference.

Calories 149	Total Fat 3 g	Fiber 8 g
Protein 8 g	Saturated 0 g	Sodium 45 mg
Carbohydrates 27 g	Polyunsaturated 0 g	Potassium 616 mg
Cholesterol 1 mg	Monounsaturated 2 g	Calcium 103 mg

Lentil Soup with Lemon

Serves 9 • 1 cup per serving

Lentils and potatoes provide wholesome fiber in this hearty main-dish soup. Try serving it with Corn Muffins (page 242) and a dessert of Spiced Fruit (page 284).

	Olive oil spray
1	teaspoon olive oil
1/2	cup chopped onion
2	medium cloves garlic, minced, or 1 teaspoon bottled minced garlic
2	quarts Vegetable Broth (page 24), commercial low-sodium broth, or water
2	cups dried lentils, sorted for stones or shriveled lentils, rinsed and drained (about 1 pound)
1	medium potato, diced (about 1 cup)
1/2	teaspoon dried oregano, crumbled
1/4	teaspoon salt
2	to 3 tablespoons fresh lemon juice
	Pepper to taste

Heat a stockpot or Dutch oven over medium-high heat. Remove pot from heat and spray with olive oil spray (being careful not to spray near a gas flame). Return to heat and add oil, swirling to coat bottom. Cook onion and garlic for 2 to 3 minutes, or until onion is translucent, stirring occasionally.

Stir in broth, lentils, potato, oregano, and salt. Simmer, covered, for 45 minutes, or until lentils are soft (no stirring needed).

Stir in remaining ingredients.

Calories 179	Total Fat 1 g	Fiber 14 g
Protein 14 g	Saturated 0 g	Sodium 112 mg
Carbohydrates 30 g	Polyunsaturated 0 g	Potassium 531 mg
Cholesterol 0 mg	Monounsaturated 0 g	Calcium 34 mg

Curried Split Pea Soup

Serves 6 • about 1 cup per serving

*With half a sandwich, this soup—unusual with curry and cumin—
makes a hearty, filling lunch.*

1	cup dried split peas, sorted for stones and shriveled peas and rinsed (about ½ pound)
6	cups Chicken Broth (page 23), Beef Broth (page 22), Vegetable Broth (page 24), commercial low-sodium broth, or water
1	cup chopped carrot
1	large onion, chopped (about 1 cup)
1½	teaspoons sugar
1½	teaspoons curry powder
1	teaspoon ground cumin
⅛	teaspoon garlic powder
⅛	teaspoon cayenne
¾	teaspoon salt

In a Dutch oven or large saucepan, combine all ingredients except
salt. Bring to a boil over high heat. Reduce heat and simmer, covered,
for 1 hour to 1 hour 30 minutes, or until peas are tender (no stirring
needed).

Whisk in salt. Continue to whisk vigorously to puree peas a bit to
give soup a thicker consistency.

Calories 122	Total Fat 1 g	Fiber 8 g
Protein 7 g	Saturated 0 g	Sodium 309 mg
Carbohydrates 23 g	Polyunsaturated 0 g	Potassium 420 mg
Cholesterol 0 mg	Monounsaturated 0 g	Calcium 33 mg

New England Fish Chowder with Thyme

Serves 6 • 1 cup per serving

This creamy chowder boasts chunks of potato and mild white fish.
For a different twist, top it with crumbled low-sodium pretzels.

1	pound fish fillets (haddock, cod, orange roughy, or other firm white fish)
1	tablespoon light stick margarine
1/2	cup chopped onion
3	cups low-sodium fish stock, Chicken Broth (page 23), or commercial low-sodium broth
2	medium potatoes, peeled and cut into 1/2-inch cubes (about 1 1/2 cups)
3/4	teaspoon dried thyme, crumbled
1/8	teaspoon pepper (white preferred)
1	cup fat-free evaporated milk
1/4	cup all-purpose flour

Cut fish into 1/2-inch cubes. Set aside.

In a large saucepan, melt margarine over medium-high heat. Cook onion for 2 to 3 minutes, or until translucent, stirring occasionally.

Add fish stock, potatoes, thyme, and pepper and bring to a simmer. Reduce heat to medium-low and cook, covered, for 20 to 25 minutes, or until potatoes are tender (no stirring needed).

In a small bowl, whisk together evaporated milk and flour. Whisk into stock mixture. Cook over medium-high heat for about 5 minutes, or until mixture thickens, stirring occasionally. Reduce heat to medium.

Add fish and cook for 6 to 7 minutes, or until fish is opaque, stirring occasionally.

Calories 167	Total Fat 2 g	Fiber 1 g
Protein 20 g	Saturated 0 g	Sodium 128 mg
Carbohydrates 17 g	Polyunsaturated 1 g	Potassium 659 mg
Cholesterol 45 mg	Monounsaturated 0 g	Calcium 159 mg

Turkey Vegetable Soup

Serves 9 • 1 cup per serving

Here's a good way to use up that leftover Thanksgiving turkey.

	Vegetable oil spray
1	teaspoon acceptable margarine
1/2	cup chopped onion
1/4	cup diced celery
6	cups Chicken Broth (page 23) or commercial low-sodium broth
1	cup canned no-salt-added tomatoes
1	cup chopped cooked turkey breast, all visible fat and skin removed
1/2	cup frozen peas
1/2	cup frozen no-salt-added whole-kernel corn
1/2	teaspoon pepper
1/4	teaspoon red hot-pepper sauce

Heat a stockpot or Dutch oven over medium heat. Remove from heat and spray with vegetable oil spray (being careful not to spray near a gas flame). Add margarine and swirl to coat bottom. Cook onion and celery for 3 to 4 minutes, or until onion is translucent, stirring occasionally.

Stir in remaining ingredients. (No need to thaw frozen vegetables.) Simmer, covered, for 20 minutes, or until vegetables are tender.

Calories 56	Total Fat 1 g	Fiber 1 g
Protein 7 g	Saturated 0 g	Sodium 46 mg
Carbohydrates 6 g	Polyunsaturated 0 g	Potassium 227 mg
Cholesterol 13 mg	Monounsaturated 0 g	Calcium 20 mg

Vegetable Beef Soup

Serves 6 • 1 cup per serving

Here's a comforting and effortless way to work toward your five or more servings of vegetables a day.

Vegetable oil spray
- ½ cup chopped onion
- ½ cup diced celery
- ½ cup sliced carrots
- 1½ teaspoons chopped fresh oregano or ½ teaspoon dried oregano, crumbled
- 2 medium cloves garlic, minced, or 1 teaspoon bottled minced garlic
- ½ teaspoon dried thyme, crumbled
- 4 cups Beef Broth (page 22) or commercial low-sodium broth
- 1 cup chopped cooked lean roast beef, all visible fat removed
- ½ cup cut fresh or frozen no-salt-added green beans
- 1 medium tomato, chopped (about ½ cup)
  Pepper to taste

Spray a Dutch oven or large saucepan with vegetable oil spray. Cook onion, celery, carrots, oregano, garlic, and thyme over medium heat for 3 to 4 minutes, or until onion is translucent, stirring occasionally.

Add remaining ingredients. Reduce heat and simmer, covered, for 30 minutes, or until vegetables are tender.

Cook's Tip on Thickening Soup: To thicken and enrich most kinds of soup, either add some vegetables if none are called for or add more vegetables than the recipe specifies. Once they've cooked, remove some or all of the vegetables from the soup and puree them in a food processor or a blender, adding a little liquid if needed. Mix the pureed vegetables back into the soup.

Calories 70	Total Fat 2 g	Fiber 1 g
Protein 9 g	Saturated 1 g	Sodium 49 mg
Carbohydrates 5 g	Polyunsaturated 0 g	Potassium 314 mg
Cholesterol 20 mg	Monounsaturated 1 g	Calcium 27 mg

Salads &
Salad Dressings

garden coleslaw

cucumber raita

balsamic-marinated vegetables

granny apple and cranberry salad

mediterranean couscous

cilantro couscous

macaroni salad

summer pasta salad

southwestern black-eyed pea salad

red-potato salad

waldorf tuna salad

sole salad

spicy shrimp salad

chicken salad

balsamic vinaigrette

cider vinaigrette

italian dressing

russian dressing

tomato french dressing

ranch dressing with fresh herbs

creamy black pepper and garlic dressing

thousand island dressing

lemon and poppy seed dressing

orange-yogurt dressing

apricot-yogurt dressing

Garden Coleslaw

Serves 7 • ½ cup per serving

Because it doesn't contain mayonnaise, this slaw is a good picnic dish. It keeps well in the refrigerator for several days, so you can make it in advance.

Slaw

	10-ounce package shredded cabbage (8 to 9 cups)
½	cup chopped onion
½	large green bell pepper, sliced into thin strips (about ½ cup)
½	cup shredded carrot

Dressing

3	to 4 tablespoons sugar
⅜	cup white vinegar
2½	tablespoons water
1½	tablespoons acceptable vegetable oil
	Pepper to taste

For slaw, in a large bowl, stir together all ingredients.

For dressing, in a small bowl, whisk together all ingredients. Pour over slaw. Toss to combine well. Cover and refrigerate for at least 1 hour before serving, if possible, to let the flavors develop.

Calories 73	Total Fat 3 g	Fiber 2 g
Protein 1 g	Saturated 0 g	Sodium 11 mg
Carbohydrates 12 g	Polyunsaturated 1 g	Potassium 166 mg
Cholesterol 0 mg	Monounsaturated 2 g	Calcium 25 mg

Cucumber Raita

Serves 10 • ¹/₂ cup per serving

You can prepare this delightful Indian-inspired raita (RI-tah) up to two hours ahead of time. Try serving it with a spicy entrée for contrast or using it to top Poached Salmon (page 75).

    3   cups fat-free or low-fat plain yogurt
    2   medium cucumbers, peeled, seeded, and finely diced (about
        2 cups)
    2   green onions (green and white parts), finely chopped
   ¹/₈ teaspoon cayenne

In a medium bowl, whisk yogurt until smooth.

Whisk in remaining ingredients. Cover and refrigerate until ready to serve.

Cook's Tip: Use 1 English cucumber instead of 2 medium cucumbers and skip the peeling and seeding steps. English, or hothouse, cucumbers are long and slender and are tightly wrapped in plastic. They don't require peeling and are virtually seedless. Remove the plastic before storing in the refrigerator so they will keep longer.

Calories 47	Total Fat 0 g	Fiber 0 g
Protein 5 g	Saturated 0 g	Sodium 57 mg
Carbohydrates 7 g	Polyunsaturated 0 g	Potassium 254 mg
Cholesterol 1 mg	Monounsaturated 0 g	Calcium 154 mg

Balsamic-Marinated Vegetables

Serves 5 • 1 cup per serving

Even your vegetable-phobes will love this. It's pretty, quick to prepare, and tastes divine. Vary vegetables and dressings for different flavors.

1½	cups diced raw broccoli florets
1½	cups diced raw cauliflower florets
1	medium zucchini, sliced (about 1 cup)
12	baby carrots, sliced (about 1 cup)
½	cup matchstick-size slices yellow onion
1	recipe Balsamic Vinaigrette (page 59) or 1 cup low-fat, low-sodium Italian dressing

Combine broccoli, cauliflower, zucchini, carrots, and onion in a large glass or ceramic bowl.

Pour dressing over vegetables, stirring well. Cover and refrigerate for 6 to 24 hours, stirring occasionally.

Calories 50	Total Fat 3 g	Fiber 1 g
Protein 1 g	Saturated 0 g	Sodium 17 mg
Carbohydrates 6 g	Polyunsaturated 1 g	Potassium 195 mg
Cholesterol 0 mg	Monounsaturated 2 g	Calcium 21 mg

Granny Apple and Cranberry Salad

Serves 6 • ¹/₂ cup per serving

Refreshing and crunchy, this fruit salad makes a good brunch dish with Turkey Sausage Patties (page 125).

    2   tablespoons chopped pecans
    2   Granny Smith apples, cut into ¹/₄-inch pieces (about 1¹/₂ cups)
    ¹/₂   cup sweetened dried cranberries
    ¹/₂   teaspoon grated orange zest
    ¹/₄   cup fresh orange juice
    ¹/₄   teaspoon ground cinnamon

Heat a large nonstick skillet over medium-high heat. Add pecans and cook for 2 to 5 minutes, or until just browned and fragrant, stirring frequently. Remove skillet from heat and set aside to let pecans cool.

In a medium bowl, stir together all ingredients. Serve immediately for peak flavor.

Cook's Tip on Apples: Chop the apples up to 2 hours in advance, then stir in 1 to 2 teaspoons of fresh lemon juice to keep them from turning brown.

Calories 81	Total Fat 2 g	Fiber 3 g
Protein 0 g	Saturated 0 g	Sodium 0 mg
Carbohydrates 17 g	Polyunsaturated 1 g	Potassium 97 mg
Cholesterol 0 mg	Monounsaturated 1 g	Calcium 5 mg

Mediterranean Couscous

Serves 7 • ½ cup per serving

Couscous is a quick-cooking Moroccan staple made of coarsely ground wheat. Try serving it hot or cold.

⅓	cup uncooked couscous
	14.5-ounce can artichoke quarters, drained and chopped
4	ounces Italian plum tomatoes, chopped (about 1 cup)
½	medium cucumber, peeled and diced (about ½ cup)
2	tablespoons finely chopped red onion
2	tablespoons snipped fresh parsley
2	tablespoons fresh lemon juice
1	tablespoon chopped fresh oregano or 1 teaspoon dried, crumbled
1	tablespoon minced fresh mint or 1 teaspoon dried, crumbled
1	ounce blue cheese, crumbled

Cook couscous using package directions, omitting salt. Fluff with a fork and set aside to cool.

Meanwhile, in a medium bowl, stir together remaining ingredients except blue cheese. Gently stir in cooled couscous, then blue cheese. Serve immediately for peak flavor.

Cilantro Couscous

Substitute radishes for onion; 2 tablespoons snipped fresh cilantro for oregano and mint; and 2.25-ounce can sliced black olives, rinsed and drained, for cheese. Add 2 to 3 drops red hot-pepper sauce (optional).

MEDITERRANEAN COUSCOUS

Calories 68	Total Fat 1 g	Fiber 1 g
Protein 3 g	Saturated 1 g	Sodium 151 mg
Carbohydrates 11 g	Polyunsaturated 0 g	Potassium 104 mg
Cholesterol 3 mg	Monounsaturated 1 g	Calcium 33 mg

CILANTRO COUSCOUS

Calories 62	Total Fat 1 g	Fiber 1 g
Protein 2 g	Saturated 0 g	Sodium 168 mg
Carbohydrates 11 g	Polyunsaturated 0 g	Potassium 92 mg
Cholesterol 0 mg	Monounsaturated 1 g	Calcium 16 mg

Macaroni Salad

Serves 4 • ¹/₂ cup per serving

Lemon Chicken with Oregano (page 119) is a great mate for this traditional favorite, made low in fat. Add some grilled asparagus for a springtime treat.

> 1   cup dried macaroni

Dressing

> 2   tablespoons fat-free, cholesterol-free or low-fat mayonnaise dressing
> 2   tablespoons fat-free or low-fat plain yogurt
> 1   tablespoon sugar
> 2   teaspoons cider vinegar
> ¹/₈   teaspoon pepper

> ¹/₄   cup chopped cucumber
> ¹/₄   cup chopped celery
> 2   radishes, sliced
> 1   tablespoon finely chopped onion

Cook macaroni using package directions, omitting salt and oil. Drain well.

For dressing, in a small bowl, whisk together all ingredients.

In a large bowl, stir together macaroni, dressing, and remaining ingredients. Cover and refrigerate for at least 3 hours before serving.

Calories 125	Total Fat 1 g	Fiber 1 g
Protein 4 g	Saturated 0 g	Sodium 75 mg
Carbohydrates 26 g	Polyunsaturated 0 g	Potassium 111 mg
Cholesterol 0 mg	Monounsaturated 0 g	Calcium 26 mg

Summer Pasta Salad

Serves 10 • ½ cup per serving

Crisp, colorful vegetables highlight this salad, perfect for a picnic.

1½	cups dried pasta spirals (about 4 ounces)
1½	cups broccoli florets
½	cup sliced carrots
1	cup sliced yellow summer squash

Dressing

3	tablespoons chopped fresh basil leaves or 1 tablespoon dried, crumbled
3	tablespoons cider vinegar
1	tablespoon extra-virgin olive oil
2	medium cloves garlic, minced, or 1 teaspoon bottled minced garlic
¼	teaspoon pepper
2	tablespoons shredded or grated Parmesan cheese
⅛	teaspoon salt

In a stockpot or large saucepan, cook pasta using package directions, omitting salt and oil. When pasta has cooked for 4 minutes, add broccoli and carrots and cook for 1 minute, then add squash and cook for 30 seconds. Immediately drain in colander and run under cold water to cool quickly. Set aside.

For dressing, in a large bowl, whisk together all ingredients.

Stir pasta mixture into dressing.

Sprinkle with Parmesan and salt and toss gently. Refrigerate for 15 minutes to 4 hours before serving.

Calories 166	Total Fat 2 g	Fiber 1 g
Protein 2 g	Saturated 0 g	Sodium 59 mg
Carbohydrates 10 g	Polyunsaturated 0 g	Potassium 96 mg
Cholesterol 1 mg	Monounsaturated 1 g	Calcium 31 mg

Southwestern Black-Eyed Pea Salad

Serves 10 • ½ cup per serving

A popular dish in the Lone Star State, where it is called Texas Caviar, this flavorful salad is sure to become a favorite in your household, too. Even people who "don't like" black-eyed peas like them prepared this way.

½ cup diced green bell pepper
¼ cup diced white onion
2 tablespoons finely chopped fresh jalapeño, stem, seeds, and
   membrane ribs removed
3 tablespoons red wine vinegar
1 tablespoon acceptable vegetable oil
1 tablespoon water
1 medium clove garlic, minced, or ½ teaspoon bottled minced
   garlic
¼ teaspoon pepper
3 15.5-ounce cans no-salt-added black-eyed peas, rinsed and
   drained, or 3 10-ounce packages no-salt-added frozen black-
   eyed peas, cooked according to package directions

In a medium bowl, stir together all ingredients except peas.
Stir in peas. Chill for 2 to 24 hours before serving.

Cook's Tip on Canned Black-Eyed Peas: For more flavor, look
for canned no-salt-added "fresh" black-eyed peas rather than canned "dried" peas.

Calories 128	Total Fat 1 g	Fiber 5 g
Protein 7 g	Saturated 0 g	Sodium 1 mg
Carbohydrates 21 g	Polyunsaturated 0 g	Potassium 333 mg
Cholesterol 0 mg	Monounsaturated 1 g	Calcium 42 mg

Red-Potato Salad

Serves 9 • ¹/₂ cup per serving

An ingredient key to great potato salad is the right amount of mustard. Since prepared mustard is usually high in sodium, we used our own recipe. You could use dry mustard instead.

1¹/₂	to 2 pounds red potatoes, cooked and diced (about 5 medium)
1	or 2 medium ribs celery with leaves, chopped (about ³/₄ cup)
6	medium radishes, sliced (about ¹/₂ cup)
2	green onions, sliced (green and white parts)

Dressing

3	tablespoons fat-free or low-fat sour cream
2¹/₂	tablespoons vinegar
2	tablespoons fat-free, cholesterol-free or low-fat mayonnaise dressing
2	tablespoons fat-free or low-fat plain yogurt
1	tablespoon sugar
1	tablespoon Hot Mustard (page 216) or 1 teaspoon dry mustard
¹/₂	teaspoon celery seeds (optional)
¹/₄	teaspoon pepper
¹/₄	teaspoon turmeric

In a large bowl, combine potatoes, celery, radishes, and green onions.

In a small bowl, whisk together dressing ingredients. Pour into potato mixture, stirring gently to mix well. Cover and chill for about 2 hours before serving.

Calories 102	Total Fat 0 g	Fiber 2 g
Protein 2 g	Saturated 0 g	Sodium 46 mg
Carbohydrates 23 g	Polyunsaturated 0 g	Potassium 359 mg
Cholesterol 1 mg	Monounsaturated 0 g	Calcium 27 mg

Waldorf Tuna Salad

Serves 2 • ¾ cup per serving

Use this tuna salad as a filling for sandwiches, or serve it on lettuce with low-fat, low-sodium crackers.

>   6-ounce can no-salt-added tuna, packed in spring water or
>   distilled water, rinsed and drained
> ½ cup chopped unpeeled red apple
> ½ cup chopped celery
> 3 tablespoons fat-free, cholesterol-free or low-fat mayonnaise
>   dressing
> ½ to 1 teaspoon curry powder (optional)

In a medium bowl, flake tuna with a fork.

Stir in remaining ingredients. Serve immediately or cover and refrigerate for 1 to 3 hours before serving.

Calories 153	Total Fat 3 g	Fiber 1 g
Protein 21 g	Saturated 1 g	Sodium 249 mg
Carbohydrates 10 g	Polyunsaturated 1 g	Potassium 329 mg
Cholesterol 36 mg	Monounsaturated 1 g	Calcium 25 mg

Sole Salad

Serves 2 • 1 cup per serving

*It isn't a mistake—you really do use unthawed, uncooked frozen
vegetables in this dish. They add a pleasant crunch to the salad,
which you can eat as is or use to stuff a tomato or top either a plate of
baby greens or some sliced tomatoes on a lettuce leaf.*

1½   cups water
½   pound sole, orange roughy, or other mild fish fillets
¾   cup frozen mixed vegetables
1   rib celery, chopped (about ½ cup)
1   or 2 green onions, thinly sliced (green part only)
2   tablespoons fat-free, cholesterol-free or low-fat mayonnaise
     dressing
1   tablespoon orange juice
¼   teaspoon dried dillweed, crumbled
     Pepper to taste

In a medium skillet, bring water to a boil over high heat. Cook fish,
covered, for 5 minutes, or until fish flakes easily when tested with
a fork.

Meanwhile, in a medium bowl, combine remaining ingredients.

Drain fish in a colander and let cool for 1 minute. Add to vegetable
mixture and stir well, using a fork to break up fish evenly.

Calories 187	Total Fat 2 g	Fiber 4 g
Protein 24 g	Saturated 0 g	Sodium 273 mg
Carbohydrates 18 g	Polyunsaturated 0 g	Potassium 704 mg
Cholesterol 54 mg	Monounsaturated 0 g	Calcium 60 mg

Spicy Shrimp Salad

Serves 5 • about ³/₄ cup per serving

Forget what you think about shrimp salad. This one is shrimp with dressing, not the other way around. It's fairly spicy, but you can vary the pepper and cayenne to suit your own palate.

Dressing

¹/₂	cup fat-free, cholesterol-free or low-fat mayonnaise dressing
¹/₃	cup chopped red or green bell pepper
¹/₄	cup chopped green onions (green and white parts)
¹/₄	cup snipped fresh parsley
2	tablespoons snipped fresh dillweed or 2 teaspoons dried, crumbled
2	tablespoons lemon juice
1	medium clove garlic, minced, or ¹/₂ teaspoon bottled minced garlic
¹/₈	to ¹/₄ teaspoon pepper
¹/₈	to ¹/₄ teaspoon cayenne
12	ounces shelled, deveined cooked shrimp

For dressing, in a medium bowl, stir together all ingredients.

Gently stir in shrimp, thoroughly coating with dressing. Cover and refrigerate for 1 to 24 hours before serving.

Calories 100	Total Fat 1 g	Fiber 1 g
Protein 15 g	Saturated 0 g	Sodium 348 mg
Carbohydrates 7 g	Polyunsaturated 0 g	Potassium 194 mg
Cholesterol 133 mg	Monounsaturated 0 g	Calcium 34 mg

Chicken Salad

Serves 5 • ½ cup per serving

*The celery and green onions give this versatile salad a crunch and a
fresh taste that will make you want to use it wherever you can—to
stuff a tomato, fill a sandwich, or provide protein on a salad plate.*

Salad

> 15-ounce can no-salt-added chicken breast, canned in water,
> drained
> ½   cup chopped celery (1 to 2 ribs)
> ½   cup chopped green onions (green and white parts)

Dressing

> ½   cup fat-free, cholesterol-free or low-fat mayonnaise dressing
> ½   teaspoon Dijon mustard
> ¼   teaspoon ground ginger
> ¼   teaspoon pepper

For salad, process chicken in a food processor or blender until shredded. Put in a medium bowl.

Process celery until finely chopped and add with green onions to chicken.

In a small bowl, whisk together dressing ingredients. Pour over chicken mixture and stir until well combined. Serve immediately, or cover and refrigerate.

Cook's Tip: Garnish this salad with any of the following: seedless grapes, cut in half; pineapple chunks; Sweet Bread-and-Butter Pickles (page 220); or tomato wedges.

Calories 122	Total Fat 2 g	Fiber 1 g
Protein 18 g	Saturated 0 g	Sodium 270 mg
Carbohydrates 6 g	Polyunsaturated 1 g	Potassium 191 mg
Cholesterol 38 mg	Monounsaturated 1 g	Calcium 6 mg

Balsamic Vinaigrette

Makes 1¼ cups • Serves 10 • 2 tablespoons per serving

When tomatoes are at their peak, drizzle some with a little of this dressing for a salad that's simple perfection. It's also very good on cooked or chilled raw vegetables.

  ½ cup water
  ¼ cup plus 2 tablespoons balsamic vinegar
  ¼ cup finely snipped fresh parsley
  2 tablespoons acceptable vegetable oil
  ½ teaspoon pepper

In a jar with a tight-fitting lid, combine all ingredients. Shake well and refrigerate.

Cook's Tip: This and most other vinaigrette dressings make great marinades for beef, seafood, poultry, and vegetables to be grilled or broiled.

Calories 33	Total Fat 3 g	Fiber 0 g
Protein 0 g	Saturated 0 g	Sodium 4 mg
Carbohydrates 2 g	Polyunsaturated 1 g	Potassium 16 mg
Cholesterol 0 mg	Monounsaturated 2 g	Calcium 4 mg

Cider Vinaigrette

Makes 1 cup • Serves 8 • 2 tablespoons per serving

Fresh lemon juice and garlic intensify the flavor of this dressing. With it and the variations below, you'll be able to complement many different types of salad.

⅓   cup cider vinegar
¼   cup fresh lemon juice (1 to 2 medium lemons)
3   tablespoons water
2   tablespoons acceptable vegetable oil
1½   tablespoons Dijon mustard
2½   teaspoons sugar
2   medium cloves garlic, minced, or 1 teaspoon bottled minced garlic
½   teaspoon pepper

In a jar with a tight-fitting lid, combine all ingredients. Shake well and refrigerate.

For each variation below, follow the same instructions.

Italian Dressing
Makes 1 cup • Serves 8 • 2 tablespoons per serving

1   recipe Cider Vinaigrette
1   teaspoon dried basil, crumbled
1   teaspoon dried oregano, crumbled

Russian Dressing
Makes 1¼ cups • Serves 10 • 2 tablespoons per serving

1   recipe Cider Vinaigrette
2   tablespoons no-salt-added tomato paste
1   tablespoon finely chopped green bell pepper
¼   teaspoon Chili Powder (page 225) or commercial no-salt-added chili powder
⅛   teaspoon onion powder
    Dash of red hot-pepper sauce

Tomato French Dressing
Makes 1¼ cups • Serves 10 • 2 tablespoons per serving

1   recipe Cider Vinaigrette
3   tablespoons no-salt-added tomato paste
2   teaspoons sugar
1   tablespoon dried minced onion

CIDER VINAIGRETTE

Calories 42	Total Fat 3 g	Fiber 0 g
Protein 0 g	Saturated 0 g	Sodium 70 mg
Carbohydrates 2 g	Polyunsaturated 1 g	Potassium 25 mg
Cholesterol 0 mg	Monounsaturated 2 g	Calcium 7 mg

ITALIAN DRESSING

Calories 43	Total Fat 3 g	Fiber 0 g
Protein 0 g	Saturated 0 g	Sodium 70 mg
Carbohydrates 3 g	Polyunsaturated 1 g	Potassium 35 mg
Cholesterol 0 mg	Monounsaturated 2 g	Calcium 14 mg

RUSSIAN DRESSING

Calories 37	Total Fat 3 g	Fiber 0 g
Protein 0 g	Saturated 0 g	Sodium 59 mg
Carbohydrates 3 g	Polyunsaturated 1 g	Potassium 54 mg
Cholesterol 0 mg	Monounsaturated 2 g	Calcium 7 mg

TOMATO FRENCH DRESSING

Calories 42	Total Fat 3 g	Fiber 0 g
Protein 0 g	Saturated 0 g	Sodium 60 mg
Carbohydrates 4 g	Polyunsaturated 1 g	Potassium 72 mg
Cholesterol 0 mg	Monounsaturated 2 g	Calcium 8 mg

Ranch Dressing with Fresh Herbs

Makes 1½ cups • Serves 12 • 2 tablespoons per serving

Fresh dillweed and parsley perk up this low-salt version of a classic.

1	cup fat-free or low-fat buttermilk
½	cup nonfat or light sour cream
1	tablespoon snipped fresh dillweed or 1 teaspoon dried, crumbled
1	tablespoon snipped fresh parsley or 1 teaspoon dried, crumbled
1	tablespoon Dijon mustard
2	teaspoons dried minced onion
¼	teaspoon garlic powder
¼	teaspoon pepper

In a jar with a tight-fitting lid, combine all ingredients. Shake well to blend. Refrigerate for at least 2 hours to allow flavors to blend.

Calories 23	Total Fat 0 g	Fiber 0 g
Protein 2 g	Saturated 0 g	Sodium 62 mg
Carbohydrates 3 g	Polyunsaturated 0 g	Potassium 63 mg
Cholesterol 2 mg	Monounsaturated 0 g	Calcium 40 mg

Creamy Black Pepper and Garlic Dressing

Makes 1 cup • Serves 16 • 1 tablespoon per serving

The black pepper gives this dressing a surprising kick that contrasts with its creamy texture.

½ cup fat-free, cholesterol-free or low-fat mayonnaise dressing
½ cup fat-free milk
1 tablespoon plus 2 teaspoons cider vinegar
1 teaspoon pepper
1 medium clove garlic, minced, or ½ teaspoon bottled minced
garlic

In a small bowl, whisk together all ingredients. Cover or transfer to a jar with a tight-fitting lid and refrigerate.

Calories 16	Total Fat 1 g	Fiber 0 g
Protein 0 g	Saturated 0 g	Sodium 74 mg
Carbohydrates 3 g	Polyunsaturated 0 g	Potassium 16 mg
Cholesterol 0 mg	Monounsaturated 0 g	Calcium 10 mg

Thousand Island Dressing

Makes 1¼ cups • Serves 20 • 1 tablespoon per serving

*Creamy and just a wee bit spicy, this classic dressing will perk up
your salad creations.*

½	cup fat-free or low-fat plain yogurt
½	cup Chili Sauce (page 213) or ½ cup no-salt-added ketchup plus dash of red hot-pepper sauce
2	tablespoons fat-free, cholesterol-free or low-fat mayonnaise dressing
	White of 1 large hard-cooked egg, finely chopped
1	tablespoon finely chopped green bell pepper
1	tablespoon finely chopped celery
¼	teaspoon onion powder
	Dash of pepper

In a small bowl, whisk together all ingredients. Transfer to a jar with
a tight-fitting lid and refrigerate.

Calories 13	Total Fat 0 g	Fiber 0 g
Protein 1 g	Saturated 0 g	Sodium 21 mg
Carbohydrates 3 g	Polyunsaturated 0 g	Potassium 55 mg
Cholesterol 0 mg	Monounsaturated 0 g	Calcium 14 mg

Lemon and Poppy Seed Dressing

Makes 1 cup • Serves 8 • 2 tablespoons per serving

Remember this recipe for your summertime luncheons. The tangy-sweet flavor of this dressing is an ideal accent for juicy chunks of cantaloupe and honeydew melon.

½   cup frozen lemonade concentrate, thawed and undiluted
⅓   cup honey
1   tablespoon plus 2 teaspoons acceptable vegetable oil
1   teaspoon poppy seeds

In a small mixing bowl, whisk together all ingredients. Transfer to a jar with a tight-fitting lid and refrigerate.

Cook's Tip on Poppy Seeds: Because they contain so much oil, poppy seeds tend to become rancid quickly. Store them in an airtight container in the refrigerator for up to six months.

Calories 103	Total Fat 3 g	Fiber 0 g
Protein 0 g	Saturated 0 g	Sodium 1 mg
Carbohydrates 20 g	Polyunsaturated 1 g	Potassium 22 mg
Cholesterol 0 mg	Monounsaturated 2 g	Calcium 7 mg

Orange-Yogurt Dressing

Makes 1¼ cups • Serves 20 • 1 tablespoon per serving

Both versions of this dressing are particularly delicious served over fresh melon or fresh pineapple.

    1   cup fat-free or low-fat plain yogurt
    ¼   cup orange juice
    1   teaspoon honey

In a small bowl, whisk together all ingredients until well blended. Cover and refrigerate.

Apricot-Yogurt Dressing
Makes 1¼ cups • Serves 20 • 1 tablespoon per serving

Substitute ¼ cup all-fruit apricot spread and ½ teaspoon vanilla extract for orange juice, and increase honey to 2 teaspoons.

ORANGE-YOGURT DRESSING		
Calories 9	Total Fat 0 g	Fiber 0 g
Protein 1 g	Saturated 0 g	Sodium 9 mg
Carbohydrates 2 g	Polyunsaturated 0 g	Potassium 38 mg
Cholesterol 0 mg	Monounsaturated 0 g	Calcium 25 mg

APRICOT-YOGURT DRESSING		
Calories 14	Total Fat 0 g	Fiber 0 g
Protein 1 g	Saturated 0 g	Sodium 10 mg
Carbohydrates 3 g	Polyunsaturated 0 g	Potassium 35 mg
Cholesterol 0 mg	Monounsaturated 0 g	Calcium 26 mg

Seafood

oven-fried fish

spicy baked fish

fish steaks with thyme

mediterranean fish fillets

orange roughy roulade

southern fish fillets

poached salmon

grilled salmon fillet with fresh herbs

grilled marinated shark

cajun snapper

herbed fillet of sole

sole with vegetables and dijon dill sauce

creole tuna steak sandwich with caper tartar sauce

tuna penne casserole

scallops and bok choy with balsamic sauce

grilled shrimp on lemongrass skewers

shrimp and pasta with spinach and lemony cream sauce

risotto with shrimp and vegetables

spanish-style crab and vegetable tortilla

Oven-Fried Fish

Serves 4 • about 3 ounces per serving

The answer to your fried-fish cravings, this oven-fried version is golden brown and crispy, yet easy on your heart and oh so easy to clean up.

        Vegetable oil spray
1½   *tablespoons acceptable stick margarine, melted*
1   *tablespoon lemon juice*
½   *teaspoon dried basil, crumbled*
¼   *teaspoon salt*
¼   *teaspoon pepper*
¼   *teaspoon paprika*
⅛   *teaspoon garlic powder*
11   *fat-free, low-sodium saltine crackers, crushed (about ½ cup)*
4   *flounder, sole, or cod fillets (about 4 ounces each)*
1   *medium lemon, cut into 4 wedges*

Preheat oven to 475° F. Lightly spray a nonstick baking sheet with vegetable oil spray.

In a shallow bowl, combine margarine, lemon juice, basil, salt, pepper, paprika, and garlic powder.

Put cracker crumbs in a separate shallow bowl.

Dip fish in margarine mixture, then roll in cracker crumbs, coating well. Arrange fish in a single layer on baking sheet. Spoon remaining margarine mixture evenly over fish.

Bake, uncovered, for 15 minutes, or until fish flakes easily when tested with a fork. Serve with lemon wedges.

Calories 166	Total Fat 5 g	Fiber 1 g
Protein 20 g	Saturated 1 g	Sodium 327 mg
Carbohydrates 9 g	Polyunsaturated 2 g	Potassium 317 mg
Cholesterol 53 mg	Monounsaturated 2 g	Calcium 26 mg

Spicy Baked Fish

Serves 4 • about 3 ounces per serving

A whole-wheat crumb and parsley crust, and just a few drops of hot-pepper sauce, provide a refreshing flavor change to baked fish.

1	cup soft whole-wheat bread crumbs (2 slices bread)
	Vegetable oil spray
¼	cup snipped fresh parsley
½	teaspoon pepper
2	tablespoons fat-free, cholesterol-free or low-fat mayonnaise dressing
1	tablespoon water
4	drops red hot-pepper sauce
1	pound fish fillets, such as cod, haddock, flounder, or sole
4	lemon wedges (optional)

Preheat oven to 350° F.

In a food processor or blender, process bread crumbs until very fine. Sprinkle crumbs on an ungreased baking sheet.

Bake for 5 to 7 minutes, or until lightly browned. Transfer to a medium shallow bowl. Increase temperature to 450° F. Spray baking sheet with vegetable oil spray.

Stir parsley and pepper into bread crumbs.

In another shallow bowl, whisk together mayonnaise, water, and hot-pepper sauce.

Dip fish in mayonnaise mixture, then roll in bread crumbs.

Bake on baking sheet for 17 to 18 minutes, or until fish flakes easily when tested with a fork. Serve with lemon wedges.

Calories 137	Total Fat 1 g	Fiber 1 g
Protein 22 g	Saturated 0 g	Sodium 198 mg
Carbohydrates 8 g	Polyunsaturated 0 g	Potassium 530 mg
Cholesterol 49 mg	Monounsaturated 0 g	Calcium 35 mg

Fish Steaks with Thyme

Serves 4 • 3 ounces per serving

You'll have time to make a salad and steam some broccoli while the fish marinates.

2	tablespoons lemon juice
1	tablespoon dried parsley, crumbled
2	teaspoons olive oil
1	teaspoon dried thyme, crumbled
½	teaspoon pepper
4	fish steaks, such as tuna or shark (about 4 ounces each)
	Vegetable oil spray

In a small bowl, stir together lemon juice, parsley, oil, thyme, and pepper.

Rub fish with lemon juice mixture. Cover and refrigerate for 30 to 60 minutes.

Lightly spray grill rack with vegetable oil spray. Preheat grill to medium-high. Put fish steaks on grill at least 6 inches from heat. For tuna, cook for 3 to 5 minutes on each side, or until desired doneness. (For other fish, cook for 4 to 5 minutes on each side, or until fish is opaque or flakes easily when tested with a fork.)

Cook's Tip on Grilling Fish: For an attractive crosshatch pattern, grill fish for about one quarter of the total grilling time. Rotate the fish 90 degrees, and grill for about one quarter of the total grilling time. Turn fish over and repeat.

Calories 147	Total Fat 3 g	Fiber 0 g
Protein 27 g	Saturated 1 g	Sodium 44 mg
Carbohydrates 1 g	Polyunsaturated 1 g	Potassium 531 mg
Cholesterol 51 mg	Monounsaturated 2 g	Calcium 28 mg

Mediterranean Fish Fillets

Serves 6 • about 3 ounces per serving

*Squeezing fresh lemon juice directly on the fish provides a subtle
flavor that will please your palate.*

	Olive oil spray
6	cod fillets (about 4 ounces each)
	Juice of 1 medium lemon (about 3 tablespoons)
1/8	teaspoon pepper
2	large fresh tomatoes, sliced 1/4 inch thick (about 3 cups)
1/2	medium green bell pepper, finely chopped (about 1/3 cup)
2	tablespoons capers packed in balsamic vinegar, rinsed and drained
1/4	cup dry bread crumbs
1	tablespoon olive oil
1 1/2	teaspoons dried basil, crumbled

Preheat oven to 350° F. Lightly spray a nonstick rimmed pan (such as
a jelly-roll pan) with olive oil spray.

Put fish in pan and drizzle with lemon juice.

Sprinkle with pepper and top with tomato slices, bell pepper, and
capers.

In a small bowl, stir together remaining ingredients. Sprinkle over fish.

Bake, uncovered, for 25 minutes, or until fish flakes easily when
tested with a fork.

Calories 139	Total Fat 3 g	Fiber 1 g
Protein 20 g	Saturated 1 g	Sodium 227 mg
Carbohydrates 8 g	Polyunsaturated 1 g	Potassium 594 mg
Cholesterol 37 mg	Monounsaturated 2 g	Calcium 26 mg

Orange Roughy Roulade

Serves 4 • 1 fillet per serving

If you're looking for a spectacular yet trouble-free dish to prepare for company, this is definitely the recipe for compliments.

	Vegetable oil spray
4	cups water
4	green onions, cut into 4-inch pieces (starting from bulb end)
½	medium red bell pepper, cut into 4 × ⅛-inch strips
½	medium carrot, cut into 4 × ⅛-inch strips
½	teaspoon paprika
¼	teaspoon salt
¼	teaspoon pepper
4	orange roughy fillets (about 4 ounces each)
1	medium lime, cut into 4 wedges
2	teaspoons extra-virgin olive oil

Sauce

⅓	cup fat-free or low-fat plain yogurt
2	tablespoons low-fat or fat-free, cholesterol-free mayonnaise dressing
1	teaspoon Hot Mustard (page 216) or commercial honey mustard
1	teaspoon fat-free milk
¾	teaspoon chopped fresh tarragon or ¼ teaspoon dried, crumbled
2	teaspoons extra-virgin olive oil
2	tablespoons finely chopped green onions (green part only)

Preheat oven to 350° F. Spray a 12 × 8 × 2-inch glass baking dish with vegetable oil spray.

In a medium saucepan, bring 4 cups water to a boil over high heat. Meanwhile, fill a medium bowl with ice water. Put green onions, bell pepper, and carrot in saucepan and boil for 1 minute, or just until tender-crisp. Using a slotted spoon, immediately transfer vegetables to ice water. Let stand for 1 to 2 minutes, or until completely cooled. Transfer with slotted spoon to paper towels; let drain thoroughly.

In a small bowl, stir together paprika, salt, and pepper.

Place one fillet on a plate. Squeeze one lime wedge over fillet and sprinkle with ¼ teaspoon paprika mixture. Turn fillet over.

Leaving a ½-inch edge on narrow end, place crosswise on fillet 1 green onion, 1 bell pepper strip, and 1 carrot strip. Roll up jelly-roll style. Repeat with remaining fillets. Place rolled fillets with seam side down in baking dish. Spoon ½ teaspoon olive oil over each fillet.

Bake for 20 to 25 minutes, or until fish flakes easily when tested with a fork and center is opaque.

Meanwhile, for sauce, in a small saucepan, whisk together yogurt, mayonnaise, mustard, milk, and tarragon until smooth. Cook over medium-low heat for 2 to 3 minutes, or until thoroughly heated, whisking frequently. Do not allow to boil. Remove from heat.

Whisk in 2 teaspoons olive oil. Cover with aluminum foil to keep warm.

To serve, pour 2 tablespoons sauce in center of each of four dinner plates. Tilt each plate and swirl sauce or use back of a spoon to spread sauce into 5-inch circle. Place a rolled fillet in center of sauce on each plate; sprinkle each fillet with 1½ teaspoons green onions.

Cook's Tip on Extra-Virgin Olive Oil: Extra-virgin olive oil is considered to be the finest and fruitiest of all olive oils. It is available in a variety of colors from a crystalline champagne color to bright green. For a more intense olive flavor, choose an oil that is deeper in color.

Calories 161	Total Fat 6 g	Fiber 1 g
Protein 19 g	Saturated 1 g	Sodium 309 mg
Carbohydrates 8 g	Polyunsaturated 1 g	Potassium 508 mg
Cholesterol 23 mg	Monounsaturated 4 g	Calcium 91 mg

Southern Fish Fillets

Serves 4 • about 3 ounces per serving

This fish will remind you of an old-fashioned fish fry. Try it with Green Beans and Corn (page 183) and Drop Biscuits (page 246), which can bake at the same time.

	Vegetable oil spray
1	pound fish fillets, such as orange roughy, perch, or crappie
1/2	teaspoon pepper
1/2	cup fat-free milk
4	drops red hot-pepper sauce
1/2	cup cornmeal
1/4	cup minced fresh parsley
1	teaspoon dried tarragon, crumbled
1/4	teaspoon cayenne
4	lemon wedges (optional)

Preheat oven to 450° F. Lightly spray a 13 × 9 × 2-inch baking dish with vegetable oil spray.

Sprinkle fish with pepper.

In a shallow bowl, combine milk and hot-pepper sauce.

In a separate shallow bowl, combine remaining ingredients except lemon wedges. Dip fish in milk mixture, then roll in cornmeal mixture. Place in baking dish.

Bake for 15 to 17 minutes, or until fish flakes easily when tested with a fork. Serve with lemon wedges.

Calories 156	Total Fat 1 g	Fiber 2 g
Protein 20 g	Saturated 0 g	Sodium 91 mg
Carbohydrates 16 g	Polyunsaturated 0 g	Potassium 456 mg
Cholesterol 23 mg	Monounsaturated 1 g	Calcium 84 mg

Poached Salmon

Serves 4 • about 3 ounces per serving

This fresh salmon is so quick and easy that it will become an on-the-go favorite. The hint of cloves gives it a distinctive flavor. For a change of taste, try topping it with Yogurt Dill Sauce (page 207).

> *1-pound salmon fillet (1 to 1½ inches thick) or 4 salmon steaks (about 4 ounces each)*

Poaching Liquid
- ¾ cup water
- ¾ cup dry white wine (regular or nonalcoholic)
- 1 medium onion, chopped (about ¾ cup)
- 1 bay leaf
- ¼ teaspoon pepper
- ⅛ teaspoon ground cloves
- ⅛ teaspoon dried thyme, crumbled

- 1 medium lemon, quartered (optional)

Rinse salmon and pat dry with paper towels.

In a large skillet, combine all poaching liquid ingredients. Bring to a simmer over medium-high heat. Reduce heat to medium-low and cook, partially covered, for 5 minutes.

Add salmon. If necessary, add water to barely cover. Simmer, covered, for 10 to 15 minutes, or until fish flakes easily when tested with a fork. Remove from liquid and serve with lemon wedges.

Cook's Tip on Fresh Salmon: You may prefer salmon fillets to the steaks because fillets have very few, if any, bones. Salmon steaks, cut crosswise through the spine, contain many bones.

Calories 164	Total Fat 7 g	Fiber 0 g
Protein 23 g	Saturated 1 g	Sodium 50 mg
Carbohydrates 0 g	Polyunsaturated 3 g	Potassium 564 mg
Cholesterol 64 mg	Monounsaturated 2 g	Calcium 14 mg

Grilled Salmon Fillet with Fresh Herbs

Serves 4 • about 3 ounces per serving

Fresh salmon with fresh herbs and lemon—a stellar combination. If you prefer your fish with sauce, this entrée is also great served with Creamy Lime and Mustard Sauce (page 209). Serve with a side of parsleyed rice and green salad splashed with a fruity vinaigrette.

	Olive oil spray
1	pound fresh salmon fillet (tail end preferred)
1	medium lemon, halved
1½	teaspoons snipped fresh dillweed or ½ teaspoon dried, crumbled
12	sprigs fresh thyme, divided use

Generously spray grill rack with olive oil spray. Preheat grill to medium-high.

Rinse salmon and pat dry with paper towels. Place salmon with skin side down on a shallow plate. Squeeze juice from one-half lemon over salmon, and sprinkle salmon with dillweed.

Slice remaining lemon half and lay slices on fish.

Top with 7 sprigs of thyme.

Grill salmon with skin side down for 20 minutes (no turning), or until fish flakes easily when tested with a fork. Garnish with remaining sprigs of thyme.

Cook's Tip on Cooking Fish: When cooking fish fillets or steaks, keep in mind the 10-minute rule: Cook fish for 10 minutes per inch of thickness at its thickest part. The rule works for grilling, poaching, broiling, baking, or pan cooking. You should still test the fish for doneness, usually by testing with a fork to see whether the fish flakes easily, and cook it longer if necessary.

GRILLED SALMON FILLET WITH FRESH HERBS

Calories 134	Total Fat 4 g	Fiber 0 g
Protein 23 g	Saturated 1 g	Sodium 56 mg
Carbohydrates 0 g	Polyunsaturated 1 g	Potassium 418 mg
Cholesterol 53 mg	Monounsaturated 2 g	Calcium 43 mg

Grilled Marinated Shark

Serves 4 • about 3 ounces fish per serving

With a meaty texture similar to that of swordfish and tuna, shark is great for grilling. It's almost like eating steak—but without the bones!

1	pound shark
3	to 4 tablespoons fat-free or light Italian salad dressing
½	cup frozen chopped bell peppers
½	cup frozen chopped onion
3	or 4 fresh parsley sprigs (Italian, or flat-leaf, preferred) or 1 teaspoon dried parsley, crumbled
½	teaspoon balsamic vinegar (optional)

Put fish in a large airtight plastic bag or 11 × 7 × 1½-inch baking pan.

In a food processor or blender, process remaining ingredients until chunky, 15 to 20 seconds. Pour over fish, turning to coat evenly. Seal and let fish marinate for 5 to 30 minutes, turning several times. If marinating for more than 5 minutes, refrigerate. Remove fish from marinade; discard marinade.

Meanwhile, preheat grill on medium-high. Grill fish for 8 minutes. Turn over and grill for 7 to 12 minutes, or until cooked through but still moist in center.

Calories 152	Total Fat 5 g	Fiber 0 g
Protein 24 g	Saturated 1 g	Sodium 217 mg
Carbohydrates 1 g	Polyunsaturated 1 g	Potassium 199 mg
Cholesterol 58 mg	Monounsaturated 2 g	Calcium 39 mg

Cajun Snapper

Serves 4 • about 3 ounces per serving

A brightly colored, intensely flavored entrée, this fish is ready in less than 15 minutes. How lucky can you get? You can even prepare the Cajun rub ahead of time, making this a great dish for entertaining.

Cajun Rub

2	teaspoons fresh lemon juice
1½	teaspoons very low sodium or low-sodium Worcestershire sauce
1	teaspoon paprika
¾	teaspoon chopped fresh thyme or ¼ teaspoon dried, crumbled
½	teaspoon red hot-pepper sauce
¼	teaspoon garlic powder
¼	teaspoon onion powder
¼	teaspoon salt

1	pound red snapper fillets or other lean white fish
	Vegetable oil spray
2	teaspoons extra-virgin olive oil
2	tablespoons water

For rub, in a small bowl, stir together all ingredients. Spoon rub onto each fillet; using back of a spoon, spread rub to coat one side of each fillet.

Heat a large nonstick skillet over medium-high heat. Remove skillet from heat and spray with vegetable oil spray (being careful not to spray near a gas flame). Add oil and tilt to coat bottom. Cook fillets, coated side down, for 4 minutes. Gently turn over fillets and cook for 3 to 4 minutes, or until fish is opaque in center and flakes easily when tested with a fork. Transfer fillets to serving platter, reserving any pan residue.

Add water to skillet, stirring well. Cook for 15 to 20 seconds, or until heated thoroughly. Spoon over fish.

Calories 138	Total Fat 4 g	Fiber 0 g
Protein 23 g	Saturated 1 g	Sodium 225 mg
Carbohydrates 1 g	Polyunsaturated 1 g	Potassium 496 mg
Cholesterol 42 mg	Monounsaturated 2 g	Calcium 40 mg

Herbed Fillet of Sole

Serves 4 • 3 ounces per serving

*Fragrant herbs and tart lemon juice flavor this moist broiled sole.
Also try the seasonings with flounder or orange roughy.*

> Vegetable oil spray
> 1/4   cup fresh lemon juice (2 medium)
> 1   tablespoon dried parsley, crumbled
> 2   teaspoons dried chives, crumbled
> 1/2   teaspoon dried tarragon, crumbled
> 1/4   teaspoon dry mustard
> 2   tablespoons light tub margarine
> 4   sole fillets (about 4 ounces each)

Spray a broiler pan and rack with vegetable oil spray. Preheat broiler.
In a small bowl, combine lemon juice, parsley, chives, tarragon, and
dry mustard.

Spread margarine in a 13 × 9 × 2-inch broilerproof baking dish.
Place fish in baking dish. Pour half the lemon juice mixture over fish.

Broil about 4 inches from heat with oven door partially open for
4 minutes. Pour remaining lemon juice mixture over fish. Broil for 4 to
6 minutes, or until fish flakes easily when tested with a fork.

Cook's Tip on Broiling: Leaving the oven door partially open when broiling keeps the oven from retaining heat, which can overcook the food.

Calories 121	Total Fat 3 g	Fiber 0 g
Protein 19 g	Saturated 1 g	Sodium 119 mg
Carbohydrates 3 g	Polyunsaturated 1 g	Potassium 310 mg
Cholesterol 53 mg	Monounsaturated 1 g	Calcium 23 mg

Sole with Vegetables and Dijon Dill Sauce

Serves 4 • 3 ounces fish and ½ cup vegetables per serving

A citrusy aroma will fill your kitchen as this fish dish bakes. Carefully open the foil packets keeping the fish and vegetables moist, and you'll have a colorful surprise. Spoon the sauce on and enjoy!

1	teaspoon olive oil
2	medium leeks (white part only), thinly sliced (about ⅓ cup)
1	cup golden Italian or button mushrooms, quartered (about 4 ounces)
1	medium carrot, thinly sliced (about ¾ cup)
½	medium red bell pepper, thinly sliced (about ½ cup)
1	cup fresh or frozen sugar snap peas (no thawing needed if frozen)
½	teaspoon very low sodium chicken bouillon granules
	Vegetable oil spray
1	small lemon, cut into 8 slices and seeded
1	small lime, cut into 8 slices and seeded
4	sole fillets (about 4 ounces each)
1	teaspoon dried marjoram or dried oregano, crumbled
¼	teaspoon pepper

Dijon Dill Sauce

½	cup fat-free or low-fat plain yogurt
1	tablespoon Dijon mustard
1	teaspoon snipped fresh dillweed or ¼ teaspoon dried, crumbled
½	teaspoon grated lemon zest
1	teaspoon lemon juice
½	teaspoon sugar

Heat a large nonstick skillet over medium heat. Add oil and swirl to coat bottom. Cook leeks, mushrooms, carrot, and bell pepper for 2 to 3 minutes, or until carrot slices are tender-crisp, stirring occasionally.

Stir in peas and chicken bouillon granules. Remove from heat.

Preheat oven to 400° F.

To assemble packets, lightly spray four 12-inch square pieces of aluminum foil with vegetable oil spray. Put 2 slices of lemon and 2 slices of lime in middle of each piece of foil. Place each fillet on citrus slices. Season with marjoram and pepper.

Spoon about ½ cup vegetable mixture onto each fillet. Seal foil tightly. Put packets on a baking sheet.

Bake for 20 minutes, or until fish flakes easily when tested with a fork. To prevent steam burns, open packets carefully.

Meanwhile, for sauce, whisk together all ingredients in a small bowl. (Sauce can be made ahead and refrigerated for up to 4 days.) If desired, heat sauce in a small saucepan over low heat for 1 to 2 minutes, or until heated through, stirring occasionally. Or microwave sauce in a microwave-safe bowl covered with vented plastic wrap. Cook on 100 percent power (high) for 30 to 45 seconds, stirring once.

To serve, place foil package on a plate and open carefully. Spoon 2 tablespoons sauce on top. Repeat with remaining packets and sauce.

Calories 211	Total Fat 3 g	Fiber 4 g
Protein 28 g	Saturated 1 g	Sodium 226 mg
Carbohydrates 18 g	Polyunsaturated 1 g	Potassium 841 mg
Cholesterol 60 mg	Monounsaturated 1 g	Calcium 150 mg

Creole Tuna Steak Sandwich with Caper Tartar Sauce

Serves 4 • ½ pita per serving

Serve this highly seasoned grilled tuna and cool, crisp vegetable sandwich either warm or chilled. You can make the Creole Seasoning ahead.

Caper Tartar Sauce

¼	cup fat-free, cholesterol-free or low-fat mayonnaise dressing
1	tablespoon capers packed in balsamic vinegar, rinsed and drained
1	tablespoon creole mustard or Hot Mustard (page 216)
1	teaspoon lemon juice
¼	teaspoon Creole Seasoning (page 226), Chili Powder (page 225), or commercial no-salt-added chili powder
	8-ounce tuna steak, about 1 inch thick
	Vegetable oil spray
1	to 1½ teaspoons Creole Seasoning (page 226), Chili Powder (page 225), or commercial no-salt-added chili powder, divided use
2	6-inch whole-wheat pita breads, halved
2	medium Italian plum tomatoes or 2 small yellow tomatoes, thinly sliced
½	cup sprouts, such as alfalfa, spicy, wheat berry, or lentil
½	cup thinly sliced cucumber

For tartar sauce, in a medium bowl, combine all ingredients. (Mixture can be covered and refrigerated for up to 4 days.)

Preheat grill to medium-high.

Lightly spray one side of fish with vegetable oil spray. Sprinkle with ½ to ¾ teaspoon Creole Seasoning. Turn fish over and repeat with vegetable oil spray and seasoning.

Grill fish for 4 to 5 minutes per side, or until desired doneness (4 minutes per side for pink center, 5 minutes per side for a blush of pink in center; if grilled longer, fish will be dry). Let stand for 5 minutes. Slice fish into about 12 strips.

While fish cooks, wrap pita bread halves in aluminum foil and heat on grill for 3 to 4 minutes.

To assemble, spread 1 tablespoon tartar sauce inside each pita half. Add tuna, tomatoes, alfalfa sprouts, and cucumber to each.

Cook's Tip on Yellow Tomatoes: Whenever you see yellow tomatoes, put them in your shopping basket. They add great color to your sandwiches and are not as acidic as red tomatoes.

Calories 191	Total Fat 4 g	Fiber 3 g
Protein 17 g	Saturated 1 g	Sodium 348 mg
Carbohydrates 23 g	Polyunsaturated 1 g	Potassium 305 mg
Cholesterol 21 mg	Monounsaturated 1 g	Calcium 19 mg

Tuna Penne Casserole

Serves 5 • 1 cup per serving

Here's a new twist on the old pantry standby—tuna casserole.

1⅓	cups dried penne or macaroni
	Vegetable oil spray
1	teaspoon acceptable vegetable oil
¼	cup chopped onion
1½	cups fat-free milk
1	tablespoon finely snipped fresh parsley or 1 teaspoon dried parsley flakes, crumbled
½	to 1 teaspoon curry powder
¼	teaspoon salt
⅛	teaspoon pepper
1	tablespoon cornstarch
3	tablespoons water
	6-ounce can tuna packed in distilled or spring water
½	cup drained no-salt-added canned diced tomatoes
1	tablespoon acceptable margarine, melted
½	cup rice square cereal crumbs

Cook penne using package directions, omitting salt and oil. Drain well and set aside.

Preheat broiler to 400° F. Lightly spray a 1½-quart broilerproof casserole dish with vegetable oil spray. Set aside.

Heat a large nonstick skillet over medium-high heat. Add oil and swirl to coat bottom. Cook onion for 2 to 3 minutes, or until translucent, stirring occasionally.

Whisk in milk, parsley, curry powder, salt, and pepper.

Put cornstarch in a small bowl. Add water, whisking to dissolve.

When milk mixture is hot, gently whisk in cornstarch mixture. Continue to whisk gently for 3 to 5 minutes, or until slightly thickened. Remove from heat.

Drain tuna. If using tuna packed in spring water, rinse and drain again. Flake with a fork. Stir tuna, penne, and tomatoes into sauce. Pour into casserole dish.

In a small bowl, combine margarine and crumbs. Sprinkle evenly over casserole.

Broil for 5 minutes, or until crumbs are lightly browned.

Time-Saver: If you're in a hurry, you can leave off the crumb topping and thus the broiling step. Omitting the crumbs also saves using (and washing) the casserole dish and preheating the broiler, since you can serve this dish right from the skillet. If you want to use the topping and have a broilerproof skillet, spray it with vegetable oil spray, prepare the casserole as directed, then top it with the crumbs. Put the skillet under the broiler to brown the crumbs.

Cook's Tip on Cornstarch: Cornstarch needs gentle treatment. Too much heat or stirring will cause a cornstarch-thickened sauce to become thin.

Calories 243	Total Fat 5 g	Fiber 1 g
Protein 15 g	Saturated 1 g	Sodium 259 mg
Carbohydrates 34 g	Polyunsaturated 2 g	Potassium 335 mg
Cholesterol 16 mg	Monounsaturated 2 g	Calcium 114 mg

Scallops and Bok Choy with Balsamic Sauce

Serves 4 • ½ cup per serving

On their own, scallops have a rich, sweet flavor. When topped with this bold balsamic sauce, they're transformed into an extraordinary dish fit for company. Serve over steamed rice for a delectable dinner.

4	stalks bok choy
2	green onions
½	cup bottled roasted red bell peppers, rinsed and drained
1	teaspoon olive oil
1	pound bay scallops, rinsed and patted dry with paper towels (about 2 cups)
¼	cup Chicken Broth (page 23) or commercial low-sodium broth
2	medium cloves garlic, minced, or 1 teaspoon bottled minced garlic
⅛	teaspoon pepper
2	tablespoons balsamic vinegar

Trim ends off bok choy and green onions. Cut stalks and leaves of bok choy horizontally into ½-inch slices. Cut green onions into 1-inch pieces. Cut roasted peppers into thin strips.

Heat a large nonstick skillet over medium-high heat. Add oil and swirl to coat bottom. Cook scallops for 1 minute, stirring occasionally after 30 seconds. If scallops have been previously frozen, they may release liquid in the skillet and need to cook an additional 1 to 2 minutes to evaporate extra liquid.

Stir in all ingredients except vinegar. Cook, covered, for 1 to 2 minutes, or until scallops are cooked through (white and opaque, not translucent, in center), stirring occasionally. Watch carefully; scallops become rubbery when overcooked. With a slotted spoon, transfer scallops and vegetables to a serving platter. Cover with aluminum foil to keep warm.

Add vinegar to liquid in skillet. Cook, uncovered, over medium-high heat for 1 to 2 minutes, or until liquid is reduced by half. Pour over scallops and serve warm.

Cook's Tip on Bok Choy: Look for bok choy, with its long white stalks and large dark green leaves, near the cabbage in the produce section. Slices of raw bok choy stalks add a pleasant crunch to salads. Both the stalks and the leaves are good in stir-fry dishes and soups.

Cook's Tip on Scallops: Either sea or bay scallops can be used whenever scallops are called for. You can substitute them for shrimp in most recipes. Bay scallops (as many as 40 per pound) are milder—and more expensive—than sea scallops (12 to 15 per pound). To reduce cooking time or to substitute sea scallops for bay, cut sea scallops in halves, quarters, or slices.

Because scallops are delicate, they need gentle handling. Overcooking scallops, even for an extra minute or two, can cause them to shrink and become tough and chewy. Dry them well before cooking, have the oil hot before adding the scallops, and don't overcrowd (no more than one layer, with some space between pieces). Otherwise, the scallops will steam and won't brown.

Calories 128	Total Fat 2 g	Fiber 0 g
Protein 20 g	Saturated 0 g	Sodium 227 mg
Carbohydrates 6 g	Polyunsaturated 0 g	Potassium 434 mg
Cholesterol 37 mg	Monounsaturated 1 g	Calcium 51 mg

Grilled Shrimp on Lemongrass Skewers

Serves 4 • 2 ounces per serving

These lemon-flavored shrimp are delicious paired with Asian Fried Rice with Peas (page 199) and steamed green Asian vegetables. The lemongrass skewers are more flexible than bamboo skewers, but they're strong enough to handle the job.

Marinade
      1   fresh stalk lemongrass, outer leaf removed
     ½   cup mirin (see Cook's Tip on Mirin), or sweet wine
      2   tablespoons minced gingerroot
      2   tablespoons light soy sauce or reduced-sodium teriyaki sauce
      2   tablespoons acceptable vegetable oil
      2   tablespoons fresh lemon juice
      1   tablespoon finely snipped fresh cilantro
     ⅛   teaspoon crushed red pepper flakes

      1   pound raw medium shrimp, shells on (36 to 40)
      4   fresh stalks lemongrass, outer leaf removed

For marinade, use only the tender bottom part (4 to 6 inches) of lemongrass stalk. Cut it off, peel to inside layers, and discard outer layers. Thinly slice inner layers. Put in a large airtight plastic bag; add remaining marinade ingredients.

Peel and devein shrimp, leaving tails intact. Rinse, drain, and pat dry with paper towels. Add shrimp to marinade and turn to coat. Seal and refrigerate for 1 to 12 hours, turning bag occasionally.

Preheat grill to medium-high.

Peel remaining four lemongrass stalks to the size of heavy-duty bamboo skewers. Thread shrimp on each lemongrass stalk, with tails facing in same direction.

Grill skewers for 5 minutes on each side or until shrimp turn pink. Don't overcook shrimp, or they'll become tough.

Variations:
Replace shrimp with 1 pound scallops or 1 pound salmon, cubed, or use ⅓ pound of each for a mixed seafood grill.

Cook's Tip on Lemongrass: An herb, lemongrass is somewhat like a green onion in structure, but the fibrous outer leaves and tops are too tough to eat. The lower white part is tender and edible. You can use the tops to impart a fragrant lemon flavor to marinades, soups, and sauces. When making chicken soup, tie 3 chopped lemongrass stalks in a small piece of cheesecloth and place it in the pot with the broth (about 8 cups of broth for 3 stalks of lemongrass). It is customary in Asian cooking to leave the cheesecloth bag in the soup and ladle around it while serving. When making sauce, place the lemongrass in cheesecloth as directed for soup. Simmer the lemongrass in the sauce for 5 to 10 minutes, then remove the bag. Finish the sauce as directed in your recipe.

Cook's Tip on Mirin: Mirin is a sweet Japanese rice wine. It's available in some supermarkets and most Asian markets. When shopping for mirin, be sure to purchase regular mirin, not cooking mirin, which has salt added.

Calories 73	Total Fat 1 g	Fiber 0 g
Protein 15 g	Saturated 0 g	Sodium 350 mg
Carbohydrates 1 g	Polyunsaturated 0 g	Potassium 146 mg
Cholesterol 135 mg	Monounsaturated 0 g	Calcium 28 mg

Shrimp and Pasta with Spinach and Lemony Cream Sauce

Serves 5 • about 1 cup per serving

This is the easiest and tastiest cream sauce you'll ever make. Don't worry about leftovers! There won't be any.

1	pound raw medium shrimp, shells on, peeled and deveined (36 to 40)
1/3	cup sliced almonds
1/4	cup dry white wine (regular or nonalcoholic)
	Vegetable oil spray
1/4	teaspoon garlic powder
1/4	teaspoon ground white pepper, or to taste
6	ounces dried vermicelli noodles
3/4	cup nonfat or light sour cream
1	tablespoon light stick margarine
2	teaspoons fresh lemon juice
1/4	teaspoon salt
1	tablespoon light stick margarine
4	ounces fresh whole baby spinach leaves or regular spinach leaves, stems removed and leaves coarsely chopped
2	tablespoons finely chopped green onions (green and white parts)

Rinse shrimp and pat dry with paper towels. Set aside.

Heat a large nonstick skillet over medium-high heat. Dry-roast almonds in skillet for 3 to 4 minutes, or until they are just beginning to lightly brown, stirring frequently. Transfer almonds to a small bowl. Set aside.

In a small saucepan, bring wine to a boil over high heat. Continue to boil for about 1 minute, or until reduced to 2 tablespoons. Remove from heat; pour into a small bowl and let cool completely.

Heat same skillet over medium heat. Remove skillet from heat and spray with vegetable oil spray (being careful not to spray near a gas flame). Return to heat and add shrimp.

Sprinkle shrimp with garlic powder and pepper. Cook for 8 to 10 minutes, or until opaque in center, stirring frequently.

Meanwhile, cook noodles using package directions, omitting salt and oil. Drain well.

In saucepan used for wine, heat sour cream and 1 tablespoon margarine over medium-low heat for 2 to 3 minutes, or until margarine has melted and mixture is thoroughly heated, stirring frequently. Remove from heat.

Whisk in cooled wine, lemon juice, and salt. Cover to keep warm.

When shrimp is cooked, stir in 1 tablespoon margarine.

Add spinach and stir until wilted, about 2 minutes.

To assemble, spread drained pasta on serving platter, spoon sour cream mixture over pasta, and top with shrimp mixture. Sprinkle green onions and almonds over all.

Calories 310	Total Fat 7 g	Fiber 2 g
Protein 23 g	Saturated 1 g	Sodium 347 mg
Carbohydrates 36 g	Polyunsaturated 2 g	Potassium 461 mg
Cholesterol 132 mg	Monounsaturated 3 g	Calcium 121 mg

Risotto with Shrimp and Vegetables

Serves 5 • 1 cup per serving

*Arborio rice gives risotto its creamy texture, and onion, red bell
pepper, and garlic give it plenty of taste in this attractive dish. The
delicate crunch of snow peas and the burst of flavor from lemon zest
add interesting surprises. (See photo on cover.)*

1	small lemon
1	teaspoon olive oil
1/2	medium onion, sliced
1/2	medium red bell pepper, chopped
2	medium cloves garlic, minced, or 1 teaspoon bottled minced garlic
1	cup uncooked arborio rice (about 8 ounces)
1 1/2	cups Chicken Broth (page 23) or commercial low-sodium broth
1/8	teaspoon pepper
1	cup dry white wine (regular or nonalcoholic)
1/2	cup Chicken Broth (page 23) or commercial low-sodium broth
1	pound large shrimp in shells, rinsed, peeled, and deveined
6	ounces fresh snow peas, trimmed and halved crosswise (about 2 cups)
1/2	cup water
3	tablespoons shredded or grated Romano cheese
1	tablespoon snipped fresh dillweed
1	tablespoon thinly sliced green onions (green part only)

Using a vegetable peeler or sharp knife, remove the zest from the
lemon. Cut into very thin strips. Set aside.

Heat a medium saucepan over medium heat. Add olive oil and swirl
to coat bottom. Cook onion, bell pepper, and garlic for 2 to 3 minutes,
or until vegetables are tender-crisp, stirring frequently.

Stir in rice. Cook for 5 minutes, stirring frequently.

Add 1 1/2 cups broth and pepper. Increase heat to high and bring to a
boil, stirring occasionally. Reduce heat and simmer, uncovered, for
5 minutes, stirring occasionally. (Rice will be slightly plump, liquid
will not be entirely absorbed, and mixture will have a thick, soupy or
stewlike consistency.)

Stir in wine and 1/2 cup broth. Increase heat to high and bring to a simmer. Reduce heat to medium-high and cook for 8 to 10 minutes, stirring constantly (a small amount of liquid should remain).

Add shrimp, peas, and water. Reduce heat to medium and cook until liquid is almost absorbed, 2 to 3 minutes, stirring constantly. Rice should be just tender and slightly creamy, and shrimp should be pink.

Stir in lemon zest and remaining ingredients. Remove from heat and serve.

Cook's Tip on Shrimp: For a decorative look, leave the tails on the shrimp. When the shrimp cooks, the tail will become a brilliant pink color.

Cook's Tip on Risotto: For proper consistency, carefully regulate the cooking temperature so the risotto boils lightly, not vigorously. If the liquid is absorbed before the rice reaches the just-tender stage, gradually add more broth, wine, or water. Arborio rice is usually used in risottos, but you can substitute a medium-grain rice if you prefer. It won't be quite as creamy, however.

Calories 307	Total Fat 3 g	Fiber 2 g
Protein 18 g	Saturated 1 g	Sodium 184 mg
Carbohydrates 42 g	Polyunsaturated 0 g	Potassium 335 mg
Cholesterol 112 mg	Monounsaturated 1 g	Calcium 107 mg

Spanish-Style Crab and Vegetable Tortilla

Serves 4 • 1 wedge per serving

In Mexico, a tortilla is a type of unleavened bread, but in Spain, a tortilla is an omelet, often served open-face.

> 1   cup frozen no-salt-added vegetables, such as artichoke hearts
>   or asparagus (½ 10-ounce package), peas and carrots, or
>   mixed vegetables
>   Olive oil spray
>   Egg substitute equivalent to 6 eggs
> 4   ounces crab (fresh, frozen, or canned), all cartilage and shell
>   removed (about ¾ cup)
> ¼   teaspoon dried dillweed, crumbled
>   Pepper to taste

If using artichoke hearts or asparagus, cut into bite-size pieces.

Heat a medium skillet over medium-low heat. Remove from heat and spray with olive oil spray (being careful not to spray near a gas flame). Cook vegetables for 3 minutes, stirring occasionally.

Add remaining ingredients. Cook for 1 minute, constantly scrambling lightly with a fork. Cover and cook for 11 to 14 minutes, or until center of tortilla is firm and doesn't run. Cut into four wedges.

Calories 85	Total Fat 0 g	Fiber 1 g
Protein 17 g	Saturated 0 g	Sodium 298 mg
Carbohydrates 3 g	Polyunsaturated 0 g	Potassium 335 mg
Cholesterol 22 mg	Monounsaturated 0 g	Calcium 57 mg

Poultry

roast chicken
oven-fried chicken
chicken dijon
chicken cacciatore
chicken marengo
glazed raspberry-ginger chicken
lemon chicken with oregano
chicken with yogurt-cilantro sauce
grilled sesame chicken
chicken with ginger and snow peas
chicken paprikash
spicy chicken saté with peanut dipping sauce
arroz con pollo (chicken with rice)
chicken primavera
chicken enchiladas
savory roasted turkey
roasted lemon-herb turkey breast
turkey tenderloins with rosemary
pork tenderloins with rosemary
tarragon turkey medallions
tarragon pork medallions
turkey picadillo
turkey sausage patties
new-style turkey club sandwich for one
honey-mustard turkey wraps
turkey stew

Roast Chicken

Serves 8 • 3 ounces chicken per serving

To complete the meal, serve this with Rice and Vegetable Pilaf (page 200) and steamed asparagus. A nice touch is to heat the serving platter before placing the chicken on it.

    4-pound roasting chicken
½   **teaspoon poultry seasoning or Savory Herb Blend (page 224)**
¼   **teaspoon pepper**
¼   **teaspoon paprika**
1   **medium lemon**

Preheat oven to 350° F.

Remove giblets and neck from chicken; save for other use or discard. Carefully remove any fat you can reach under skin. Sprinkle with seasonings and place whole lemon inside cavity. Put chicken with breast side up on rack in a deep roasting pan.

Bake for 1 hour 15 minutes to 1 hour 30 minutes, or until clear juices run from thigh when pierced with a sharp skewer or meat thermometer inserted in thigh registers 180° F. Remove skin before eating chicken.

Cook's Tip on Thermometers: A thermometer is your best bet to ensure the safe preparation and cooking of meat, including poultry. If you have the regular type of meat thermometer, insert it into the meat before putting the meat in the oven. The instant-read type, however, would melt in the oven. You insert it into the meat only when you think the meat may be done. Whichever type you use, be sure to insert the thermometer into a thicker area of the meat. If it pushes against gristle or bone, it will not give you an accurate reading.

Calories 160	Total Fat 6 g	Fiber 0 g
Protein 24 g	Saturated 2 g	Sodium 72 mg
Carbohydrates 0 g	Polyunsaturated 2 g	Potassium 222 mg
Cholesterol 72 mg	Monounsaturated 2 g	Calcium 13 mg

Oven-Fried Chicken

Serves 6 • 3 ounces chicken per serving

*Serve this moist chicken in its crisp herb "crust" with Green Beans
and Corn (page 183) and Garden Coleslaw (page 46).*

> Vegetable oil spray
> 1/2   cup fat-free or low-fat plain yogurt
> 2   medium cloves garlic, minced, or 1 teaspoon bottled minced
>   garlic
> 2   cups whole-wheat or plain dry bread crumbs
> 1/4   cup minced fresh parsley
> 2   tablespoons shredded or grated Parmesan cheese
> 1   teaspoon dried basil, crumbled
> 1   teaspoon dried oregano, crumbled
> 1/4   teaspoon pepper
> 2 1/2- to 3-pound chicken cut into serving pieces, skin and all visible
>   fat removed

Preheat oven to 400° F. Lightly spray a 13 × 9 × 2-inch baking pan
with vegetable oil spray.

In a shallow bowl, combine yogurt and garlic.

In a separate shallow bowl, combine remaining ingredients except
chicken.

Dip each piece of chicken in yogurt mixture, then roll it in bread
crumb mixture. Put chicken pieces in baking pan. Lightly spray top of
chicken with vegetable oil spray.

Bake for 55 to 60 minutes, or until no longer pink in center.

Cook's Tip on Whole-Wheat Bread Crumbs: To make your
own whole-wheat bread crumbs, lightly toast six slices of whole-wheat bread. Process
toast in a food processor or blender for 15 to 20 seconds, or until desired texture.

Calories 240	Total Fat 8 g	Fiber 2 g
Protein 27 g	Saturated 2 g	Sodium 270 mg
Carbohydrates 15 g	Polyunsaturated 2 g	Potassium 358 mg
Cholesterol 68 mg	Monounsaturated 3 g	Calcium 115 mg

Chicken Dijon

Serves 6 • 3 ounces chicken, ⅓ cup vegetables, and
2 tablespoons sauce per serving

*A smooth Dijon sauce enhances the combination of chicken breasts
and colorful vegetables. Serve this dish with couscous and melon
slices.*

6	*boneless, skinless chicken breast halves (about 4 ounces each), all visible fat removed*
¼	*teaspoon pepper*
2	*teaspoons olive oil*
½	*cup Chicken Broth (page 23) or commercial low-sodium broth*
2	*medium carrots, sliced (about 1½ cups)*
1	*medium zucchini, sliced (about 1 cup)*
½	*medium red bell pepper, cut into strips (about ½ cup)*
1	*medium clove garlic, minced, or ½ teaspoon bottled minced garlic*
½	*cup fat-free milk*
2	*tablespoons all-purpose flour*
2	*tablespoons light tub margarine*
1	*to 2 teaspoons Dijon mustard*
1	*tablespoon snipped fresh parsley or 1 teaspoon dried, crumbled*

Put chicken smooth side up between two sheets of plastic wrap. Using a tortilla press or smooth side of a meat mallet, lightly flatten chicken to ½-inch thickness, being careful not to tear meat. Sprinkle both sides of chicken with pepper.

Heat a large nonstick skillet over medium-high heat. Add olive oil and swirl to coat bottom. Cook chicken for 2 to 3 minutes on each side, or until browned.

Add broth, carrots, zucchini, bell pepper, and garlic. Cook, covered, for 5 to 8 minutes, or until chicken is no longer pink in center and vegetables are tender, stirring occasionally. Using a slotted spoon, transfer chicken and vegetables to a serving platter. Cover with aluminum foil to keep warm.

In a small bowl, whisk together milk and flour. Add with margarine and mustard to liquid in skillet. Bring to a simmer over medium-high heat, whisking occasionally. Cook for 2 to 3 minutes, or until thickened, whisking occasionally. Pour over chicken and vegetables; sprinkle with parsley.

Calories 191	Total Fat 4 g	Fiber 1 g
Protein 28 g	Saturated 1 g	Sodium 150 mg
Carbohydrates 8 g	Polyunsaturated 1 g	Potassium 521 mg
Cholesterol 66 mg	Monounsaturated 2 g	Calcium 55 mg

Chicken Cacciatore

Serves 6 • 3 ounces chicken per serving

Cacciatore *refers to a style of preparation that includes onions, tomatoes, herbs, often wine, and sometimes mushrooms. Serve this dish over rice or with polenta. Buon appetito!*

1	tablespoon acceptable vegetable oil
1	medium clove garlic, minced, or 1/2 teaspoon bottled minced garlic
6	boneless, skinless chicken breast halves (about 4 ounces each), all visible fat removed
1	medium onion, chopped (about 3/4 cup)
2	tablespoons chopped green bell pepper
4	medium tomatoes, peeled if desired and chopped (about 2 cups)
1/4	cup dry white wine (regular or nonalcoholic)
1/4	teaspoon dried rosemary, crushed
1/4	teaspoon dried basil, crumbled
1/8	teaspoon pepper
1	bay leaf
8	ounces sliced fresh mushrooms (about 2 1/2 cups)

In a large nonstick skillet, heat oil and garlic over medium-high heat. Brown chicken on both sides. Transfer to a plate.

Reduce heat to medium and cook onion and green pepper for 2 to 3 minutes, or until onion is translucent, stirring occasionally.

Return chicken to skillet. Add remaining ingredients except mushrooms. Simmer, covered, for 30 minutes, or until chicken is tender, adding mushrooms after 20 minutes.

Remove bay leaf before serving chicken.

Calories 187	Total Fat 5 g	Fiber 2 g
Protein 25 g	Saturated 1 g	Sodium 65 mg
Carbohydrates 8 g	Polyunsaturated 1 g	Potassium 569 mg
Cholesterol 63 mg	Monounsaturated 2 g	Calcium 28 mg

Chicken Marengo

Serves 6 • 3 ounces chicken and ½ cup sauce per serving

This European dish stars chicken that is seared, then cooked in an herbed tomato and wine sauce, so it stays moist and tender.

6	boneless, skinless chicken breast halves (about 4 ounces each), all visible fat removed
½	teaspoon pepper
2	teaspoons olive oil
8	ounces fresh mushrooms, sliced (about 2½ cups)
1	medium red onion, chopped (about ¾ cup)
2	medium cloves garlic, minced, or 1 teaspoon bottled minced garlic
	14.5-ounce can diced no-salt-added tomatoes, undrained
½	cup marsala, dry white wine (regular or nonalcoholic), Chicken Broth (page 23), or commercial low-sodium broth
1	teaspoon sugar
1	teaspoon dried oregano, crumbled
½	teaspoon dried thyme, crumbled
¼	to ½ teaspoon crushed red pepper flakes (optional)

Season both sides of chicken with pepper.

Heat a large nonstick skillet over medium-high heat. Add oil and swirl to coat bottom. Cook chicken for 2 to 3 minutes on each side, or until golden brown. Transfer chicken to a plate.

Reduce heat to medium and add mushrooms, onion, and garlic to skillet. Cook for 3 to 4 minutes, or until vegetables are tender, stirring occasionally.

Stir in remaining ingredients. Return chicken to skillet and spoon sauce over chicken. Bring to a simmer over medium-high heat. Reduce heat to medium-low; cook, covered, for 25 to 30 minutes, or until chicken is no longer pink in center (no stirring needed).

Calories 203	Total Fat 3 g	Fiber 2 g
Protein 29 g	Saturated 1 g	Sodium 83 mg
Carbohydrates 10 g	Polyunsaturated 1 g	Potassium 638 mg
Cholesterol 66 mg	Monounsaturated 2 g	Calcium 46 mg

Glazed Raspberry-Ginger Chicken

Serves 4 • 3 ounces chicken and ¾ cup sweet potato per serving

A showpiece, this incredibly easy and elegant entrée is rich in color and in flavor.

    2   *teaspoons sugar*
  ⅛   *teaspoon ground cinnamon*

Glaze
  ½   *cup seedless all-fruit raspberry spread*
    3   *tablespoons cider vinegar*
    1   *teaspoon grated gingerroot or ¼ teaspoon ground ginger*
  ⅛   *to ¼ teaspoon crushed red pepper flakes*
  ¼   *teaspoon salt*

       Vegetable oil spray
    4   *boneless, skinless chicken breast halves (about 4 ounces each), all visible fat removed*
    1   *pound sweet potatoes, peeled and cut horizontally into ½-inch slices*

In a small bowl, stir together sugar and cinnamon. Set aside.

In another small bowl, stir together all glaze ingredients.

Heat a large nonstick skillet over medium-high heat. Remove skillet from heat and spray with vegetable oil spray (being careful not to spray near a gas flame). Add chicken, immediately reduce heat to medium, and cook for 6 minutes. Turn chicken, top each piece with 1 tablespoon glaze, and cook for 7 minutes, or until no longer pink in center.

Meanwhile, put potato slices in a steamer basket in a medium saucepan over a small amount of simmering water. Cook, tightly covered, for 10 to 12 minutes, or until tender. Arrange potatoes on a serving platter and cover with aluminum foil to keep warm.

Place chicken on a separate plate. Add remaining glaze to skillet. Increase heat to high and bring mixture to a boil. Continue boiling for 2 minutes, or until mixture begins to thicken slightly, scraping bottom and side of skillet frequently.

Add chicken pieces and cook for 2 to 2½ minutes, turning constantly with a fork and spoon, until richly glazed and beginning to darken intensely. Remove from heat and arrange chicken on platter with potatoes.

Sprinkle potatoes with cinnamon sugar.

Calories 256	Total Fat 2 g	Fiber 3 g
Protein 27 g	Saturated 0 g	Sodium 231 mg
Carbohydrates 32 g	Polyunsaturated 0 g	Potassium 544 mg
Cholesterol 66 mg	Monounsaturated 0 g	Calcium 94 mg

Lemon Chicken with Oregano

Serves 4 • 3 ounces chicken per serving

Serve this beautifully browned chicken over steamed rice with green beans on the side.

	Vegetable oil spray
2	teaspoons acceptable vegetable oil
½	teaspoon grated lemon zest
2	tablespoons lemon juice
1	pound chicken breast tenders, all visible fat removed
2	to 3 tablespoons chopped fresh oregano or 2 to 3 teaspoons dried, crumbled
1	medium clove garlic, minced, or ½ teaspoon bottled minced garlic
¼	teaspoon paprika
2	tablespoons snipped fresh parsley

Heat a large nonstick skillet over medium-high heat. Remove skillet from heat and spray with vegetable oil spray (being careful not to spray near a gas flame). Return to heat and add oil, lemon zest, and lemon juice, swirling to coat bottom.

Add chicken, oregano, and garlic to skillet; cook, covered, for 3 to 5 minutes, or until chicken begins to turn white. Turn chicken over; cook for 3 to 5 minutes, or until completely white on surface. With lid on skillet, pour all pan liquid into a small bowl, reserving liquid.

Cook chicken, uncovered, for 2 minutes, or until lightly brown. Turn chicken over; cook for 3 to 5 minutes, or until lightly brown.

Sprinkle paprika over chicken and return pan liquid to skillet. Cook for 3 to 5 minutes, or until chicken is no longer pink in center, stirring frequently. Garnish with parsley.

Calories 152	Total Fat 4 g	Fiber 0 g
Protein 26 g	Saturated 1 g	Sodium 75 mg
Carbohydrates 2 g	Polyunsaturated 1 g	Potassium 328 mg
Cholesterol 66 mg	Monounsaturated 2 g	Calcium 29 mg

Chicken with Yogurt-Cilantro Sauce

Serves 4 • 3 ounces chicken and 2 tablespoons sauce per serving

This dish is so scrumptious that even low-salt skeptics will be clamoring for a sample. You won't have to spend much time in the kitchen, but remember to allow time for marinating.

Marinade
- 1 tablespoon olive oil
- 2 tablespoons lime juice (1 to 2 medium)
- 1/4 teaspoon pepper

- 4 boneless, skinless chicken breast halves (about 4 ounces each), all visible fat removed

Sauce
- 4 ounces fat-free or low-fat plain yogurt
- 1 tablespoon snipped fresh cilantro
- 1 tablespoon snipped fresh mint
- 1/2 teaspoon ground cumin

- 1 medium lime, quartered (optional)

For marinade, combine all ingredients in an airtight plastic bag. Add chicken and turn to coat. Seal and refrigerate for 30 minutes to 8 hours, turning bag occasionally.

Meanwhile, for sauce, stir together all ingredients in a small bowl. Set aside.

Remove chicken from refrigerator 5 to 10 minutes before cooking.

Preheat broiler or grill to medium-high. Broil or grill chicken for 4 to 5 minutes on each side, or until chicken is no longer pink in center.

Spoon 2 tablespoons sauce over each breast half and garnish with lime.

Calories 142	Total Fat 2 g	Fiber 0 g
Protein 28 g	Saturated 0 g	Sodium 97 mg
Carbohydrates 2 g	Polyunsaturated 0 g	Potassium 376 mg
Cholesterol 66 mg	Monounsaturated 0 g	Calcium 75 mg

Grilled Sesame Chicken

Serves 4 • 3 ounces chicken per serving

Tired of the same old grilled chicken? Sesame seeds give it a crunchy difference.

> Vegetable oil spray
> 4   boneless, skinless chicken breast halves (about 4 ounces each), all visible fat removed
>   Dash of paprika
>   Dash of cayenne
> 1/4   cup fresh lemon juice (2 medium)
> 1/4   cup honey
> 1   tablespoon dry-roasted sesame seeds

Preheat grill on medium-high or preheat broiler. If using broiler, spray broiler rack and pan with vegetable oil spray.

Season chicken lightly with paprika and cayenne.

In a small microwave-safe bowl, whisk together lemon juice and honey. Microwave on 100 percent power (high) for 1 minute, or until honey has dissolved. Reserve 2 tablespoons mixture for sauce; stir sesame seeds into reserved mixture.

Coat chicken pieces with 3 tablespoons remaining lemon mixture.

Grill chicken for 5 minutes, or broil 4 to 5 inches from heat for 5 minutes, leaving oven door partially open, basting occasionally with lemon mixture, not sauce. To prevent transferring harmful bacteria, wash basting brush after each use. Turn pieces over and cook for 5 to 6 minutes, or until no longer pink in center, basting occasionally.

Spoon sauce over chicken just before serving.

Cook's Tip on Dry-Roasting Seeds or Nuts: Put seeds or nuts in a single layer in a small skillet. Cook over medium-high heat for 2 to 5 minutes, or until seeds darken and begin to pop, or until nuts brown, stirring frequently.

Calories 205	Total Fat 2 g	Fiber 1 g
Protein 27 g	Saturated 1 g	Sodium 76 mg
Carbohydrates 19 g	Polyunsaturated 1 g	Potassium 329 mg
Cholesterol 66 mg	Monounsaturated 1 g	Calcium 18 mg

Chicken with Ginger and Snow Peas

Serves 5 • 1 cup per serving

Serve this Asian-inspired dish over rice with fruit salad or steamed squash on the side.

6	ounces fresh snow peas (about 2 cups)
1/2	cup Chicken Broth (page 23) or commercial low-sodium broth
1	tablespoon cornstarch
1	tablespoon light soy sauce
1	teaspoon pepper
2	teaspoons acceptable vegetable oil
1 1/4	pounds boneless, skinless chicken breast tenders, all visible fat removed
2	medium cloves garlic, minced, or 1 teaspoon bottled minced garlic
1/2	teaspoon minced gingerroot
1	to 2 tablespoons Chicken Broth (page 23) or commercial low-sodium broth (optional)

Trim ends off snow peas.

In a small bowl, whisk together broth, cornstarch, soy sauce, and pepper.

Heat a wok or large, heavy nonstick skillet over high heat, add oil, and swirl to coat bottom. Cook chicken for 4 to 5 minutes, stirring frequently.

Add snow peas, garlic, and gingerroot. Cook for 2 to 3 minutes, stirring constantly.

Add chicken broth mixture and cook for 2 to 3 minutes, or until sauce thickens and chicken is no longer pink in center, stirring constantly. If mixture begins to burn, remove wok or skillet from heat momentarily, or add 1 to 2 tablespoons broth or water.

Calories 166	Total Fat 3 g	Fiber 1 g
Protein 28 g	Saturated 1 g	Sodium 185 mg
Carbohydrates 5 g	Polyunsaturated 1 g	Potassium 380 mg
Cholesterol 66 mg	Monounsaturated 1 g	Calcium 31 mg

Chicken Paprikash

Serves 6 • 1 cup per serving

Rich and full-bodied with strong tones of paprika, this traditional Hungarian entrée will satisfy even the most ravenous appetite. This goes well with a green salad with Cider Vinaigrette (page 60).

2½	cups dried no-yolk noodles
6	boneless, skinless chicken breast halves (about 4 ounces each), all visible fat removed
	Vegetable oil spray
1	medium red onion, thinly sliced (about 1 cup)
2	tablespoons paprika (sweet Hungarian paprika preferred)
1	medium tomato, peeled if desired and chopped (about ½ cup)
½	cup Chicken Broth (page 23) or commercial low-sodium broth
½	cup fat-free or low-fat plain yogurt
2	tablespoons nonfat or light sour cream
2	tablespoons all-purpose flour

Cook noodles using package directions, omitting salt and oil. Drain well and set aside.

Cut chicken into bite-size pieces.

Heat a large nonstick skillet over medium heat. Remove skillet from heat and spray with vegetable oil spray (being careful not to spray near a gas flame). Add chicken and brown lightly on all sides, stirring occasionally; remove from skillet.

Add onion and paprika to skillet; cook for 2 to 3 minutes, or until onion is translucent, stirring constantly.

Stir in tomato and broth; cook for 2 to 3 minutes, or until hot, stirring occasionally.

Return chicken to skillet. Reduce heat and simmer, covered, for 30 minutes, or until tender.

Meanwhile, in a small bowl, whisk together yogurt and sour cream. Set aside.

Using a slotted spoon, remove chicken and vegetables from skillet. Set aside.

Sprinkle flour into skillet; cook for 2 to 3 minutes, or until sauce has thickened, whisking constantly.

Whisk in yogurt mixture.

Return chicken and vegetables to skillet; stir.
Put noodles on a large platter and top with chicken mixture.

Calories 342	Total Fat 2 g	Fiber 3 g
Protein 35 g	Saturated 1 g	Sodium 123 mg
Carbohydrates 42 g	Polyunsaturated 1 g	Potassium 601 mg
Cholesterol 69 mg	Monounsaturated 0 g	Calcium 83 mg

Spicy Chicken Saté with Peanut Dipping Sauce

Serves 4 • 2 skewers and 2 tablespoons peanut sauce per serving

A generous combination of interesting flavors makes this saté (sah-TAY) dish a standout. Serve it with a side of rice or Asian noodles. The dipping sauce is too good to limit to just one recipe. Use it also as a salad dressing on fresh spinach or kale or as a dipping sauce for spring rolls.

Marinade

- ⅓ cup sliced lemongrass (see Cook's Tip on Lemongrass, page 89)
- ¼ cup plus 1 tablespoon fresh lemon juice (2 medium)
- 2 tablespoons light brown sugar
- 2 tablespoons mirin (see Cook's Tip on Mirin, page 89) or sweet wine
- 2½ teaspoons light soy sauce or reduced-sodium teriyaki sauce
- 2 medium cloves garlic, minced, or 1 teaspoon bottled minced garlic
- ⅛ teaspoon crushed red pepper flakes, or to taste

- 4 boneless, skinless chicken breast halves (about 4 ounces each), all visible fat removed, cubed

Peanut Dipping Sauce

- 2 tablespoons acceptable vegetable oil
- ⅓ cup green onions, finely chopped (green and white parts)
- 1 tablespoon grated gingerroot
- 1 medium clove garlic, finely chopped, or ½ teaspoon bottled minced garlic
- ½ cup water
- ¼ cup plus 1 tablespoon reduced-fat creamy peanut butter
- 2 tablespoons tarragon wine vinegar or white vinegar
- 1½ tablespoons light brown sugar
- 1 tablespoon light soy sauce or reduced-sodium teriyaki sauce
- ⅛ teaspoon crushed red pepper flakes

- 16 large mushrooms, stems removed, halved

For marinade, combine all ingredients in an airtight plastic bag.

Add chicken and turn to coat. Seal and refrigerate for 1 to 12 hours, turning bag occasionally.

For sauce, heat oil in a small saucepan over medium-high heat. Cook green onions, gingerroot, and garlic for 1 minute, or until fragrant and glossy, stirring occasionally.

Stir in remaining sauce ingredients. Reduce heat and simmer until smooth, stirring occasionally. Remove from heat and let cool to room temperature.

Preheat grill to medium-high.

Thread chicken and 4 mushroom halves alternately on each of eight skewers, beginning and ending with chicken.

Grill skewers for 5 minutes on each side, or until chicken is no longer pink in center.

Serve skewers with peanut dipping sauce.

Cook's Tip: You can make the peanut dipping sauce several days ahead. Put it in a bowl, cover with plastic wrap, and refrigerate.

Cook's Tip on Food Rasps: Food rasps work well for grating gingerroot, garlic, and citrus zest. You can find them in most specialty kitchen shops.

Calories 244	Total Fat 9 g	Fiber 2 g
Protein 31 g	Saturated 1 g	Sodium 337 mg
Carbohydrates 11 g	Polyunsaturated 3 g	Potassium 727 mg
Cholesterol 66 mg	Monounsaturated 4 g	Calcium 24 mg

Arroz con Pollo (Chicken with Rice)

Serves 7 • 1 cup per serving

This savory one-dish meal will make you think of Spanish sunshine!

	Vegetable oil spray
6	*boneless, skinless chicken breast halves (about 4 ounces each), all visible fat removed, cut into bite-size pieces*
1	*tablespoon light stick margarine, melted*
1	*medium clove garlic, minced, or ½ teaspoon bottled minced garlic*
¼	*teaspoon pepper*
¼	*teaspoon paprika*
1	*teaspoon olive oil*
¼	*cup chopped onion*
¼	*cup chopped green bell pepper*
1	*cup uncooked rice*
2	*cups Chicken Broth (page 23) or commercial low-sodium broth*
1	*cup chopped fresh tomatoes (2 medium)*
⅛	*teaspoon turmeric*
1	*cup frozen green peas*

Preheat oven to 350° F. Lightly spray a 13 × 9 × 2-inch casserole dish with vegetable oil spray.

Put chicken in casserole dish.

In a small bowl, combine margarine, garlic, pepper, and paprika. Brush mixture on chicken.

Bake, uncovered, for 15 to 20 minutes, or until cooked through.

Meanwhile, heat a large nonstick skillet over medium heat. Add oil and swirl to coat bottom. Cook onion and bell pepper for 3 to 4 minutes, or until soft.

Stir in rice; cook for 2 to 3 minutes, or until rice begins to brown, stirring frequently.

Stir in broth, tomatoes, and turmeric. Simmer, covered, for 20 minutes.

Add peas and chicken; simmer, covered, for 10 minutes.

Calories 253	Total Fat 3 g	Fiber 2 g
Protein 26 g	Saturated 1 g	Sodium 108 mg
Carbohydrates 27 g	Polyunsaturated 1 g	Potassium 421 mg
Cholesterol 56 mg	Monounsaturated 1 g	Calcium 37 mg

Chicken Primavera

Serves 8 • 1 cup fettuccine and ¾ cup sauce per serving

Simmer spring vegetables and chunks of chicken in a rich tomato sauce, then serve over warm fettuccine.

1	teaspoon olive oil
1	medium zucchini, chopped (about 1 cup)
1	medium yellow summer squash, chopped (about 1 cup)
1	medium red onion, chopped (about ½ cup)
½	cup sliced fresh mushrooms (golden Italian preferred)
2	medium cloves garlic, minced, or 1 teaspoon bottled minced garlic
	14.5-ounce can no-salt-added diced tomatoes, undrained
½	cup Chicken Broth (page 23) or commercial low-sodium broth
1	teaspoon dried oregano, crumbled
¼	teaspoon pepper
¼	teaspoon crushed red pepper flakes
1	pound dried fettuccine
2	cups cubed cooked chicken breast
1	cup frozen green peas

Heat a large saucepan over medium heat. Add olive oil and swirl to coat bottom. Cook zucchini, yellow summer squash, onion, mushrooms, and garlic for 3 to 4 minutes, or until vegetables are tender-crisp, stirring occasionally.

Add tomatoes with liquid, broth, oregano, pepper, and red pepper flakes. Bring to a simmer over medium-high heat. Reduce heat to medium-low and cook, uncovered, for 15 to 20 minutes, or until flavors are blended, stirring occasionally.

Meanwhile, cook fettuccine using package directions, omitting salt and oil. Drain well. Pour into a large bowl and cover with a dry dish towel to keep warm.

Add chicken and peas to tomato mixture. Increase heat to medium and cook, uncovered, for 5 to 10 minutes, or until peas and chicken are warmed through, stirring occasionally. Spoon sauce over warm fettuccine.

Calories 312	Total Fat 3 g	Fiber 4 g
Protein 20 g	Saturated 1 g	Sodium 59 mg
Carbohydrates 50 g	Polyunsaturated 1 g	Potassium 472 mg
Cholesterol 30 mg	Monounsaturated 1 g	Calcium 50 mg

Chicken Enchiladas

Serves 4 • 2 enchiladas per serving

Cheesy, gooey, and zesty—what more could you ask for in an enchilada? You don't even need salsa or sour cream with these. ¡Olé!

  Vegetable oil spray

Sauce
  1   cup fat-free milk
  ½   cup Chicken Broth (page 23) or commercial low-sodium broth
  2   tablespoons all-purpose flour
  ¼   teaspoon pepper
  ½   cup reduced-fat Monterey Jack cheese or Mexican cheese
       blend
  1   teaspoon lime juice

  8   6-inch corn tortillas
  2   cups cubed cooked chicken breast (10 ounces cooked)
  ¼   cup thinly sliced green onions (green and white parts)
  1   medium clove garlic, minced, or ½ teaspoon bottled minced
       garlic
  ½   teaspoon ground cumin
  ¼   teaspoon Chili Powder (page 225) or commercial no-salt-
       added chili powder
  ½   cup reduced-fat Monterey Jack cheese or Mexican cheese
       blend
  2   to 3 tablespoons canned chopped mild green chiles, rinsed
       and drained

Preheat oven to 350° F. Lightly spray a 13 × 9 × 2-inch baking dish with vegetable oil spray. Set aside.

For sauce, in a medium saucepan, whisk together milk, broth, flour, and pepper. Bring mixture to a simmer over medium-high heat. Reduce heat and simmer for 5 to 6 minutes, or until mixture thickens slightly, whisking occasionally. Add ½ cup cheese and lime juice; remove from heat. Set aside.

To soften tortillas, wrap in aluminum foil and warm in oven for 5 minutes.

In a medium bowl, combine chicken, green onions, garlic, cumin, and chili powder.

To assemble, place tortillas on a flat surface. Spread ¼ cup chicken mixture and 1 tablespoon cheese in center of each. Roll jelly-roll style and place with seam side down in baking dish. Pour sauce over enchiladas and sprinkle with chiles. Bake, uncovered, for 20 to 25 minutes, or until filling is warmed through.

Calories 303	Total Fat 9 g	Fiber 2 g
Protein 34 g	Saturated 4 g	Sodium 346 mg
Carbohydrates 21 g	Polyunsaturated 1 g	Potassium 388 mg
Cholesterol 76 mg	Monounsaturated 2 g	Calcium 433 mg

Savory Roasted Turkey

Serves 20; about 3 ounces turkey per serving

Roast a turkey stuffed with aromatic vegetables and fresh rosemary any time of the year. Unless you're serving a crowd, you'll have wonderful leftovers to use in sandwiches, such as Honey Mustard Turkey Wraps (page 127), casseroles, and soups.

	12-pound fresh or frozen turkey, not injected with a basting solution
	Vegetable oil spray
2	tablespoons Herb Seasoning (page 222), Lemon Herb Seasoning (page 223), Savory Herb Blend (page 224), or commercial no-salt-added herb seasoning
	Vegetable oil spray
1	rib celery, cut into 1-inch pieces
1	medium carrot, unpeeled, cut into 1-inch pieces
½	medium onion, sliced
1	small lime, quartered
4	sprigs fresh rosemary
½	cup Chicken Broth (page 23) or commercial low-sodium broth (optional)
3	cups Easy Gravy (optional; see page 117)

If cooking a frozen turkey, thaw completely, using package directions.

Preheat oven to 325° F. Lightly spray rack for roasting pan with vegetable oil spray. Don't spray bottom of pan.

Remove giblets and neck from turkey cavity; save for another use or discard. Rinse turkey and pat dry with paper towels. Rub outside of turkey with herb mixture. Put turkey with breast side up on rack in roasting pan. Lightly spray surface of turkey with vegetable oil spray. Put celery, carrot, onion, lime, and rosemary in turkey cavity.

Roast for 3 hours 30 minutes to 3 hours 45 minutes, basting once every hour with pan juices (or up to ½ cup broth). Turkey is done if juices run clear when you pierce a thigh with a sharp skewer or if an instant-read meat thermometer registers 180° F when you insert it between thigh and breast meat (be sure thermometer doesn't touch bone). Remove from oven and let stand for 15 minutes before carving. Discard vegetables in cavity. Remove skin before serving turkey.

Easy Gravy

Makes 12 servings • ¼ cup per serving

Using a turkey baster, skim fat from pan drippings in roasting pan, leaving caramelized brown bits and juices in bottom of pan. Pour 1 cup water into pan; scrape pan with a wooden spoon to loosen brown bits from bottom of pan. Pour this mixture into a medium saucepan, along with 2 cups Chicken Broth (page 23) or commercial low-sodium broth. Bring to a simmer over medium-high heat. In a small bowl, whisk together ½ cup cold water and ⅓ cup all-purpose flour. Pour into broth mixture. Cook over medium-high heat for 3 to 4 minutes, or until mixture is thickened, whisking occasionally. Season with pepper to taste.

Cook's Tip: The reason you don't spray the turkey roasting pan is that the caramelized brown bits that stick to the bottom of the pan will make a delicious gravy. The pan will virtually clean itself when it is deglazed with water.

Cook's Tip on Turkeys Injected with Basting Solutions: Most turkeys sold in supermarkets have been injected with a basting solution to enhance the flavor and keep the bird moist while roasting. These solutions are almost always high in sodium. If you can't find a noninjected turkey at your regular grocery store, check specialty grocery stores, butcher shops, health food stores, and natural food markets. You may need to order your turkey a few days ahead of time. Baste your turkey with pan juices or chicken broth during roasting to help keep it moist, and be sure not to overcook.

SAVORY ROASTED TURKEY		
Calories 150	Total Fat 5 g	Fiber 0 g
Protein 25 g	Saturated 2 g	Sodium 57 mg
Carbohydrates 0 g	Polyunsaturated 1 g	Potassium 259 mg
Cholesterol 62 mg	Monounsaturated 1 g	Calcium 24 mg

EASY GRAVY*		
Calories 14	Total Fat 0 g	Fiber 0 g
Protein 1 g	Saturated 0 g	Sodium 5 mg
Carbohydrates 3 g	Polyunsaturated 0 g	Potassium 20 mg
Cholesterol 0 mg	Monounsaturated 0 g	Calcium 2 mg

*Nutrient analysis is based only on water, broth, and flour. Amount of fat will vary according to amount of drippings left in the pan. Although the amount of fat in Easy Gravy will be more than is listed here, it will be much lower than the amount in traditional turkey gravy.

Roasted Lemon-Herb Turkey Breast

Serves 12 • 3 ounces per serving

Fresh lemon, fresh parsley, and lots of herbs tucked between the skin and the meat infuse this turkey with sensational flavors.

Vegetable oil spray
5-pound turkey breast with skin
2   medium lemons
1/2 cup snipped fresh parsley
2   tablespoons Lemon Herb Seasoning (page 223)
1   tablespoon extra-virgin olive oil
1   tablespoon Dijon mustard
    Paprika

Preheat oven to 325° F. Spray a roasting pan and baking rack with vegetable oil spray.

Rinse turkey and pat dry with paper towels.

Cut lemons in half and squeeze about 1/4 cup juice into a small mixing bowl. Set aside lemon halves.

Whisk remaining ingredients except paprika into lemon juice.

Using a tablespoon or your fingers, carefully separate skin from meat of turkey. Spread lemon juice mixture between skin and meat over as much area as possible, being careful not to tear skin. Gently pull skin over top and sides. Put turkey breast on rack in pan. Put reserved lemon halves in pan, directly under turkey cavity. Sprinkle turkey with paprika.

Roast turkey, uncovered, for 1 hour 30 minutes to 1 hour 45 minutes, or until no longer pink in center or a meat thermometer registers 170° F (see Cook's Tip on Thermometers, page 96).

Let stand for 10 to 15 minutes for easier slicing. Remove and discard skin before serving turkey.

Cook's Tip: If you prefer, replace the Lemon Herb Seasoning with 1 tablespoon dried basil, crumbled; 2 teaspoons dried oregano, crumbled; 1/4 teaspoon garlic powder; and 1/2 teaspoon coarsely ground pepper.

Cook's Tip on Turkey Breast: If you're not serving a crowd or don't want to have leftovers, ask the butcher to cut a frozen uncooked turkey breast in half and wrap it separately. Cook one piece and freeze the remaining piece for later use.

Calories 135	Total Fat 2 g	Fiber 0 g
Protein 26 g	Saturated 1 g	Sodium 79 mg
Carbohydrates 1 g	Polyunsaturated 0 g	Potassium 277 mg
Cholesterol 73 mg	Monounsaturated 1 g	Calcium 28 mg

Turkey Tenderloins with Rosemary

Serves 4 • 3 ounces turkey per serving

What an ideal way to season, bake, and make a sauce—all in one dish. It's great when you're in a hurry, and even greater when you're the one cleaning up.

	1-pound turkey breast tenderloin, all visible fat removed
	Vegetable oil spray
1	*tablespoon olive oil*
1	*tablespoon chopped fresh rosemary or 1 teaspoon dried, crushed*
1	*teaspoon lemon juice*
1	*medium clove garlic, minced, or ½ teaspoon bottled minced garlic*
¾	*teaspoon no-salt-added lemon pepper*
¼	*cup Chicken Broth (page 23) or commercial low-sodium broth*
1	*tablespoon dry white wine (regular or nonalcoholic), Chicken Broth (page 23), or commercial low-sodium broth*

Preheat oven to 350° F.

Rinse turkey and pat dry with paper towels. Set aside.

Spray a 12 × 8 × 2-inch glass baking dish with vegetable oil spray. Combine olive oil, rosemary, lemon juice, garlic, and lemon pepper in baking dish. Roll turkey in mixture, coating well. Tuck ends under.

Bake for 20 minutes. Turn over and bake for another 20 to 25 minutes, or until turkey registers 170° F on a meat thermometer. Transfer turkey to a cutting board, retaining liquid in baking dish and leaving oven on. Let turkey stand for 5 minutes. Thinly slice turkey diagonally across grain. Arrange on a serving platter.

Meanwhile, add broth and wine to liquid in baking dish, scraping bottom and sides of dish and stirring until well blended. Return dish to oven for 3 to 4 minutes, or until broth is heated throughout. Pour over turkey slices.

Pork Tenderloins with Rosemary

Substitute a 1-pound pork tenderloin for turkey; cook as directed above. Before removing it from the oven, make sure the pork registers 160° F for medium or 170° F for well-done on a meat thermometer.

Cook's Tip on Fresh Rosemary: Sprigs of rosemary are hardy and will keep for about two weeks in an airtight plastic bag in the refrigerator.

TURKEY TENDERLOINS WITH ROSEMARY

Calories 161	Total Fat 5 g	Fiber 0 g
Protein 27 g	Saturated 1 g	Sodium 134 mg
Carbohydrates 1 g	Polyunsaturated 1 g	Potassium 266 mg
Cholesterol 77 mg	Monounsaturated 3 g	Calcium 17 mg

PORK TENDERLOINS WITH ROSEMARY

Calories 175	Total Fat 8 g	Fiber 0 g
Protein 24 g	Saturated 2 g	Sodium 132 mg
Carbohydrates 1 g	Polyunsaturated 1 g	Potassium 389 mg
Cholesterol 67 mg	Monounsaturated 4 g	Calcium 9 mg

Tarragon Turkey Medallions

Serves 4 • 3 ounces turkey per serving

This is a very fast-paced dish. Be sure to prepare the side dishes before cooking the entrée. This goes well with Rice and Vegetable Pilaf (page 200) and mixed salad greens topped with Cider Vinaigrette (page 60).

Sauce
   2   tablespoons fresh lemon juice
   2   tablespoons water
1½   teaspoons fresh tarragon leaves or ½ teaspoon dried,
        crumbled
   1   medium clove garlic, minced, or ½ teaspoon bottled minced
        garlic
 ¼   teaspoon salt
 ⅛   teaspoon pepper

        1-pound turkey tenderloin, all visible fat removed
        Vegetable oil spray
   2   teaspoons extra-virgin olive oil

In a small bowl, whisk together all sauce ingredients. Set aside.

Rinse turkey and pat dry with paper towels. Cut turkey crosswise into ¼-inch slices.

Heat a large nonstick skillet over high heat. Remove skillet from heat and spray with vegetable oil spray (being careful not to spray near a gas flame). Add oil and tilt to coat bottom. Arrange turkey in a single layer in skillet and cook for 2 minutes. Turn slices over and cook for 3 minutes, or until no longer pink in center. Remove skillet from heat and transfer turkey to serving platter.

Return skillet to heat and add sauce mixture. Cook over high heat for 15 to 20 seconds, or until mixture reduces to 2 tablespoons, stirring constantly with a flat spatula. Drizzle sauce over turkey.

Tarragon Pork Medallions
Substitute a 1-pound pork tenderloin for turkey; cook as directed above.

TARRAGON TURKEY MEDALLIONS

Calories 149	Total Fat 3 g	Fiber 0 g
Protein 27 g	Saturated 1 g	Sodium 196 mg
Carbohydrates 1 g	Polyunsaturated 1 g	Potassium 265 mg
Cholesterol 77 mg	Monounsaturated 2 g	Calcium 17 mg

TARRAGON PORK MEDALLIONS

Calories 163	Total Fat 6 g	Fiber 0 g
Protein 24 g	Saturated 2 g	Sodium 194 mg
Carbohydrates 1 g	Polyunsaturated 1 g	Potassium 388 mg
Cholesterol 67 mg	Monounsaturated 3 g	Calcium 9 mg

Turkey Picadillo

Serves 6 • 1 cup per serving

Serve this spicy turkey mixture, pronounced pee-kah-DEE-yoh, mixed with rice or wrap it in a tortilla. Leftovers freeze and reheat beautifully.

2	teaspoons olive oil
1	large red bell pepper, diced (about 1 cup)
1	medium onion, chopped (about ¾ cup)
2	teaspoons bottled minced garlic or 4 medium cloves garlic, minced
1½	pounds ground turkey breast, skin removed before grinding
	28-ounce can no-salt-added crushed tomatoes
⅓	cup dried currants or coarsely chopped raisins
¼	cup coarsely chopped green olives
1	teaspoon ground cumin
½	teaspoon crushed red pepper flakes

Heat a large skillet over medium-high heat. Add oil and swirl to coat bottom. Increase heat to high and cook bell pepper and onion for 2 to 3 minutes, or until onion is translucent, stirring frequently.

Add garlic, reduce heat to medium-low, and cook for 3 to 4 minutes.

Add turkey, breaking it up with a fork, and cook until it whitens, about 5 minutes.

Add remaining ingredients; bring to a boil over high heat. Reduce heat to medium and cook, uncovered, for 10 minutes, stirring occasionally.

Calories 208	Total Fat 4 g	Fiber 3 g
Protein 29 g	Saturated 1 g	Sodium 239 mg
Carbohydrates 15 g	Polyunsaturated 1 g	Potassium 694 mg
Cholesterol 77 mg	Monounsaturated 2 g	Calcium 73 mg

Turkey Sausage Patties

Serves 4 • 1 patty per serving

These flavorful patties are a leaner version of the breakfast staple.
Serve them with French Toast, Pancakes, or Apple-Filled Crepes
(pages 241, 250, and 282).

	Vegetable oil spray
12	ounces ground turkey breast, skin removed before grinding
2	tablespoons water
	White of 1 large egg
1/4	teaspoon pepper
1/4	teaspoon dried basil, crumbled
1/4	teaspoon dried sage
1/4	teaspoon dried oregano, crumbled
1/8	teaspoon ground allspice
1/8	teaspoon ground nutmeg
1/8	teaspoon dried dillweed, crumbled
1/8	teaspoon garlic powder
1/8	teaspoon Chili Powder (page 225) or commercial no-salt-added variety (optional)
1/8	teaspoon red hot-pepper sauce (optional)

Preheat broiler. Spray a broiler pan and rack or a roasting pan and
baking rack with vegetable oil spray.

In a medium bowl, thoroughly combine all ingredients. Shape into
4 patties and put on rack in pan.

Broil 2 to 4 inches from heat for 10 minutes. Turn patties over and
broil for 5 to 10 minutes, or until no longer pink in center.

Cook's Tip on Allspice: Use allspice for a piquant flavor in all kinds of
foods from soups, stews, and meats to cakes and fruit dishes. Allspice is used in the
liqueurs Chartreuse and Bénedictine.

Calories 100	Total Fat 1 g	Fiber 0 g
Protein 21 g	Saturated 0 g	Sodium 52 mg
Carbohydrates 1 g	Polyunsaturated 0 g	Potassium 208 mg
Cholesterol 58 mg	Monounsaturated 0 g	Calcium 17 mg

New-Style Turkey Club Sandwich for One

Serves 1 • 2 pita halves per serving

Turn a popular sandwich into a heart-healthy, low-sodium lunch by making a few simple substitutions.

1	whole pita bread, cut in half crosswise
2	to 3 ounces Savory Roasted Turkey (page 116), sliced
1	medium Italian plum tomato, sliced (about ½ cup)
¼	cup shredded carrots
¼	cup finely shredded cabbage
1	teaspoon Hot Mustard (page 216) or commercial honey mustard
½	teaspoon imitation bacon bits

Stuff each pita half with turkey, tomato, carrots, and cabbage. Spread mustard on stuffing and sprinkle with bacon bits.

Cook's Tip on Low-Sodium Sandwiches: One flavorful way to cut down on the sodium in sandwiches is by using your own home-baked low-sodium breads (pages 228–235). Add leftover meats such as Savory Roasted Turkey (page 116) or Easy Roast Beef (page 130) and plenty of vegetables. Our recipes for condiments, such as Roasted Tomato Chipotle Salsa, Hot Mustard, Horseradish (pages 215–217), Ketchup (page 212), Easy Dill Pickles, Sweet Bread-and-Butter Pickles, or Sweet Relish (pages 218–220), are designed to add lots of flavor without much sodium.

Calories 331	Total Fat 6 g	Fiber 4 g
Protein 28 g	Saturated 1 g	Sodium 300 mg
Carbohydrates 43 g	Polyunsaturated 2 g	Potassium 508 mg
Cholesterol 52 mg	Monounsaturated 1 g	Calcium 93 mg

Honey-Mustard Turkey Wraps

Serves 6 • 1 wrap per serving

If you want a break from the usual turkey sandwich, try this spicy wrap. For extra kick, top it with thin slices of fresh jalapeños. Leftovers from Roasted Lemon-Herb Turkey Breast (page 118) or Savory Roasted Turkey (page 116) are terrific here.

3	tablespoons Hot Mustard (page 216) or 5 tablespoons honey mustard
2	tablespoons honey (omit if using honey mustard)
1/4	to 1/2 teaspoon red hot-pepper sauce
1	pound 2 ounces Roasted Lemon-Herb Turkey Breast (page 118) or low-sodium cooked turkey breast, shredded
6	6-inch reduced-fat flour tortillas, warmed
1 1/2	cups shredded lettuce
3/4	cup thinly sliced green bell pepper or Anaheim pepper
3/8	cup thinly sliced red onion
1	cup alfalfa sprouts
1	fresh jalapeño, stemmed, seeded, and thinly sliced crosswise (optional)

In a small bowl, whisk together mustard, honey, and hot-pepper sauce until smooth.

Put turkey in center of each tortilla. Drizzle mustard mixture over turkey. Top with remaining ingredients. Roll tortilla jelly-roll style, secure with toothpicks, and cut in half crosswise.

Calories 280	Total Fat 5 g	Fiber 2 g
Protein 30 g	Saturated 1 g	Sodium 222 mg
Carbohydrates 29 g	Polyunsaturated 1 g	Potassium 390 mg
Cholesterol 73 mg	Monounsaturated 2 g	Calcium 75 mg

Turkey Stew

Serves 12 • 1 cup per serving

If you have a household with people eating at different times, this one-pot meal is perfect.

    2   teaspoons fat-free tub margarine
    1   medium onion, chopped (about ¾ cup)
    4   cups Chicken Broth (page 23) or commercial low-sodium broth
 1¼   pounds cooked turkey breast, cooked without salt, skin and all
        visible fat removed, cut into bite-size pieces
    ¼   cup water
    2   tablespoons all-purpose flour
    6   medium ribs celery, coarsely chopped (about 3 cups)
    6   medium carrots, coarsely chopped (about 4 cups)
    1   teaspoon poultry seasoning
    1   bay leaf
    ½   teaspoon garlic powder
    ¼   to ½ teaspoon pepper
    6   medium potatoes, coarsely chopped (about 5 cups)
 1½   cups frozen green peas

In a stockpot, melt margarine over medium-high heat. Cook onion for 2 to 3 minutes, or until translucent, stirring occasionally.

Add broth and bring to a boil, stirring occasionally.

In a small bowl, whisk together water and flour. Add to broth and cook for 5 minutes, or until broth just begins to thicken, whisking constantly.

Stir in turkey, celery, carrots, poultry seasoning, bay leaf, garlic powder, and pepper. Bring to a boil. Reduce heat and cook for 15 minutes, or until heated through.

Add potatoes and cook, covered, for 30 minutes, or until vegetables are tender, stirring occasionally.

Stir in peas and cook for 5 minutes. Remove bay leaf before serving stew.

Calories 164	Total Fat 1 g	Fiber 5 g
Protein 19 g	Saturated 0 g	Sodium 120 mg
Carbohydrates 22 g	Polyunsaturated 0 g	Potassium 716 mg
Cholesterol 41 mg	Monounsaturated 0 g	Calcium 46 mg

Meats

easy roast beef
lime-marinated steak
beef stroganoff
beef bourguignon
meat loaf
beef and pasta portobello
spaghetti with meat sauce
middle eastern beef casserole
southwestern beef pita-tacos
chili
caribbean jerk pork
grilled pork medallions with apple cider sauce
grilled chicken with apple cider sauce
pork chops with herb rub
hungarian pork chops
chunky joes
chunky joe burritos
lemon veal with spinach
lemon chicken with spinach
buffalo baked in pumpkin
grilled lamb chops with rhubarb mint chutney
lamb curry

Easy Roast Beef

Serves 18 • 3 ounces beef and 2 tablespoons sauce per serving

You'll be transported back to Grandma's kitchen when you smell this homey dish. The leftovers are excellent for sandwiches and for recipes calling for cooked lean beef.

	Vegetable oil spray (olive oil preferred)
	5-pound beef rump roast, all visible fat removed
2	*tablespoons olive oil*
1	*tablespoon Chili Powder (page 225) or commercial no-salt-added variety*
1	*medium onion, thinly sliced (about ¾ cup)*
2	*medium carrots, thinly sliced (about 1½ cups)*
1	*large rib celery, thinly sliced (about ½ cup)*
½	*cup dry red wine (regular or nonalcoholic), plus more as needed*
1	*tablespoon very low sodium or low-sodium Worcestershire sauce*
½	*teaspoon salt*

Preheat oven to 350° F. Spray a roasting pan with vegetable oil spray. Rub meat with oil and sprinkle with chili powder; put in roasting pan. Arrange onion, carrots, and celery around meat.

In a small bowl, combine wine and Worcestershire sauce and pour over meat.

Bake, uncovered, for 1 hour 30 minutes, or until meat thermometer inserted in thickest part of meat registers desired degree of doneness. If meat begins to dry out during cooking, baste with additional wine. Don't use drippings from roast for basting. Remove roast from pan, retaining pan juices. Lightly cover roast with aluminum foil and let sit for 10 to 15 minutes.

Skim fat from pan juices or remove juices with bulb baster and discard fat.

Stir salt into pan juices.

Thinly slice roast; arrange on serving platter. Spoon pan juices over roast.

Cook's Tip on Beef Temperatures: Use a meat thermometer or an instant-read thermometer to determine internal temperature. To be safe, beef should be cooked to at least 160° F. For well-done, cook to 170° F.

Cook's Tip on Separating Fat from Pan Juices: A gravy separator makes this so easy! It looks like a measuring cup with a spout coming out from the bottom. Pour all the pan juices into the separator. The fat rises to the top, and you simply pour the fat-free juice out of the bottom until the fat layer falls to the level of the spout. Discard what remains in the separator.

Calories 195	Total Fat 6 g	Fiber 1 g
Protein 30 g	Saturated 2 g	Sodium 129 mg
Carbohydrates 2 g	Polyunsaturated 0 g	Potassium 477 mg
Cholesterol 78 mg	Monounsaturated 3 g	Calcium 14 mg

Lime-Marinated Steak

Serves 4 • 3 ounces per serving

Fresh lime juice adds a distinctive flavor to this grilled sirloin.

Marinade
- 1/2   cup fresh lime juice (5 medium)
- 2   tablespoons acceptable vegetable oil
- 1   tablespoon honey
- 1/2   teaspoon garlic powder
- 1/2   teaspoon red hot-pepper sauce

  16-ounce boneless sirloin steak, all visible fat removed
- 1/2   teaspoon pepper
- 1   medium lime (optional)

For marinade, combine all ingredients in an airtight plastic bag.

Add steak and turn to coat. Seal and refrigerate for 6 to 8 hours, turning bag occasionally.

Preheat grill to medium-high or preheat broiler.

Remove steak from marinade and sprinkle with pepper. Discard marinade.

Grill steak for 4 to 5 minutes on each side, or until tender and to desired doneness.

Meanwhile, slice lime into wedges or twists for garnish.

Cook's Tip on Marinating: Because marinades frequently call for acidic ingredients, such as vinegar or lemon juice, it's best to marinate in a plastic bag or a glass, ceramic, or stainless steel container. If you use an aluminum or a copper bowl, the acid can react with the bowl and add a metallic taste to the food. A plastic bowl may absorb the flavors and odors of your marinade. A large self-sealing plastic bag is very handy for marinating. Just put the food in the bag, seal it tightly, and turn the bag over from time to time so the marinade covers all the ingredients. Discard the bag to keep from encouraging bacterial growth.

Calories 164	Total Fat 6 g	Fiber 0 g
Protein 26 g	Saturated 2 g	Sodium 59 mg
Carbohydrates 0 g	Polyunsaturated 0 g	Potassium 342 mg
Cholesterol 75 mg	Monounsaturated 3 g	Calcium 11 mg

Beef Stroganoff

Serves 4 • 1 cup per serving

Sour cream sauce is a must in this classic, which was named for a 19th-century Russian diplomat.

1	pound beef tenderloin or sirloin steak, all visible fat removed
1/8	teaspoon pepper
1	teaspoon acceptable vegetable oil
1/2	pound fresh mushrooms, sliced (about 2 1/2 cups)
1	medium onion, sliced
2	cups Beef Broth (page 22) or commercial low-sodium broth, heated
3	tablespoons all-purpose flour
2	tablespoons no-salt-added tomato paste
2	tablespoons dry sherry
1	teaspoon dry mustard
1/8	teaspoon dried oregano, crumbled
1/8	teaspoon dried dillweed, crumbled
1/4	cup nonfat or light sour cream

Cut meat into thin strips about 2 inches long. Sprinkle with pepper.

Heat a large nonstick skillet over medium-high heat. Add oil and swirl to coat bottom. Cook meat for 1 minute.

Add mushrooms and onion; cook for 2 to 3 minutes, or until onion is translucent, stirring occasionally.

In a medium bowl, whisk together broth and flour. Add to skillet; bring to a boil. Reduce heat and simmer for 2 to 3 minutes, or until thickened, stirring constantly.

In a small bowl, whisk together remaining ingredients except sour cream. Stir into meat mixture. Simmer, covered, for 5 to 10 minutes, or until beef is tender.

Transfer 1/4 cup sauce to a small bowl; whisk in sour cream. Stir into skillet and cook for 5 minutes, or until warmed.

Calories 276	Total Fat 10 g	Fiber 2 g
Protein 29 g	Saturated 3 g	Sodium 92 mg
Carbohydrates 16 g	Polyunsaturated 1 g	Potassium 804 mg
Cholesterol 72 mg	Monounsaturated 4 g	Calcium 51 mg

Beef Bourguignon

Serves 8 • 1 cup per serving

*Even though this fancy stew takes a while to prepare, it's well worth
the time. Packed with meat and vegetables, it's a complete meal in
a bowl.*

2	tablespoons all-purpose flour
	Pepper to taste
1	pound lean beef chuck roast, all visible fat removed, cut into 1-inch cubes
	Vegetable oil spray
1	teaspoon acceptable vegetable oil
¼	cup chopped onion
1	medium clove garlic, minced, or ½ teaspoon bottled minced garlic
2	cups small whole fresh mushrooms (about 1 pound)
2	cups finely chopped fresh tomatoes (4 medium) or 14.5-ounce can no-salt-added diced tomatoes, undrained
1½	cups water, plus more as needed
½	cup dry red wine (regular or nonalcoholic)
1½	tablespoons Herb Seasoning (page 222) or the following:
1	tablespoon snipped fresh parsley
¼	teaspoon dried thyme, crumbled
¼	teaspoon dried basil, crumbled
¼	teaspoon dried oregano, crumbled
⅛	teaspoon dried rosemary, crushed
⅛	teaspoon dried marjoram, crumbled
3	cups peeled, coarsely diced potatoes (4 medium)
2	cups coarsely diced carrots (4 medium)

In a large bowl, stir together flour and pepper.

Add beef, turning to coat.

Heat a Dutch oven over medium-high heat. Remove from heat and
spray with vegetable oil spray (being careful not to spray near a gas
flame). Add oil, swirling to coat bottom. When oil is hot, cook beef for
1 to 2 minutes, stirring frequently.

Add onion and garlic; cook for 2 to 3 minutes, or until onion is
translucent, stirring frequently.

Stir in mushrooms and cook for 1 to 2 minutes, or until mushrooms absorb liquid.

Stir in tomatoes, water, wine, and herb seasoning. Reduce heat and simmer, covered, for 2 hours, stirring occasionally and adding water if necessary to keep bottom of pot covered.

Add potatoes and carrots; simmer, covered, for 30 minutes, or until beef and vegetables are tender.

Slow-Cooker Method

Omit vegetable oil spray and vegetable oil. Put coated beef cubes in a 3½- to 4-quart electric slow cooker. Add remaining ingredients and cook, covered, on high for 4 to 5 hours or on low for 8 to 9 hours.

Calories 204	Total Fat 6 g	Fiber 4 g
Protein 16 g	Saturated 2 g	Sodium 46 mg
Carbohydrates 22 g	Polyunsaturated 1 g	Potassium 791 mg
Cholesterol 41 mg	Monounsaturated 3 g	Calcium 36 mg

Meat Loaf

Serves 8 • 3 ounces per serving

Capers contribute Mediterranean flavor to this tried-and-true classic. Serve with garlic mashed potatoes and steamed green beans. Don't forget to save some of the meat loaf for sandwiches.

> *Vegetable oil spray*
> 1/2   *cup uncooked quick-cooking oatmeal*
> 1/4   *cup fat-free or low-fat plain yogurt*
> 1   *pound lean ground beef*
> 1/2   *cup chopped onion*
> 1   *medium rib celery, chopped (about 1/2 cup)*
> 1   *small parsnip or carrot, peeled and shredded (about 1/2 cup)*
>   *Egg substitute equivalent to 1 egg, or 1 large egg*
> 1   *tablespoon capers packed in balsamic vinegar, rinsed and drained*
> 1   *tablespoon fresh lemon juice*
> 1/2   *teaspoon dried thyme, crumbled*
> 1/4   *teaspoon pepper*
> 1/4   *teaspoon garlic powder*

Preheat oven to 375° F. Lightly spray a 9-inch square baking pan with vegetable oil spray.

In a large bowl, stir together oatmeal and yogurt; let stand for 5 minutes.

Add remaining ingredients, combining with your hands or a spoon. Form into a loaf about 8 × 5 inches and place in baking pan.

Bake, uncovered, for about 1 hour 15 minutes, or until internal temperature registers 165° F on a meat or instant-read thermometer. Remove from oven and let stand for 5 to 10 minutes. Cut into 16 slices; serve 2 slices to each person.

Cook's Tip on Gourmet Meat Loaf Sandwich: For leftovers with style, raise the classic meat loaf sandwich to new heights. Serve it in low-sodium buns or on low-sodium bread. Top the meat loaf with a mixture of 1 tablespoon Ketchup (page 212) or commercial no-salt-added ketchup and 1/2 teaspoon Horseradish (page 217) or dried horseradish. For a different flavor, spread the meat loaf with Roasted

Tomato Chipotle Salsa (page 215) or a commercial fat-free variety with the lowest
sodium available.

Calories 139	Total Fat 6 g	Fiber 1 g
Protein 13 g	Saturated 2 g	Sodium 100 mg
Carbohydrates 7 g	Polyunsaturated 0 g	Potassium 288 mg
Cholesterol 33 mg	Monounsaturated 2 g	Calcium 33 mg

Beef and Pasta Portobello

Serves 4 • 1 cup per serving

Portobello mushrooms have a meaty texture that's perfect for this classic meat-lovers' dish.

1	cup dried small shell macaroni
1	pound lean ground beef
1	medium portobello mushroom, stem trimmed, cut into ¾-inch cubes (about 1 cup)
1	cup chopped onion
1	medium clove garlic, minced, or 1 teaspoon bottled minced garlic
	14.5-ounce can no-salt-added diced tomatoes, undrained
	8-ounce can no-salt-added tomato sauce
½	cup water
1	bay leaf
1	teaspoon sugar
1	teaspoon salt-free Italian seasoning
½	teaspoon pepper
½	teaspoon crushed red pepper flakes (optional)

Cook macaroni using package directions, omitting salt and oil. Drain well and set aside.

Meanwhile, heat a large nonstick saucepan over medium-high heat. Add ground beef, mushroom, onions, and garlic. Cook for 8 to 10 minutes, or until meat is no longer pink and vegetables are tender, stirring occasionally. Put in a colander and drain well. Blot with paper towels to remove excess fat. Wipe skillet with paper towels; return drained mixture to skillet. Stir in remaining ingredients. Bring to a simmer over medium-high heat. Reduce heat and simmer for 15 minutes, stirring occasionally.

Add macaroni and cook, uncovered, for 2 to 3 minutes, or until macaroni is warmed through. Remove bay leaf before serving.

Calories 303	Total Fat 9 g	Fiber 4 g
Protein 23 g	Saturated 3 g	Sodium 68 mg
Carbohydrates 34 g	Polyunsaturated 1 g	Potassium 878 mg
Cholesterol 56 mg	Monounsaturated 3 g	Calcium 64 mg

Spaghetti with Meat Sauce

Serves 12 • 1 cup spaghetti and ⅔ cup sauce per serving

When you want to serve a crowd an entrée, this great recipe is the answer. Once you start the sauce cooking, it'll take care of itself while you take care of party preparations.

1	pound lean ground beef
1	28-ounce can no-salt-added diced tomatoes, undrained
2	small zucchini, diced
	6-ounce can no-salt-added tomato paste
1	medium onion, chopped (about ¾ cup)
½	cup dry red wine (regular or nonalcoholic)
1½	teaspoons chopped fresh oregano, or ½ teaspoon dried, crumbled
1½	teaspoons chopped fresh basil, or ½ teaspoon dried, crumbled
1	medium clove garlic, minced, or ½ teaspoon bottled minced garlic
½	teaspoon fennel seeds
⅛	teaspoon pepper
24	ounces dried spaghetti

Heat a large saucepan over medium-high heat. Cook beef until brown, 3 to 4 minutes, stirring occasionally. Put beef in a colander and rinse with hot water to remove excess fat; drain well. Wipe saucepan with paper towels; return beef to saucepan.

Stir in remaining ingredients except spaghetti. Cover and simmer for 1 hour 30 minutes, stirring occasionally. If sauce appears too thick, add water.

Cook spaghetti, using package directions, omitting salt and oil. Drain well. Spoon about 1 cup spaghetti onto each plate and top with about ⅔ cup sauce.

Calories 222	Total Fat 2 g	Fiber 3 g
Protein 13 g	Saturated 1 g	Sodium 39 mg
Carbohydrates 36 g	Polyunsaturated 0 g	Potassium 529 mg
Cholesterol 17 mg	Monounsaturated 1 g	Calcium 44 mg

Middle Eastern Beef Casserole

Serves 6 • 1 cup per serving

This dish is made in a fraction of the time and with a lot less effort than traditional moussaka. Once you pop the casserole into the oven, you have time to go for a walk or a bike ride while it's cooking.

14.5-ounce can no-salt-added tomatoes, well drained
1/2   cup finely chopped onion
2   teaspoons sugar
3/4   to 1 teaspoon ground cinnamon
1/2   teaspoon ground allspice or nutmeg
1/2   teaspoon salt
       Vegetable oil spray
8   ounces lean ground beef
8   to 10 ounces eggplant, cut crosswise into 1/2-inch slices
       (peeled, if desired)
4   ounces low-fat cream cheese
1/2   cup fat-free or low-fat plain yogurt
       Whites of 2 large eggs, egg substitute equivalent to 1 egg,
       or 1 large egg
       Paprika

Preheat oven to 350° F.

In a large bowl, combine tomatoes, onion, sugar, cinnamon, allspice, and salt. Set aside.

Heat a large nonstick skillet over high heat. Remove from heat and spray with vegetable oil spray (being careful not to spray near a gas flame). Cook beef for 3 minutes, or until brown, stirring constantly. Put in a colander and rinse with hot water to remove excess fat; drain well. Stir into tomato mixture. Wipe skillet with paper towels.

Put eggplant slices in one layer in skillet and top with beef mixture.

In a food processor or blender, combine remaining ingredients except paprika and process until smooth. Pour over beef mixture and sprinkle with paprika.

Cover handle of skillet with aluminum foil and bake for 1 hour, uncovered. Remove from oven and let stand for 10 to 30 minutes for eggplant to absorb liquid. If serving after 10 minutes, use a slotted spatula.

Cook's Tip: If you can, make this casserole early in the day. The longer it stands, the more flavorful it gets. It's best served the day you prepare it, however.

Calories 132	Total Fat 5 g	Fiber 2 g
Protein 12 g	Saturated 3 g	Sodium 307 mg
Carbohydrates 10 g	Polyunsaturated 0 g	Potassium 413 mg
Cholesterol 28 mg	Monounsaturated 2 g	Calcium 90 mg

Southwestern Beef Pita-Tacos

Serves 6 • 1 pita per serving

*Are they pita pockets or tacos? However you think of them, they're
fun to eat. They're especially good when served with slices of chilled
watermelon.*

Filling

1	pound lean ground beef
1	tablespoon all-purpose flour
1	cup water
1	teaspoon Chili Powder (page 225) or commercial no-salt-added variety
1/2	teaspoon ground cumin
1/4	teaspoon garlic powder
1/4	teaspoon onion powder
1/4	teaspoon pepper

6	6-inch whole-wheat pita breads, halved
1 1/2	cups shredded lettuce
2	medium tomatoes, chopped (about 1 cup)
1/2	cup chopped green bell pepper
1/2	cup chopped onion

If heating pitas, preheat oven to 350° F.

For filling, in a large nonstick skillet, cook beef over medium-high
heat until brown, 8 to 10 minutes, stirring occasionally. Put beef in a
colander and rinse with hot water to remove excess fat; drain well. Wipe
skillet with paper towels; return beef to skillet.

Sprinkle flour over meat, stirring to combine.

Stir in remaining filling ingredients. Bring to a simmer over medium-
high heat, stirring occasionally. Cook for 3 to 4 minutes, or until mixture has thickened, stirring occasionally.

If desired, wrap pitas in aluminum foil and heat in oven for 5 minutes
to soften.

To serve, spoon about 2 tablespoons meat mixture into each pita half.
Sprinkle with remaining ingredients.

Calories 269	Total Fat 5 g	Fiber 6 g
Protein 21 g	Saturated 1 g	Sodium 357 mg
Carbohydrates 39 g	Polyunsaturated 1 g	Potassium 452 mg
Cholesterol 34 mg	Monounsaturated 1 g	Calcium 27 mg

Chili

Serves 4 • 1 cup per serving

What could be easier or more welcome during the first cold weekend of the season than a bowl of big red? Before or after the football game, it's a sure winner.

1	pound lean ground beef
½	cup chopped onion
1	to 2 tablespoons chopped fresh jalapeño, stems, seeds, and membrane removed
	14.5-ounce can no-salt-added stewed tomatoes, undrained
	15-ounce can no-salt-added pinto beans, undrained
½	cup water (more as needed)
¼	cup stout or beer (regular, light, or nonalcoholic)
1	tablespoon Chili Powder (page 225) or commercial no-salt-added variety
2	teaspoons ground cumin
½	teaspoon dried oregano, crumbled
¼	teaspoon salt
⅛	teaspoon pepper
⅛	teaspoon cayenne (optional)

Heat a Dutch oven over high heat. Cook beef until brown, 3 to 4 minutes, stirring frequently. Put beef in a colander and rinse with hot water to remove excess fat; drain well. Wipe Dutch oven with paper towels.

Reduce heat to medium-high. Return beef to Dutch oven and add onion and jalapeño. Cook for 2 to 3 minutes, or until onion is translucent, stirring occasionally.

Stir in remaining ingredients. Reduce heat and simmer, covered, for 1 hour 30 minutes, stirring occasionally. Add water as needed for desired consistency.

Calories 261	Total Fat 5 g	Fiber 8 g
Protein 27 g	Saturated 2 g	Sodium 220 mg
Carbohydrates 25 g	Polyunsaturated 0 g	Potassium 778 mg
Cholesterol 51 mg	Monounsaturated 2 g	Calcium 114 mg

Caribbean Jerk Pork

The tropical flavor of thyme blended with spices and citrus comes through whether you broil the pork chops over an open grill or in your broiler. Vary the heat to taste by the amount of jalapeño you use.

> *Vegetable oil spray*

Jerk Seasoning

1	or 2 fresh jalapeños, stems removed, seeded if desired
2	tablespoons chopped onion
1	teaspoon grated orange zest
2	tablespoons fresh orange juice
1	tablespoon honey
2	teaspoons steak sauce
1	tablespoon ground allspice
1	tablespoon chopped fresh thyme or 1 teaspoon dried, crumbled
½	teaspoon ground cinnamon

4	boneless center-cut pork chops (about 4 ounces each), all visible fat removed
¼	teaspoon salt
1	medium lime, cut in 8 wedges (optional)

Spray grill rack with vegetable oil spray. Preheat grill to high. Or if using broiler, preheat broiler. Spray broiler rack and pan with vegetable oil spray.

In a food processor or blender, process all jerk seasoning ingredients until smooth. Put jerk seasoning in an airtight plastic bag.

Add pork to bag and turn to coat. Seal and refrigerate for 15 to 20 minutes, turning bag occasionally.

Grill pork for 5 minutes. Turn meat and grill for another 5 to 6 minutes, or until no longer pink in center.

If using broiler, put pork on rack and broil about 4 inches from heat for 5 minutes. Turn meat and broil for another 5 to 6 minutes, or until no longer pink in center. Transfer to serving platter; sprinkle with salt and serve with lime wedges.

Cook's Tip on Handling Hot Peppers: Wear rubber gloves when handling hot peppers, or wash your hands thoroughly with warm, soapy water after handling them. Your skin, especially around your eyes, is sensitive to oil from hot peppers.

Calories 195	Total Fat 6 g	Fiber 1 g
Protein 27 g	Saturated 2 g	Sodium 233 mg
Carbohydrates 8 g	Polyunsaturated 1 g	Potassium 390 mg
Cholesterol 78 mg	Monounsaturated 3 g	Calcium 35 mg

Grilled Pork Medallions with Apple Cider Sauce

Serves 8 • 3 ounces per serving

This delightful entrée is perfect for a dinner party or a special family dinner, but keep in mind that the pork marinates for three days. Leftover roast makes great sandwiches.

Marinade

1	cup fresh apple cider
¾	cup cider (draft cider preferred)
½	cup apple-flavored liqueur
3	tablespoons sugar
2	tablespoons whole mustard seeds
2	tablespoons olive oil (light preferred) (see Cook's Tip on Light Olive Oil, page 26)
1	tablespoon fresh rosemary, crushed, or 1 teaspoon dried, crushed
2	teaspoons fresh thyme or 1 teaspoon dried, crumbled
3	medium cloves garlic, minced, or 1½ teaspoons bottled minced garlic

2	pounds pork tenderloin, all visible fat removed, cut into eight medallions
6	cups fresh apple cider

Combine marinade ingredients in a medium skillet. Bring to a boil over medium heat. Boil for 4 to 5 minutes. Reduce heat and simmer for 30 minutes, or until reduced by half. Remove from heat and let cool for 30 minutes, or until at room temperature.

Pour marinade into an airtight plastic bag. Add pork and turn to coat. Seal and refrigerate for three days, turning bag occasionally.

In a medium saucepan, boil 6 cups apple cider over high heat for 40 to 50 minutes, or until reduced to ⅔ cup and thick enough to coat back of a spoon. Be careful not to let sauce boil over. If necessary, reduce heat to medium-high.

Preheat grill to medium-high. Grill tenderloin for 10 to 12 minutes; turn and grill for 10 to 12 minutes, or until pork registers 160° F for medium or 170° F for well-done on an instant-read thermometer.

To serve, drizzle each medallion with a tablespoon of sauce.

Grilled Chicken with Apple Cider Sauce

Replace pork tenderloin with eight 4-ounce boneless, skinless chicken breast halves or 2 pounds turkey breast medallions, all visible fat removed, adjusting grilling time to 6 to 8 minutes per side, or until no longer pink in center.

Cook's Tip: You can buy draft cider at most specialty beer and wine stores; many grocery stores also carry it.

Cook's Tip: You can make the cider sauce three days ahead and reheat it in a glass container set in a pan of hot water or in the microwave set on 25 percent power (low) until the sauce is pouring consistency.

GRILLED PORK MEDALLIONS WITH APPLE CIDER SAUCE

Calories 227	Total Fat 4 g	Fiber 0 g
Protein 24 g	Saturated 1 g	Sodium 66 mg
Carbohydrates 22 g	Polyunsaturated 0 g	Potassium 593 mg
Cholesterol 67 mg	Monounsaturated 2 g	Calcium 18 mg

GRILLED CHICKEN WITH APPLE CIDER SAUCE

Calories 212	Total Fat 2 g	Fiber 0 g
Protein 26 g	Saturated 0 g	Sodium 92 mg
Carbohydrates 22 g	Polyunsaturated 0 g	Potassium 511 mg
Cholesterol 66 mg	Monounsaturated 0 g	Calcium 26 mg

GRILLED TURKEY MEDALLIONS WITH APPLE CIDER SAUCE

Calories 213	Total Fat 1 g	Fiber 0 g
Protein 27 g	Saturated 0 g	Sodium 69 mg
Carbohydrates 22 g	Polyunsaturated 0 g	Potassium 470 mg
Cholesterol 77 mg	Monounsaturated 0 g	Calcium 27 mg

Pork Chops with Herb Rub

Serves 4 • 3 ounces per serving

Marjoram, an aromatic herb that tastes like a mild version of oregano, is the key ingredient in the rub that makes these grilled pork chops so tasty.

Rub

- 1/2 teaspoon dried marjoram, crumbled
- 1/8 teaspoon garlic powder
- 1/8 teaspoon onion powder
- 1/8 teaspoon pepper

- 4 loin pork chops, all visible fat removed, cut 1/2 inch thick (about 4 ounces each if boneless, 6 ounces each if bone in)

Preheat grill or broiler on medium-high.

In a small bowl, combine all rub seasoning ingredients. Rub on both sides of pork.

Grill for 6 minutes, or until brown. Turn and grill for 6 minutes, or until tender and no longer pink in center.

If using broiler, broil about 4 inches from heat for 5 minutes. Turn meat and broil for another 5 to 6 minutes, or until no longer pink in center.

Calories 144	Total Fat 6 g	Fiber 0 g
Protein 21 g	Saturated 2 g	Sodium 43 mg
Carbohydrates 0 g	Polyunsaturated 0 g	Potassium 269 mg
Cholesterol 58 mg	Monounsaturated 3 g	Calcium 24 mg

Hungarian Pork Chops

Serves 4 • 3 ounces meat and 3 tablespoons sauce per serving

Here's an Old World comfort dish without the work.

Rub
1   teaspoon paprika
¾   teaspoon dried dillweed, crumbled
½   teaspoon caraway seeds
½   teaspoon onion powder
½   teaspoon garlic powder

Vegetable oil spray
*4   loin pork chops, cut ½ inch thick (about 4 ounces each), all
        visible fat removed*
½   cup water
½   cup nonfat or light sour cream
¼   teaspoon salt
*2   tablespoons finely chopped green onions (green and
        white parts)*

In a small bowl, stir together all rub ingredients. Rub half the mixture on one side of pork chops.

Heat a large, heavy nonstick skillet over medium-high heat. Remove from heat and spray with vegetable oil spray (being careful not to spray near a gas flame). Cook pork chops with seasoned side down over medium heat for 4 minutes. Rub top side with remaining mixture. Turn pork chops over and cook for 4 to 5 minutes, or until no longer pink in center. Transfer to a platter and cover with aluminum foil.

Increase heat to high. Add water, scraping skillet. Boil for 1 to 2 minutes, or until liquid is reduced to ¼ cup. Reduce heat to low. When boiling stops, whisk in sour cream and salt. Cook for 2 to 3 minutes, or until heated through, whisking constantly. Don't boil.

To serve, spoon sauce over pork and sprinkle with green onions.

Calories 187	Total Fat 6 g	Fiber 0 g
Protein 25 g	Saturated 2 g	Sodium 219 mg
Carbohydrates 7 g	Polyunsaturated 0 g	Potassium 409 mg
Cholesterol 60 mg	Monounsaturated 3 g	Calcium 71 mg

Chunky Joes

Serves 6 • ²/₃ cup pork mixture and 1 bun per serving

Chunks of lean pork replace ground beef in this delightfully messy sandwich. Add some corn for crunch.

1	pound pork tenderloin or other lean boneless pork, all visible fat removed
	Vegetable oil spray
1	cup finely chopped onion
1	medium green bell pepper, finely chopped (about 1 cup)
	14.5-ounce can no-salt-added diced tomatoes, undrained
½	cup frozen no-salt-added whole-kernel corn, thawed (optional)
1½	tablespoons cider vinegar
1	tablespoon sugar
1½	tablespoons Chili Powder (page 225) or commercial no-salt-added variety
⅛	teaspoon salt
6	hamburger buns

Cut pork into ¼-inch cubes.

Heat a large nonstick skillet over high heat. Remove from heat and spray with vegetable oil spray (being careful not to spray near a gas flame). Cook pork for 3 minutes, or until it just begins to brown and liquid evaporates, stirring constantly. Transfer pork to a plate. Set aside.

Spray skillet with vegetable oil spray and return to heat. Reduce heat to medium-high. Cook onion and bell pepper for 2 to 3 minutes, or until onion is translucent, stirring frequently.

Stir in reserved meat, any accumulated juices, tomatoes, corn, vinegar, sugar, and chili powder. Cook, uncovered, for 10 minutes, or until mixture has thickened, stirring occasionally. Stir in salt.

Meanwhile, split and toast buns. Spoon pork mixture over buns.

Chunky Joe Burritos

Replace hamburger buns with six 6-inch reduced-fat flour tortillas, warmed. Before rolling the mixture up in the tortilla, top each serving with 1 tablespoon nonfat or light sour cream.

Cook's Tip: For a moister consistency, add 2 to 3 tablespoons of water with the salt.

CHUNKY JOES

Calories 259	Total Fat 5 g	Fiber 3 g
Protein 21 g	Saturated 2 g	Sodium 330 mg
Carbohydrates 32 g	Polyunsaturated 2 g	Potassium 587 mg
Cholesterol 45 mg	Monounsaturated 2 g	Calcium 98 mg

CHUNKY JOE BURRITOS

Calories 248	Total Fat 5 g	Fiber 3 g
Protein 21 g	Saturated 2 g	Sodium 240 mg
Carbohydrates 29 g	Polyunsaturated 1 g	Potassium 599 mg
Cholesterol 46 mg	Monounsaturated 2 g	Calcium 95 mg

Lemon Veal with Spinach

Serves 6 • 1 cup per serving

*Bake some Whole-Wheat Bread (page 228) to complete this
tasty meal.*

2	teaspoons olive oil
1½	pounds top round veal, all visible fat removed, cut into cubes
1	large onion, chopped (about 1 cup)
¼	cup water, plus more as needed
1	tablespoon fresh lemon juice
½	teaspoon crushed fennel seeds
¼	teaspoon pepper
2	10-ounce packages frozen spinach
3	green onions, chopped (green and white parts)
1	lemon, cut into 6 wedges (optional)

Heat oil in a Dutch oven over medium-high heat. Cook veal and
onion for 5 minutes, or until veal is brown and onion is translucent, stirring frequently. Use a slotted spoon to transfer to a plate or bowl; drain
off any fat. Wipe Dutch oven with paper towels. Return veal and onion
to pot.

Stir in ¼ cup water, lemon juice, fennel seeds, and pepper. Simmer,
covered, for 1 hour, or until veal is tender, stirring occasionally. If mixture begins to get too dry, add small amount of water.

Add spinach and green onions. Simmer, covered, for 5 to 10 minutes,
or until spinach is tender. Transfer to a serving platter and garnish with
lemon wedges.

Lemon Chicken with Spinach

Substitute 6 boneless, skinless chicken breast halves (about 4 ounces
each) for the veal. Remove all visible fat from chicken. Substitute 1 teaspoon dried basil, crumbled, for the fennel seeds. Reduce simmering
time from 1 hour to 20 minutes.

LEMON VEAL WITH SPINACH

Calories 173	Total Fat 4 g	Fiber 4 g
Protein 28 g	Saturated 1 g	Sodium 145 mg
Carbohydrates 8 g	Polyunsaturated 1 g	Potassium 800 mg
Cholesterol 89 mg	Monounsaturated 2 g	Calcium 126 mg

LEMON CHICKEN WITH SPINACH

Calories 182	Total Fat 3 g	Fiber 4 g
Protein 31 g	Saturated 1 g	Sodium 149 mg
Carbohydrates 8 g	Polyunsaturated 1 g	Potassium 685 mg
Cholesterol 68 mg	Monounsaturated 2 g	Calcium 136 mg

Buffalo Baked in Pumpkin

Serves 10 • 1 cup pumpkin plus 1 cup stuffing per serving

An ideal one-dish meal for the fall and winter months, this stuffed pumpkin makes a dramatic presentation. Widely available in specialty meat stores and health food stores, buffalo is lower in total fat and saturated fat than beef or pork. If buffalo isn't available, use extra-lean ground beef or turkey breast ground without skin.

1	cup uncooked wild rice, rinsed and drained
6	pound pumpkin or winter squash (you may need several squash)
¼	cup honey mustard
1	tablespoon acceptable vegetable oil
2½	cups chopped onion (2 to 3 large)
2	to 3 fresh jalapeño peppers, seeded and finely chopped
3	large cloves garlic, minced, or 2¼ teaspoons bottled minced garlic
1½	pounds ground buffalo
¾	cup snipped fresh parsley
2	roasted yellow or red bell peppers, chopped (⅔ cup)
¼	cup unsalted shelled pumpkin seeds or toasted pine nuts
1	tablespoon dried thyme, crumbled
1	tablespoon dried cilantro, crumbled
⅛	to ¼ teaspoon cayenne
3	finely chopped green onions (green and white parts) (optional)

Cook rice using package directions, omitting salt, but don't cook rice until puffy. Keep it al dente (slightly firm); it will cook more during baking.

Meanwhile, cut off top of pumpkin as you would for a jack-o'-lantern. Remove and discard seeds and stringy fibers; rinse pumpkin well and pat dry with paper towels. Using a pastry brush, paint inside of pumpkin and lid with honey mustard. Set aside.

Place oven rack in lowest position. Preheat oven to 325° F.

Heat a large nonstick skillet over medium-high heat. Add oil and swirl to coat bottom. Cook onion for 2 to 3 minutes, or until translucent, stirring occasionally.

Add jalapeño peppers and garlic. Cook for 2 minutes, stirring occasionally.

Break up buffalo into pieces and add to onion mixture. Cook for 5 minutes, or until meat is lightly browned, stirring occasionally. Transfer meat mixture to a large bowl.

Add rice and remaining ingredients except green onions; stir well.

Gently spoon mixture into pumpkin; cover with lid. Place in a roaster or large baking pan; gently pour in water to a depth of 1½ inches.

Bake for 2 to 2½ hours, or until pumpkin shell is soft to the touch. If top of squash begins to brown too quickly, cover with aluminum foil. Be sure to check water level in baking pan, adding water, if necessary, to keep it at a depth of 1½ inches.

Bring whole stuffed pumpkin to table; slice, adding a spoonful of stuffing and a sprinkle of green onions to each portion.

Cook's Tip: Try adding 1 cup fresh diced tomatoes to the stuffing for a change of flavor.

Cook's Tip on Pumpkin Seeds: If you can't find unsalted pumpkin seeds, simply rinse the salted seeds and let them dry on paper towels.

Calories 265	Total Fat 5 g	Fiber 4 g
Protein 21 g	Saturated 1 g	Sodium 52 mg
Carbohydrates 35 g	Polyunsaturated 2 g	Potassium 1152 mg
Cholesterol 42 mg	Monounsaturated 2 g	Calcium 74 mg

Grilled Lamb Chops with Rhubarb Mint Chutney

Serves 6 • 2 chops and 2 tablespoons chutney per serving

Serve this exotic dish with mashed or roasted potatoes and a spinach salad. The chutney recipe makes twice the amount you need for the chops, so you'll have plenty left over to spice up other meals.

Marinade
- ⅔   cup balsamic vinegar
- 2   tablespoons fresh lemon juice
- 2   teaspoons dried rosemary, crushed
- 4   medium cloves garlic, minced, or 2 teaspoons bottled minced garlic
- 1   teaspoon pepper

- 12   4-ounce loin lamb chops, bone in, all visible fat removed

Rhubarb Mint Chutney

Makes 1½ cups

- 1   tablespoon light stick margarine
- 1   small onion, minced
- 3   cups frozen chopped rhubarb
- 1   ounce fresh mint, chopped (about 1 cup)
- ⅓   cup sugar
- ⅓   cup firmly packed light brown sugar
- 1   tablespoon grated lemon zest (2 medium)
- ¼   cup fresh lemon juice (2 medium)

In a large airtight plastic bag, combine all marinade ingredients. Add lamb and turn to coat. Seal and refrigerate for 3 to 4 hours, turning bag occasionally.

Meanwhile, for chutney, melt margarine in a medium saucepan over medium heat. Cook onion for 3 to 4 minutes, or until translucent, stirring occasionally.

Stir in remaining chutney ingredients. Bring to a boil over medium-high heat, about 5 minutes. Reduce heat and simmer, uncovered, for 10 minutes, or until thickened.

Preheat grill to medium-high. Drain chops, reserving marinade.

In a small saucepan, bring marinade to a boil over high heat. Boil for 5 minutes.

Grill chops on a covered grill to desired doneness, 4 to 5 minutes per side for medium-rare, basting with marinade often. Transfer to serving platter and serve with warm or room temperature chutney.

Cook's Tip: When grilling the lamb chops, watch them carefully. The marinade tends to make the fire flare up. Avoid total charring.

Cook's Tip: Chutney can be prepared up to two days ahead, covered with plastic wrap, and refrigerated. For an appetizer or snack, use leftover chutney to top salt-free crackers spread with fat-free cream cheese.

Calories 309	Total Fat 10 g	Fiber 1 g
Protein 31 g	Saturated 4 g	Sodium 102 mg
Carbohydrates 22 g	Polyunsaturated 1 g	Potassium 510 mg
Cholesterol 95 mg	Monounsaturated 4 g	Calcium 114 mg

Lamb Curry

Serves 8 • 3 ounces per serving

Serve this spicy lamb over rice with small side bowls of raisins and sliced green onions to sprinkle on top.

3	tablespoons all-purpose flour
1/8	teaspoon pepper
2	pounds boneless lamb chuck roast, all visible fat removed, cut into cubes
2	teaspoons acceptable vegetable oil
3	cups water
1/2	cup finely chopped onion
1/2	cup unsweetened applesauce
2	to 3 teaspoons curry powder
2	teaspoons fresh lemon juice

In a medium plastic or paper bag, combine flour and pepper.

Add lamb, a few pieces at a time, and shake to coat. Shake off any excess flour.

In a large nonstick skillet, heat oil over medium-high heat. Cook lamb for about 5 minutes, or until brown on all sides, stirring occasionally. Using a slotted spoon, transfer lamb to a plate; pour off excess fat. Wipe skillet clean with paper towels. Return lamb to skillet.

Stir in remaining ingredients except lemon juice. Simmer, covered, for 1 hour, or until meat is tender, stirring occasionally.

Stir in lemon juice right before serving.

Calories 179	Total Fat 6 g	Fiber 1 g
Protein 24 g	Saturated 2 g	Sodium 74 mg
Carbohydrates 5 g	Polyunsaturated 1 g	Potassium 370 mg
Cholesterol 73 mg	Monounsaturated 3 g	Calcium 15 mg

Vegetarian Entrées

grilled pizza with grilled vegetables
pizza muffins
spaghetti with wild mushroom sauce
eggplant lasagna
alfredo lasagna with broccoli and cauliflower
fettuccine alfredo
zucchini frittata
stir-fried noodles with tofu and vegetables
pasta e fagioli supremo
polenta and cheese with fresh mushrooms
spicy polenta
gorgonzola portobello rounds
pizza portobellos
crustless garden quiche
vegetarian chili

Grilled Pizza with Grilled Vegetables

Serves 8 • ¹/₂ 8-inch pizza per serving

Serve these pizzas as an appetizer, entrée, or side dish. Get creative by adding your favorite grilled vegetables or by cutting the dough into interesting shapes with cookie cutters.

Dough
1   cup warm water (105° F to 115° F)
1   teaspoon sugar
    ¹/₄-ounce package active dry yeast (2¹/₂ teaspoons)
3   cups all-purpose flour
2   tablespoons olive oil (light preferred) (see Cook's Tip on Light
    Olive Oil, page 26)
¹/₈ teaspoon salt

    Vegetable oil spray
2   medium red bell peppers
2   medium thin zucchini, sliced (about 2 cups)
1   bunch medium asparagus, trimmed (about 16 medium
    stalks)
3   very large fresh button mushrooms
    Cornmeal for rolling out dough
2   to 3 tablespoons no-salt-added tomato paste
8   large fresh basil leaves, coarsely chopped
1¹/₄ cups shredded part-skim mozzarella cheese

For dough, in a glass measuring cup, stir together water, sugar, and yeast. Let stand for about 5 minutes, or until foamy.

In a food processor, combine yeast mixture and remaining dough ingredients (see Cook's Tip, page 161). Process for about 1 minute, or until dough comes together and forms a ball. Transfer dough to a flat surface and knead gently for about 30 seconds; dough should be light, smooth, and elastic.

Spray a large glass bowl with vegetable oil spray; place dough in bowl. With a sharp knife, cut a big "x" into top surface of dough (¹/₁₆ to ¹/₈ inch deep). Cover bowl tightly with plastic wrap and let stand in a warm, draft-free area for 45 to 60 minutes, or until dough doubles in size.

Remove plastic wrap and punch dough down; transfer dough to a flat surface and lightly knead.

Divide dough into four equal pieces and pat into balls. Cover dough balls individually with plastic wrap and refrigerate until ready to use.

Spray grill rack generously with vegetable oil spray. Preheat grill to medium-high. Place vegetables on rack and grill for 30 to 35 minutes, turning peppers to char evenly. Turn zucchini, asparagus, and mushrooms after 15 minutes. When cooked through, bell peppers should be totally blackened, and zucchini and asparagus should be well marked.

Seal peppers in an airtight plastic bag or put in a large bowl and cover with plastic wrap. Let peppers cool for 20 to 30 minutes.

Meanwhile, cut off asparagus tips; reserve stalks for another use. Slice mushrooms. Set aside.

When cooled, slice peppers in half and remove stems, seeds, and veins. Gently peel skin off peppers, using your fingers or rubbing with paper towels, or scrape skin off with a knife. Discard skin (see Cook's Tip on Roasted Bell Peppers, page 10). Slice peppers to desired thickness and place in a bowl. Set aside.

Sprinkle a flat surface with cornmeal; remove dough from refrigerator. Pat dough down. Roll into desired shape, keeping dough about ¼ inch thick.

With grill lid closed or with dough loosely covered with heavy aluminum foil, grill dough with cornmeal side up for 4 minutes, or until top of crust is lightly browned. Remove from grill.

With fingers or a pastry brush, coat each grilled side with 1½ to 2 teaspoons tomato paste, rubbing it into surface of dough. Top with zucchini, mushrooms, asparagus tips, and bell pepper. Sprinkle with basil and cheese.

Grill for 5 to 6 minutes, or until cheese melts. Remove from grill and let sit for about 2 minutes before serving.

Cook's Tip: If you don't have a food processor, you can prepare the dough with a large electric mixer that has a dough hook. Put the yeast mixture and the remaining dough ingredients in a large bowl and beat until combined. You can also combine the ingredients with a fork or a spoon, transfer dough to a flat surface, and knead it for about 3 minutes, or until it feels elastic and smooth.

Calories 283	Total Fat 7 g	Fiber 4 g
Protein 12 g	Saturated 2 g	Sodium 128 mg
Carbohydrates 44 g	Polyunsaturated 1 g	Potassium 444 mg
Cholesterol 10 mg	Monounsaturated 3 g	Calcium 144 mg

Pizza Muffins

Zesty and satisfying, this sandwich version of a veggie pizza is so trouble-free to make it will become an after-school favorite for kids as well as an entrée for grown-ups.

    2   English muffins
    ¼   cup Spaghetti Sauce (page 208) or commercial no-salt-added
        spaghetti sauce
    1   ounce shredded part-skim mozzarella cheese
    ¼   cup sliced fresh mushrooms
    4   thin slices onion
    4   green bell pepper rings

Preheat oven to 400° F.

Split muffins in half and put on baking sheet, cut sides up. Spread spaghetti sauce over muffins.

Top with remaining ingredients.

Place pizzas in oven and heat for about 5 minutes, or until cheese melts.

Calories 195	Total Fat 4 g	Fiber 3 g
Protein 9 g	Saturated 2 g	Sodium 303 mg
Carbohydrates 34 g	Polyunsaturated 0 g	Potassium 356 mg
Cholesterol 8 mg	Monounsaturated 1 g	Calcium 222 mg

Spaghetti with Wild Mushroom Sauce

Serves 4 • 1 cup spaghetti and ½ cup sauce per serving

We've jazzed up this classic with exotic mushrooms. Use your favorite mushroom, whatever the market is featuring, or a mixture.

1	tablespoon olive oil
1	cup sliced fresh mushrooms, such as shiitake, cremini, or portobello, or a combination
⅓	cup chopped onion
1	medium clove garlic, minced, or ½ teaspoon bottled minced garlic
	16-ounce can no-salt-added diced tomatoes, undrained
	6-ounce can no-salt-added tomato paste
½	cup water
1	tablespoon sugar
1	bay leaf
¾	teaspoon chopped fresh basil or ¼ teaspoon dried, crumbled
¾	teaspoon chopped fresh oregano, or ¼ teaspoon dried, crumbled
⅛	teaspoon pepper
⅛	teaspoon cayenne (optional)
8	ounces dried spaghetti

Heat a large nonstick skillet over medium-high heat. Add oil and swirl to coat bottom. Cook mushrooms, onion, and garlic for 3 to 5 minutes, or until onion is translucent, stirring occasionally.

Stir in remaining ingredients except spaghetti. Simmer, covered, for 1 to 2 hours, stirring occasionally. If sauce is too thick, add water. Remove bay leaf.

Cook spaghetti using package directions, omitting salt and oil. Drain well. Spoon about 1 cup spaghetti onto each plate and top with about ½ cup sauce.

Calories 267	Total Fat 5 g	Fiber 4 g
Protein 9 g	Saturated 1 g	Sodium 54 mg
Carbohydrates 50 g	Polyunsaturated 1 g	Potassium 816 mg
Cholesterol 0 mg	Monounsaturated 3 g	Calcium 64 mg

Eggplant Lasagna

Serves 6 • 4 × 4-inch piece per serving

If you can, prepare this hearty lasagna a day ahead. Its flavors will be enhanced, plus all you'll need to do for dinner is toss a salad and make a quick fruit dessert while the casserole bakes.

	Vegetable oil spray
6	dried lasagna noodles
3	cups peeled, chopped eggplant
1	medium green bell pepper, diced (about 1 cup)
1	large onion, chopped (about 1 cup)
¼	cup chopped fresh basil or 1 tablespoon plus 1 teaspoon dried, crumbled
3	medium cloves garlic, minced, or 1½ teaspoons bottled minced garlic
2	8-ounce cans no-salt-added tomato sauce
2	teaspoons very low sodium or low-sodium Worcestershire sauce
⅛	teaspoon salt
¼	teaspoon fennel seeds (optional)
1	cup fat-free or low-fat cottage cheese
1	cup part-skim mozzarella cheese, shredded
2	tablespoons shredded or grated Parmesan cheese

Preheat oven to 350° F. Spray a 12 × 8 × 2-inch glass baking dish with vegetable oil spray.

In a large stockpot, cook noodles using package directions, omitting salt and oil.

Meanwhile, heat a large nonstick skillet over medium-high heat. Remove skillet from heat and spray with vegetable oil spray (being careful not to spray near a gas flame). Cook eggplant, bell pepper, onion, dried basil (if using fresh basil, add with tomato sauce), and garlic for 10 minutes, or until eggplant is tender, stirring occasionally; reduce heat to medium if mixture sticks to skillet.

Add tomato sauce, Worcestershire sauce, salt, and fennel seeds. Bring to a boil; reduce heat, and simmer, uncovered, for 15 minutes, or until sauce has slightly thickened and bell pepper is tender. Remove from heat.

To assemble, lay 2 noodles lengthwise in baking dish. Spread a scant 1 cup eggplant mixture over noodles. Spoon half the cottage cheese over sauce; spread evenly. Sprinkle with ¼ cup mozzarella. Repeat layers twice, ending with remaining ½ cup mozzarella. Tuck in ends of noodles if overhanging; cover with aluminum foil.

Bake for 30 minutes. Remove from oven; discard foil.

Sprinkle lasagna with Parmesan; let stand for 5 to 10 minutes to allow cheese to melt and to make slicing easier.

Cook's Tip on Cheese: When using fairly small amounts of cheese on top of a casserole, cover the dish with aluminum foil during the baking period to prevent the cheese from overcooking and drying out. Run the casserole under the broiler for a few seconds if you want to brown the cheese lightly.

Calories 214	Total Fat 4 g	Fiber 4 g
Protein 15 g	Saturated 2 g	Sodium 312 mg
Carbohydrates 30 g	Polyunsaturated 0 g	Potassium 522 mg
Cholesterol 16 mg	Monounsaturated 3 g	Calcium 201 mg

Alfredo Lasagna with Broccoli and Cauliflower

Serves 8 • ³/₄ to 1 cup per serving

A creamy Alfredo-type sauce binds layers of noodles, vegetables, and cheeses in this vegetarian lasagna. No tomatoes allowed!

Vegetable oil spray

Sauce

2½	cups fat-free milk
3	tablespoons all-purpose flour
¼	teaspoon pepper
⅛	teaspoon cayenne (optional)
¼	cup shredded or grated Parmesan cheese

Ricotta Mixture

1	cup fat-free or low-fat ricotta cheese
	Egg substitute equivalent to 1 egg, or 1 large egg
1	teaspoon dried oregano, crumbled
¼	teaspoon onion powder
¼	teaspoon garlic powder

4	cups water (optional)
2	cups chopped fresh (½-inch pieces) or frozen cauliflower, thawed
2	cups chopped fresh (½-inch pieces) or frozen broccoli, thawed
4	oven-ready lasagna noodles, broken in half
¼	cup roasted red bell peppers, rinsed and drained if bottled, chopped
1	cup shredded part-skim mozzarella cheese

Crumb Topping

¼	cup plain dry bread crumbs
2	teaspoons olive oil
½	teaspoon salt-free Italian seasoning

Preheat oven to 375° F. Lightly spray a 2-quart casserole dish with vegetable oil spray.

For sauce, in a medium saucepan, whisk together all ingredients except Parmesan. Cook over medium-high heat for 4 to 5 minutes, or until mixture thickens slightly, stirring occasionally. (Sauce will be somewhat thin.)

Stir in Parmesan and remove from heat. Set aside.

For ricotta mixture, in a medium bowl, combine all ingredients. Set aside.

If using fresh cauliflower and broccoli, bring water to a boil in a medium saucepan over high heat. Reduce heat to medium-high and cook cauliflower for 2 minutes. Add broccoli and cook for 1 minute. Drain well.

If using frozen cauliflower and broccoli, place in a colander and let sit under warm running water for 3 to 5 minutes. Drain well.

To assemble, pour half the sauce into casserole dish. Make a layer of four lasagna noodle halves. Spread ricotta mixture evenly over noodles. Arrange cauliflower and broccoli over ricotta mixture. Sprinkle with peppers and ½ cup mozzarella. Top with remaining noodles, sauce, and cheese. Cover dish with aluminum foil and set on a baking sheet in case lasagna bubbles over.

Bake for 30 minutes.

Meanwhile, in a small bowl, combine crumb topping ingredients. After 30 minutes, remove foil from lasagna and sprinkle with crumb topping. Bake, uncovered, for 8 to 10 minutes, or until topping is toasted and noodles are tender. Let stand for 5 to 10 minutes before cutting.

Calories 187	Total Fat 5 g	Fiber 2 g
Protein 15 g	Saturated 2 g	Sodium 282 mg
Carbohydrates 20 g	Polyunsaturated 0 g	Potassium 383 mg
Cholesterol 15 mg	Monounsaturated 2 g	Calcium 386 mg

Fettuccine Alfredo

Serves 8 • 1 cup per serving

*Now you can have all the richness of Alfredo sauce with only a
fraction of the fat and sodium. The addition of lemon gives this dish a
fresh twist.*

1	pound dried fettuccine
¼	cup fat-free milk
2	tablespoons all-purpose flour
1¼	cups fat-free milk
¼	cup shredded or grated Parmesan cheese
2	teaspoons fresh lemon juice
⅛	teaspoon white pepper
2	tablespoons finely snipped fresh parsley
1½	tablespoons shredded or grated Parmesan cheese
¼	teaspoon salt
4	lemon wedges (optional)

Cook fettuccine using package directions, omitting salt and oil.
Drain and cover with aluminum foil to keep warm.

Meanwhile, heat a medium saucepan over medium heat. In a small
bowl, whisk together ¼ cup milk and flour until smooth. Whisk mixture
into saucepan.

Whisk in remaining milk. Bring to a boil. Cook for 15 minutes, or
until thickened, stirring constantly with a flat spatula to keep sauce from
sticking to bottom of pan.

Add ¼ cup Parmesan, lemon juice, and pepper. Pour sauce over
warm fettuccine.

Sprinkle with parsley, remaining Parmesan, and salt. Garnish with
lemon wedges.

Calories 254	Total Fat 2 g	Fiber 1 g
Protein 11 g	Saturated 1 g	Sodium 181 mg
Carbohydrates 46 g	Polyunsaturated 0 g	Potassium 182 mg
Cholesterol 4 mg	Monounsaturated 1 g	Calcium 128 mg

Zucchini Frittata

Serves 4 • 1 wedge per serving

Bursting with Italian flavor, this frittata is equally at home at brunch or dinner.

Whites of 6 large eggs or egg substitute equivalent to 3 eggs
4   drops yellow food coloring (optional)
Vegetable oil spray
1   medium zucchini, diced
3   medium green onions, sliced (green and white parts)
14.5-ounce can no-salt-added tomatoes, drained
2   medium cloves garlic, minced, or 1 teaspoon bottled minced garlic
½   teaspoon salt-free Italian seasoning
¼   teaspoon pepper
¼   teaspoon salt
½   cup grated part-skim mozzarella cheese (2 ounces)
1   tablespoon shredded or grated Parmesan cheese

Preheat oven to 350° F.

In a small bowl, whisk together egg whites and food coloring. Set aside.

Heat a large nonstick skillet with an ovenproof handle over medium heat. Remove skillet from heat and spray with vegetable oil spray (being careful not to spray near a gas flame). Cook zucchini for about 6 minutes, or until soft.

Add green onions; cook for 1 minute.

Add tomatoes with liquid, garlic, Italian seasoning, and pepper; cook for 5 minutes, or until vegetables are tender and mixture has slightly thickened, stirring frequently.

Stir egg whites into skillet.

Sprinkle with salt and mozzarella.

Bake for 12 minutes, or until toothpick inserted in center comes out clean. Leaving pan in oven, change setting to broil. Broil for 3 to 4 minutes, or until golden brown. Remove from oven and sprinkle with Parmesan.

Calories 100	Total Fat 3 g	Fiber 2 g
Protein 11 g	Saturated 2 g	Sodium 336 mg
Carbohydrates 8 g	Polyunsaturated 0 g	Potassium 473 mg
Cholesterol 9 mg	Monounsaturated 1 g	Calcium 164 mg

Stir-Fried Noodles with Tofu and Vegetables

Serves 6 • 1 cup per serving

Similar to a vegetarian version of pad thai, *the famous Thai dish, this dish features user-friendly ingredients to re-create the traditional flavors. Nutrient-packed Swiss chard or leafy green spinach adds dimension.*

    6   ounces dried fettuccine or dried flat rice sticks
    4   cups whole spinach leaves
    4   cups Swiss chard leaves, coarsely chopped, or an additional
        4 cups spinach leaves

Sauce
    2   tablespoons fresh or bottled lime juice (1 to 2 medium limes)
    2   tablespoons light soy sauce
    1   tablespoon sugar
    1   tablespoon dry sherry (optional)

Egg Shreds
        Vegetable oil spray
        Egg substitute equivalent to 2 eggs, or 2 large eggs

    1   teaspoon acceptable vegetable oil
    1   large red bell pepper, thinly sliced
    2   medium cloves garlic, minced, or 1 teaspoon bottled minced garlic
    ½   teaspoon crushed red pepper flakes
        10.5-ounce package light tofu (firm or extra firm), diced
    2   green onions, cut into 1-inch pieces (green and white parts)
    2   tablespoons chopped unsalted peanuts, crushed
        Lime wedges (optional)

Cook fettuccine using package directions, omitting salt and oil. If using rice sticks, see Cook's Tip on page 171. During last 2 minutes of cooking time, stir in spinach and Swiss chard. Drain well.

For sauce, in a small bowl, combine all ingredients. Set aside.

For egg shreds, heat a 12-inch nonstick skillet over medium heat. Remove from heat and lightly spray with vegetable oil spray (being careful not to spray near a gas flame). Pour egg substitute into pan, tilting to cover bottom. Cook for 20 to 30 seconds, or until egg is set (doesn't jiggle when skillet is gently shaken).

Using a spatula, "scramble" egg substitute while cooking for 10 to 15 seconds, or until cooked through. Remove from pan and set aside.

Increase heat to medium-high. Add oil and swirl to coat bottom. Cook bell pepper, garlic, and red pepper flakes for 1 minute, or until bell pepper is tender, stirring occasionally.

Add tofu and green onions; cook for 2 to 3 minutes, or until tofu is lightly browned and warmed through, stirring occasionally.

Add reserved sauce; cook for 15 seconds.

Stir in noodle mixture and egg shreds; cook for 1 to 2 minutes, or until warmed through, stirring occasionally.

Spoon mixture onto a large serving platter and top with peanuts. Garnish with lime wedges.

Cook's Tip on Swiss Chard: The peppery-tasting green leaf/red stem variety of Swiss chard is quite interesting in this dish—it turns the noodles slightly reddish pink. The mild-tasting green leaf/lighter green stalk variety is also delicious.

Cook's Tip on Rice Sticks: Made of rice flour and water, rice sticks, or rice-flour noodles, are available in Asian grocery stores, health food stores, and some supermarkets. To use flat rice sticks in this recipe, soak 6 ounces of dried noodles in hot tap water for 15 to 20 minutes. (You will need to cook the spinach and Swiss chard separately in boiling water for 2 minutes.) Drain the noodles and add them with the egg shreds. Be careful not to overcook rice noodles, or they will become mushy.

STIR-FRIED NOODLES WITH TOFU AND VEGETABLES (FETTUCCINE)

Calories 188	Total Fat 3 g	Fiber 3 g
Protein 11 g	Saturated 0 g	Sodium 285 mg
Carbohydrates 30 g	Polyunsaturated 1 g	Potassium 410 mg
Cholesterol 0 mg	Monounsaturated 1 g	Calcium 55 mg

STIR-FRIED NOODLES WITH TOFU AND VEGETABLES (RICE STICKS)

Calories 185	Total Fat 3 g	Fiber 2 g
Protein 9 g	Saturated 0 g	Sodium 286 mg
Carbohydrates 32 g	Polyunsaturated 1 g	Potassium 365 mg
Cholesterol 0 mg	Monounsaturated 1 g	Calcium 53 mg

Pasta e Fagioli Supremo

Serves 8 • 1³/₄ cup per serving

The traditional Italian dish of pasta and beans lightens up in this recipe. Serve it warm in the winter and cold in the summer. For unlimited possibilities, experiment with different beans, pasta, and herbs every time you make this dish.

2	teaspoons olive oil (light preferred) (see Cook's Tip on Light Olive Oil, page 26)
1	large sweet onion, chopped (preferably Vidalia or Maui Sweet)
1	cup finely chopped celery (3 medium ribs)
3	medium cloves garlic, minced, or 1¹/₂ teaspoons bottled minced garlic
1	cup diced mushrooms
³/₄	cup no-salt-added canned navy beans, rinsed and drained
³/₄	cup no-salt-added canned fava beans (broad beans), rinsed and drained
³/₄	cup no-salt-added canned chick-peas (garbanzo beans), rinsed and drained
¹/₂	cup medium-dry white wine (regular or nonalcoholic), or Vegetable Broth (page 24), or commercial low-sodium broth
5	oil-packed sun-dried tomatoes, well drained and finely chopped (about ¹/₄ cup)
¹/₄	cup balsamic vinegar
1	tablespoon dried oregano, crumbled
1	teaspoon dried basil, crumbled
3	bay leaves
¹/₄	to ¹/₂ teaspoon crushed dried red pepper flakes, or to taste
1	pound dried pasta (ziti preferred)
¹/₂	cup snipped fresh parsley
³/₄	cup grated Parmesan or Parmigiano-Reggiano cheese, divided use

In a stockpot, heat oil over medium-high heat. Cook onion, celery, and garlic for 2 to 3 minutes, or until onion is translucent, stirring occasionally.

Stir in mushrooms, navy and fava beans, chick-peas, wine, tomatoes, vinegar, oregano, basil, and bay leaves; increase heat to high and bring to a boil.

Stir in red pepper flakes and simmer, covered, for 10 minutes, or until flavors are combined.

Meanwhile, cook pasta using package directions, omitting salt and oil. Drain well.

In a large bowl, stir together all ingredients except ½ cup Parmesan. Top with remaining Parmesan.

Calories 387	Total Fat 6 g	Fiber 7 g
Protein 17 g	Saturated 2 g	Sodium 208 mg
Carbohydrates 63 g	Polyunsaturated 1 g	Potassium 469 mg
Cholesterol 7 mg	Monounsaturated 2 g	Calcium 199 mg

Polenta and Cheese with Fresh Mushrooms

Serves 8 • ½ cup per serving

Decorate your dinner plate with rosemary sprigs to give a fresh look to this fancy polenta.

	Butter-flavor vegetable oil spray
1¾	cups chopped mixed fresh mushrooms, such as chanterelles and oyster
5	cups Vegetable Broth (page 24) or commercial low-sodium broth
1½	cups cornmeal (100% stone-ground preferred)
¼	cup plus 4 tablespoons shredded or grated Parmesan cheese, divided use
1	tablespoon olive oil (light preferred) (see Cook's Tip on Light Olive Oil, page 26)
1	to 1½ teaspoons chopped fresh rosemary (leaves only)
	Fresh rosemary sprigs (optional)

Preheat oven to 375° F. Spray a 13 × 9 × 2-inch baking dish with vegetable oil spray.

Spray a large nonstick skillet with vegetable oil spray. Cook mushrooms over medium heat for 5 minutes, or until cooked through, stirring occasionally. Set aside.

In a medium saucepan, bring broth to a boil over medium heat.

Slowly add cornmeal, stirring constantly with a wooden spoon. Cook for 20 to 25 minutes, or until thickened and beginning to pull away from pan, stirring constantly. Remove from heat.

Stir in mushrooms, ¼ cup plus 1 tablespoon Parmesan cheese, olive oil, and chopped rosemary. Pour into baking dish, smoothing top.

Sprinkle with remaining 3 tablespoons Parmesan.

Bake for 20 minutes, or until firm to the touch.

Let cool for 5 to 6 minutes. Cut into squares or use cookie cutters to cut into your favorite shapes. Garnish with rosemary sprigs.

Spicy Polenta

Cook two fresh jalapeño peppers, seeded and finely chopped, with mushrooms; substitute Chicken Broth (page 23) or commercial low-sodium broth for Vegetable Broth; and add yolk of one large egg, slightly beaten, when stirring in olive oil.

Cook's Tip: If you're having trouble cutting the polenta into shapes, it may have cooled too much. Just reheat it briefly in a microwave oven on 100 percent power (high) for about 3 minutes.

Cook's Tip: Substitute dried mushrooms that have been reconstituted for fresh mushrooms. A .35-ounce package of chanterelles and a 1-ounce package of oyster mushrooms make a great combination. Reconstitute the mushrooms by soaking them in hot water for 20 to 30 minutes. Use the soaking broth as part of the 5 cups broth for cooking the cornmeal.

POLENTA AND CHEESE WITH FRESH MUSHROOMS

Calories 141	Total Fat 5 g	Fiber 2 g
Protein 6 g	Saturated 2 g	Sodium 154 mg
Carbohydrates 20 g	Polyunsaturated 1 g	Potassium 163 mg
Cholesterol 5 mg	Monounsaturated 2 g	Calcium 93 mg

SPICY POLENTA

Calories 145	Total Fat 5 g	Fiber 2 g
Protein 6 g	Saturated 2 g	Sodium 142 mg
Carbohydrates 19 g	Polyunsaturated 1 g	Potassium 202 mg
Cholesterol 32 mg	Monounsaturated 2 g	Calcium 95 mg

Gorgonzola Portobello Rounds

Serves 4 • 1 stuffed mushroom per serving

Pile fresh spinach leaves, Italian-seasoned vegetables, and Gorgonzola cheese on giant mushrooms, then bake the mixture for a creamy, exotic vegetarian entrée.

4	portobello mushroom caps, stems removed (about 5 inches in diameter)
	Vegetable oil spray
2	teaspoons extra-virgin olive oil
2	medium red bell peppers, chopped (about 2 cups)
1	medium red onion, chopped (about ¾ cup)
2	medium cloves garlic, minced, or 1 teaspoon bottled minced garlic
½	teaspoon crushed red pepper flakes
½	cup chopped Italian plum tomatoes
1	tablespoon chopped fresh basil or 1 teaspoon dried, crumbled
1	ounce fresh spinach leaves, unrinsed, stems removed (about ¾ cup)
¼	cup plus 1 tablespoon blue cheese, crumbled (Gorgonzola preferred)

Preheat oven to 350° F.

Spray both sides of mushrooms with vegetable oil spray and place with cap side down on a baking sheet. Brush ½ teaspoon olive oil evenly over each mushroom.

Bake for 10 to 12 minutes, or until tender when pierced with a fork.

Meanwhile, heat a large nonstick skillet over medium-high heat. Remove skillet from heat and spray with vegetable oil spray (being careful not to spray near a gas flame). Cook bell peppers, onion, garlic, and red pepper flakes for 5 minutes, or until bell peppers are tender, stirring frequently. Remove skillet from heat.

Stir in tomatoes and basil.

Meanwhile, rinse spinach leaves and shake off excess water. Don't dry with paper towels.

Top each mushroom with spinach leaves. Carefully spoon ½ cup pepper mixture on each. Sprinkle with cheese.

Bake for 6 to 7 minutes, or until cheese begins to melt.

Pizza Portobellos

Substitute ½ cup Spaghetti Sauce (page 208) or bottled low-salt pizza sauce for spinach; substitute shredded mozzarella cheese for Gorgonzola. Sprinkle each serving with 1 teaspoon shredded or grated Parmesan cheese at serving time.

Cook's Tip on Portobello Mushrooms: Brushing a small amount of oil on portobello mushrooms before baking or broiling them prevents them from getting a "leathery" texture.

GORGONZOLA PORTOBELLO ROUNDS

Calories 107	Total Fat 6 g	Fiber 3 g
Protein 5 g	Saturated 2 g	Sodium 160 mg
Carbohydrates 11 g	Polyunsaturated 1 g	Potassium 488 mg
Cholesterol 8 mg	Monounsaturated 3 g	Calcium 81 mg

PIZZA PORTOBELLOS

Calories 114	Total Fat 5 g	Fiber 3 g
Protein 6 g	Saturated 2 g	Sodium 113 mg
Carbohydrates 14 g	Polyunsaturated 1 g	Potassium 571 mg
Cholesterol 7 mg	Monounsaturated 2 g	Calcium 114 mg

Crustless Garden Quiche

Serves 6 • 1 wedge per serving

For a rainy-night supper, serve this "sunshine on a plate." Brilliant red, green, and yellow-orange radiate from this flavor-packed quiche, which is filled with delicious vegetables.

Vegetable oil spray
8   ounces fresh mushrooms, sliced (about 2½ cups)
1   medium red bell pepper, thinly sliced (about 1 cup)
    Egg substitute equivalent to 6 eggs
¼   cup fat-free evaporated milk
1   tablespoon Dijon mustard
½   teaspoon very low sodium or low-sodium Worcestershire sauce
¼   teaspoon cayenne
1   cup shredded reduced-fat sharp Cheddar cheese, divided use
2   cups frozen no-salt-added broccoli and cauliflower, thawed and drained on paper towels (about 10 ounces)
¼   cup snipped fresh parsley

Preheat oven to 350° F. Spray a 9-inch glass deep-dish pie pan with vegetable oil spray.

Heat a large nonstick skillet over medium-high heat. Remove skillet from heat and spray with vegetable oil spray (being careful not to spray near a gas flame). Cook mushrooms for 6 minutes, or until they begin to brown slightly, stirring frequently.

Add bell pepper and cook for 2 minutes, stirring frequently. Remove skillet from heat.

Meanwhile, in a medium bowl, whisk together egg substitute, milk, mustard, Worcestershire sauce, and cayenne until well blended.

Stir in ¼ cup Cheddar.

Spoon cooked mushroom mixture evenly in pie pan. Top with broccoli and cauliflower, parsley, and ¼ cup Cheddar.

Pour egg mixture evenly over all.

Bake for 30 minutes (quiche won't be quite set). Sprinkle with remaining ½ cup Cheddar. Bake for 5 minutes, or until cheese melts. Remove from oven.

Let stand for 5 minutes to absorb liquids and for easier slicing.

Calories 122	Total Fat 4 g	Fiber 2 g
Protein 14 g	Saturated 2 g	Sodium 333 mg
Carbohydrates 8 g	Polyunsaturated 0 g	Potassium 427 mg
Cholesterol 10 mg	Monounsaturated 1 g	Calcium 251 mg

Vegetarian Chili

Serves 10 • 1 cup per serving

*When it's time to put logs in the fireplace, it's also time to fire up a big
pot of this chili, flavored with lots of cumin and brightened with
lemon juice.*

	Vegetable oil spray
2	teaspoons acceptable vegetable oil
2	cups chopped onion (2 large)
2	cups chopped green bell peppers (3 medium)
2	medium cloves garlic, minced, or 1 teaspoon bottled minced garlic
2	cups water
1	cup no-salt-added canned diced tomatoes
1	cup bulgur
2	tablespoons ground cumin
1½	tablespoons Chili Powder (page 225) or commercial no-salt-added chili powder, to taste
1	tablespoon lemon juice
½	teaspoon pepper
¼	teaspoon cayenne
2	16-ounce cans no-salt-added kidney beans, rinsed and drained

Heat a large saucepan or Dutch oven over medium-high heat. Remove from heat and spray with vegetable oil spray (being careful not to
spray near a gas flame). Add oil and swirl to coat bottom. Cook onion,
bell peppers, and garlic for 8 to 10 minutes, or until bell peppers are tender, stirring frequently. Reduce heat if necessary to prevent burning.

Stir in remaining ingredients except beans. Reduce heat and simmer,
covered, for 45 to 60 minutes, or until bulgur is done and flavors are
blended.

Stir in beans and simmer, uncovered, for 10 minutes.

Calories 167	Total Fat 2 g	Fiber 8 g
Protein 9 g	Saturated 0 g	Sodium 14 mg
Carbohydrates 33 g	Polyunsaturated 1 g	Potassium 575 mg
Cholesterol 0 mg	Monounsaturated 1 g	Calcium 81 mg

Vegetables & Side Dishes

baked beans

green beans and corn

succotash

broccoli pancakes

zucchini pancakes

stir-fried cabbage with noodles

gingered carrots

thyme-flavored cauliflower

eggplant mexicana

roasted red peppers and portobello mushrooms

hash brown potatoes

potatoes o'brien

potato pancakes

scalloped potatoes

zesty oven-fried potatoes

sweet potato casserole

asian fried rice with peas

rice and vegetable pilaf

dilled summer squash

baked tomatoes

Baked Beans

Serves 6 • ¹/₂ cup per serving

No potluck meal or barbecue is complete without baked beans. These cook for a long time, but need very little attention. The result is well worth the wait.

¹/₂	pound dried navy beans, sorted for stones and shriveled beans and rinsed (about 1 cup)
4	cups water
	Vegetable oil spray
	4-ounce loin-end pork chop, all visible fat removed
1	cup Chili Sauce (page 213) or 1 cup no-salt-added ketchup plus dash of red hot-pepper sauce
1	cup water
³/₄	cup chopped onion
2	tablespoons light molasses
1	tablespoon light brown sugar
1¹/₂	teaspoons dry mustard
¹/₄	teaspoon garlic powder

In a Dutch oven, bring beans and water to a boil over high heat. Boil for 2 minutes. Remove from heat and let stand for 1 hour. Return beans to heat and simmer, covered, for 1 hour, or until tender. Rinse and drain.

Preheat oven to 350° F. Lightly spray a 1¹/₂-quart casserole dish with vegetable oil spray. Put beans in casserole.

In a small nonstick skillet, brown pork chop over medium-high heat for 2 to 3 minutes on each side. Cut into small cubes and add to beans.

Stir in remaining ingredients.

Bake, covered, for 4 hours, or until tender. If beans begin to dry out while baking, add water about ¹/₄ cup at a time.

Calories 215	Total Fat 2 g	Fiber 7 g
Protein 10 g	Saturated 0 g	Sodium 24 mg
Carbohydrates 43 g	Polyunsaturated 1 g	Potassium 668 mg
Cholesterol 2 mg	Monounsaturated 0 g	Calcium 93 mg

Green Beans and Corn

Serves 4 • 1/2 cup per serving

This pairing of two all-time favorite vegetables is simple but colorful.

1/2   cup water
1   cup sliced fresh green beans or frozen no-salt-added French-
     style green beans
1   cup fresh or frozen no-salt-added whole-kernel corn
1   teaspoon light stick margarine
3   tablespoons chopped onion
1/2   teaspoon dried basil, crumbled
1/2   teaspoon lemon juice
     Dash of pepper

In a medium saucepan, bring water to a boil over high heat. Stir in beans and corn. Reduce heat and simmer, covered, until beans are just tender, 5 to 8 minutes. Drain well in a colander.

In same saucepan, melt margarine over medium heat. Cook onion for 3 to 4 minutes, or until translucent.

Return green beans and corn to pan; stir in remaining ingredients.

Succotash

Substitute fresh or frozen lima beans for the green beans. Simmer for 15 to 20 minutes. Substitute crumbled dried marjoram for the basil.

GREEN BEANS AND CORN		
Calories 58	Total Fat 2 g	Fiber 2 g
Protein 2 g	Saturated 0 g	Sodium 27 mg
Carbohydrates 10 g	Polyunsaturated 1 g	Potassium 182 mg
Cholesterol 0 mg	Monounsaturated 1 g	Calcium 17 mg

SUCCOTASH		
Calories 93	Total Fat 2 g	Fiber 3 g
Protein 4 g	Saturated 0 g	Sodium 29 mg
Carbohydrates 16 g	Polyunsaturated 1 g	Potassium 301 mg
Cholesterol 0 mg	Monounsaturated 1 g	Calcium 18 mg

Broccoli Pancakes

Serves 10 • 2 pancakes per serving as side dish

Topped with a dollop of nonfat sour cream, these colorful veggie pancakes make either a great side dish with meat, poultry, or seafood or a terrific vegetarian entrée. Made in a smaller version, they also serve as an appetizer.

1	pound frozen broccoli florets, chopped (about 4 cups)
1	bunch chopped green onions (green and white parts) (about 1 cup)
1	cup shredded carrot
2	tablespoons finely snipped fresh cilantro
1	tablespoon dried dillweed, crumbled
2	teaspoons dried basil, crumbled
½	teaspoon salt
¼	teaspoon white pepper
½	cup fat-free milk
½	cup all-purpose flour
	Egg substitute equivalent to 2½ eggs or 1 large egg plus whites of 3 large eggs
1¼	cups nonfat or light sour cream

In a large bowl, stir together broccoli, green onions, carrot, cilantro, dillweed, basil, salt, and pepper until thoroughly combined.

In a medium bowl, whisk together remaining ingredients except sour cream until smooth. Add to vegetable mixture and stir thoroughly.

Preheat oven to 300° F. Place baking sheet in oven.

Heat a large nonstick skillet over medium heat. Working in batches, use a ¼-cup measuring cup to drop batter into pancakes; flatten slightly with bottom of measuring cup. Cook for 7 to 10 minutes per side, or until pancakes are golden brown and cooked through. If pancakes begin to burn, reduce heat to medium-low. Transfer each batch of pancakes to baking sheet in oven to keep warm. To serve, top each pancake with 1 tablespoon sour cream.

Zucchini Pancakes

Substitute 4 cups shredded zucchini for broccoli. Squeeze excess liquid from zucchini before combining vegetables.

Cook's Tip: Serve miniature versions of these pancakes as an appetizer. Simply drop by tablespoonfuls into the skillet, and proceed as directed. Top with a dab of sour cream and a bit of black olive or dot of caviar.

BROCCOLI PANCAKES

Calories 92	Total Fat 0 g	Fiber 2 g
Protein 6 g	Saturated 0 g	Sodium 197 mg
Carbohydrates 16 g	Polyunsaturated 0 g	Potassium 302 mg
Cholesterol 3 mg	Monounsaturated 0 g	Calcium 102 mg

ZUCCHINI PANCAKES

Calories 87	Total Fat 0 g	Fiber 2 g
Protein 5 g	Saturated 0 g	Sodium 187 mg
Carbohydrates 16 g	Polyunsaturated 0 g	Potassium 334 mg
Cholesterol 3 mg	Monounsaturated 0 g	Calcium 84 mg

Stir-Fried Cabbage with Noodles

Serves 5 • ½ cup per serving

Cabbage and pasta may seem to be unlikely partners, but they work well together, especially with the addition of flavorful caraway seeds.

1	cup dried no-yolk noodles
1	tablespoon light tub margarine
3	cups finely chopped cabbage
¾	teaspoon caraway seeds
½	teaspoon onion powder

Prepare noodles using package directions, omitting salt and oil. Drain well.

Meanwhile, in a large skillet, melt margarine over medium heat. Stir-fry cabbage for 5 to 8 minutes, or until tender-crisp.

Stir in noodles and remaining ingredients.

Calories 102	Total Fat 1 g	Fiber 2 g
Protein 3 g	Saturated 0 g	Sodium 34 mg
Carbohydrates 19 g	Polyunsaturated 1 g	Potassium 173 mg
Cholesterol 0 mg	Monounsaturated 0 g	Calcium 32 mg

Gingered Carrots

Serves 5 • ¹/₂ cup per serving

This dish will make even unbelievers change their minds about vegetables.

1   *pound carrots, cut into ¹/₄-inch slices (about 4 medium) (2¹/₂ to 3 cups)*
1   *tablespoon light tub margarine, melted*
1   *teaspoon sugar*
¹/₄   *teaspoon ground ginger*
2   *tablespoons finely snipped fresh parsley or 2 teaspoons dried, crumbled*

Place carrots in a large saucepan. Add just enough water to cover. Bring to a boil over high heat; reduce heat and simmer, covered, for 10 to 12 minutes, or until barely tender. Drain well.

In a small bowl, stir together margarine, sugar, and ginger; gently stir into carrots.

Sprinkle with parsley.

Calories 52	Total Fat 1 g	Fiber 3 g
Protein 1 g	Saturated 0 g	Sodium 47 mg
Carbohydrates 11 g	Polyunsaturated 1 g	Potassium 304 mg
Cholesterol 0 mg	Monounsaturated 0 g	Calcium 27 mg

Thyme-Flavored Cauliflower

Serves 4 • ¹/₂ cup per serving

Here's the answer to what to do with cauliflower besides covering it with cheese sauce. Serve with Hungarian Pork Chops (page 149) and cinnamon applesauce.

1	medium head cauliflower (about 1¹/₂ pounds) or 10-ounce package frozen cauliflower (about 2 cups)
2	tablespoons water
1	to 2 teaspoons cider vinegar
¹/₂	medium clove garlic, minced, or ¹/₄ teaspoon bottled minced garlic
¹/₄	teaspoon dried thyme, crumbled
	Dash of pepper
2	teaspoons acceptable vegetable oil
2	teaspoons finely snipped fresh parsley or 1 teaspoon dried, crumbled

If using fresh cauliflower, break into small florets. In a medium saucepan, bring a small amount of water to a boil over high heat; boil cauliflower, covered, for 10 to 12 minutes, or until just tender. If using frozen cauliflower, prepare using package directions, omitting salt. Drain well.

Meanwhile, in a medium bowl, combine 2 tablespoons water, vinegar, garlic, thyme, and pepper. Set aside.

Heat a large skillet over medium heat. Add oil and tilt to coat bottom. Cook cauliflower for 2 to 3 minutes, stirring occasionally.

Stir in vinegar mixture. Cook, covered, for 5 to 8 minutes, or until cauliflower is tender.

Sprinkle with parsley.

Calories 50	Total Fat 2 g	Fiber 2 g
Protein 2 g	Saturated 0 g	Sodium 35 mg
Carbohydrates 6 g	Polyunsaturated 1 g	Potassium 316 mg
Cholesterol 0 mg	Monounsaturated 1 g	Calcium 25 mg

Eggplant Mexicana

Serves 8 • ¹⁄₂ cup per serving

Want a tasty new way to get vegetables into your diet? Try this eggplant and tomato side dish, which gets a flavor burst from our Chili Powder and fresh cilantro.

1	medium eggplant, peeled and cubed (about 1 pound)
4	medium tomatoes, peeled if desired and chopped, or 16-ounce can no-salt-added tomatoes (about 2 cups)
2	tablespoons chopped onion
1	medium clove garlic, minced, or ¹⁄₂ teaspoon bottled minced garlic
¹⁄₄	to ¹⁄₂ teaspoon Chili Powder (page 225) or commercial no-salt-added chili powder
¹⁄₄	teaspoon pepper
2	tablespoons snipped fresh cilantro or parsley

In a large nonstick skillet, combine all ingredients except cilantro. Simmer, covered, for 15 to 20 minutes, or until eggplant is tender.
   Sprinkle with cilantro.

Calories 30	Total Fat 0 g	Fiber 2 g
Protein 1 g	Saturated 0 g	Sodium 8 mg
Carbohydrates 7 g	Polyunsaturated 0 g	Potassium 273 mg
Cholesterol 0 mg	Monounsaturated 0 g	Calcium 10 mg

Roasted Red Peppers and Portobello Mushrooms

Serves 12 • ¹/₂ cup per serving

Since you serve this unusual side dish at room temperature, it's perfect for a party buffet. It's also a terrific appetizer when served over crostini or low-sodium wheat crackers.

     Olive oil spray
6   medium red bell peppers
4   medium portobello mushrooms, stems removed
     Olive oil spray
¹/₄ cup plain rice vinegar
2   teaspoons sugar, or to taste

Spray a broiling pan and rack or a grill rack with olive oil spray. Preheat broiler or grill.

Broil peppers 3 to 4 inches from heat on broiling rack or grill peppers until almost completely black, turning peppers to char evenly. Remove from heat. Seal in an airtight plastic bag or put in a large bowl and cover with plastic wrap. Let peppers cool for 20 to 30 minutes.

Slice peppers in half and remove stems, seeds, and veins. Gently peel skin off peppers, using your fingers or rubbing between paper towels, or scrape skin off with a knife (see Cook's Tip on Roasted Bell Peppers, page 10). Discard skin.

Slice roasted peppers to desired thickness and place in a large bowl. Set aside.

Spray mushrooms with olive oil spray. If roasting peppers on an outdoor grill, use it to cook mushrooms. Or spray a large grill pan (specially designed pan with raised ridges for indoor grilling on stovetop) with olive oil spray. Heat pan for several minutes over medium-high heat.

Grill mushrooms for about 30 minutes, or until meaty and juicy. (Cooking time will vary depending on size of mushrooms. If you cook them too long, they will dry out.) Slice mushrooms to desired thickness and add to sliced peppers.

In a small bowl, whisk together vinegar and sugar until sugar has dissolved. Pour over vegetables; stir gently. Serve at room temperature.

Calories 26	Total Fat 0 g	Fiber 1 g
Protein 1 g	Saturated 0 g	Sodium 2 mg
Carbohydrates 6 g	Polyunsaturated 0 g	Potassium 176 mg
Cholesterol 0 mg	Monounsaturated 0 g	Calcium 6 mg

Hash Brown Potatoes

Serves 6 • ½ cup per serving

No weekend breakfast or brunch is complete without the aroma and taste of hash brown potatoes. Cooking the pepper, onion powder, and garlic powder in the oil infuses it with flavor and helps spread seasoning through the potatoes. The Potatoes O'Brien variation includes onion, bell pepper, and a flavor enhancer, balsamic vinegar.

1	tablespoon olive oil
¼	teaspoon pepper
¼	teaspoon onion powder
¼	teaspoon garlic powder
3	cups fat-free frozen diced hash brown potatoes
¼	teaspoon paprika

Heat a large nonstick skillet over medium-high heat. Add oil, pepper, onion powder, and garlic powder. Cook for 10 to 15 seconds, stirring occasionally.

Add potatoes. Reduce heat to medium-low and cook, covered, for 8 to 10 minutes, stirring occasionally. Increase heat to medium-high and cook, uncovered, for 3 to 4 minutes, or until potatoes are brown and slightly crisp.

Stir in paprika.

Potatoes O'Brien

Infuse oil and cook potatoes as directed above. After 5 minutes of covered cooking, add 1 medium onion, chopped; ½ medium green bell pepper, chopped; and ½ medium red bell pepper, chopped. Reduce heat to medium-low and cook, covered, for 3 to 5 minutes. Uncover and cook over medium-high heat for 3 minutes, or until potatoes are brown and slightly crisp. Stir in paprika and 1 tablespoon balsamic vinegar.

HASH BROWN POTATOES

Calories 102	Total Fat 2 g	Fiber 2 g
Protein 2 g	Saturated 0 g	Sodium 23 mg
Carbohydrates 19 g	Polyunsaturated 0 g	Potassium 305 mg
Cholesterol 0 mg	Monounsaturated 2 g	Calcium 12 mg

POTATOES O'BRIEN

Calories 120	Total Fat 2 g	Fiber 2 g
Protein 3 g	Saturated 0 g	Sodium 25 mg
Carbohydrates 23 g	Polyunsaturated 0 g	Potassium 382 mg
Cholesterol 0 mg	Monounsaturated 2 g	Calcium 20 mg

Potato Pancakes

Serves 4 • 2 pancakes per serving

Lacy and golden, these pancakes will grace your holiday brunch table or provide comfort as a side dish for a winter supper. Topped with a tablespoon of warm applesauce and a dash of ground cinnamon, they're even good for dessert!

2	cups fat-free frozen shredded potatoes, thawed, or 2 medium potatoes (Idaho or Russet preferred)
4	cups water (for fresh potatoes)
1	teaspoon vinegar (for fresh potatoes)
	Whites of 2 large eggs
¼	cup all-purpose flour
2	tablespoons finely chopped onion
¾	teaspoon baking powder
¼	teaspoon onion powder
¼	teaspoon garlic powder
⅛	teaspoon pepper
	Vegetable oil spray
2	teaspoons olive oil, divided use

If using frozen potatoes, drain and put in a medium bowl. If using fresh potatoes, combine water and vinegar in a medium bowl (this will help keep the potatoes from turning brown). Shred potatoes and immediately put into water mixture. Let potatoes stand for 2 to 3 minutes; drain well. Spread potatoes on four layers of paper towel. Cover potatoes with two or three layers of paper towel and pat dry. Dry bowl and return potatoes to bowl.

Stir in egg whites, flour, onion, baking powder, onion powder, garlic powder, and pepper.

Heat a large nonstick skillet over medium heat. Remove from heat and spray with vegetable oil spray (being careful not to spray near a gas flame). Add 1 teaspoon oil and swirl to coat bottom. Spoon batter for four pancakes, ¼ cup each, into skillet, spreading each slightly with back of a spoon. Cook for 3 to 4 minutes, or until golden brown on bottom. Remove pan from heat and lightly spray tops of pancakes with vegetable oil spray. Turn pancakes over and cook for 3 to 4 minutes, or until golden brown. Transfer to a plate; cover with aluminum foil to keep warm. Repeat with remaining oil and potato mixture.

Cook's Tip on Thawing Frozen Vegetables: To thaw frozen vegetables quickly, put them in a colander and hold them under cold running water for about 30 seconds, or until completely thawed. Drain well.

Calories 146	Total Fat 3 g	Fiber 2 g
Protein 5 g	Saturated 1 g	Sodium 142 mg
Carbohydrates 26 g	Polyunsaturated 0 g	Potassium 344 mg
Cholesterol 0 mg	Monounsaturated 2 g	Calcium 65 mg

Scalloped Potatoes

Serves 8 • ¹/₂ cup per serving

You'll probably attract an audience when you take these yummy potatoes out of the oven.

Vegetable oil spray

Sauce
1	cup fat-free milk
3	tablespoons all-purpose flour
1	cup Chicken Broth (page 23) or commercial low-sodium broth
¹/₄	teaspoon pepper
¹/₄	teaspoon onion powder
¹/₄	teaspoon garlic powder
3	tablespoons shredded or grated Parmesan cheese

4	large potatoes, peeled and thinly sliced (about 4 cups)
¹/₂	cup chopped onion
¹/₂	cup low-fat shredded Cheddar cheese
¹/₈	teaspoon paprika

Preheat oven to 350° F. Lightly spray a 1¹/₂-quart casserole dish with vegetable oil spray.

For sauce, in a medium saucepan, whisk together milk and flour.

Whisk in remaining sauce ingredients except Parmesan. Cook over medium-high heat for 5 to 6 minutes, or until mixture is thickened, whisking occasionally.

Whisk in Parmesan and remove from heat.

Put potatoes and onion in casserole dish. Add sauce and stir lightly.

Bake, covered, for 30 minutes. Gently stir in Cheddar and sprinkle with paprika. Bake, uncovered, for 30 to 40 minutes, or until potatoes are tender and lightly browned.

Calories 109	Total Fat 1 g	Fiber 2 g
Protein 6 g	Saturated 1 g	Sodium 111 mg
Carbohydrates 19 g	Polyunsaturated 0 g	Potassium 500 mg
Cholesterol 4 mg	Monounsaturated 0 g	Calcium 108 mg

Zesty Oven-Fried Potatoes

Serves 6 • ½ cup per serving

This is finger food at its finest! Have everyone over for a meal with these oven-fries, Cajun Snapper (page 78), and Garden Coleslaw (page 46).

	Vegetable oil spray
1½	pounds medium red potatoes (4 to 5)
1	tablespoon olive oil
½	to ¾ teaspoon Creole Seasoning (page 226)
½	teaspoon pepper
2	tablespoons malt vinegar

Preheat oven to 400° F. Lightly spray a large baking sheet with vegetable oil spray.

Cut each potato lengthwise into six wedges. Put on baking sheet.

In a small bowl, combine oil, creole seasoning, and pepper. Drizzle over potatoes and stir to coat.

Bake for 30 minutes, or until potatoes are golden and tender. Remove from oven.

Sprinkle with vinegar.

Calories 99	Total Fat 2 g	Fiber 2 g
Protein 3 g	Saturated 0 g	Sodium 2 mg
Carbohydrates 20 g	Polyunsaturated 0 g	Potassium 562 mg
Cholesterol 0 mg	Monounsaturated 2 g	Calcium 18 mg

Sweet Potato Casserole

Serves 5 • ½ cup per serving

You'll soon be replacing the traditional recipe for this Southern holiday favorite with our healthful version.

4	medium sweet potatoes, or 2 15-ounce cans sweet potatoes (about 4 cups)
	Vegetable oil spray
¼	cup orange juice
2	tablespoons chopped walnuts
¼	teaspoon ground nutmeg
¼	teaspoon brandy flavoring

If using fresh sweet potatoes, boil them whole in a Dutch oven for 25 to 30 minutes, or until tender. Drain potatoes, soak in cold water until cool enough to handle, and peel. If using canned potatoes, drain thoroughly.

Meanwhile, preheat oven to 375° F. Lightly spray a 1-quart casserole dish with vegetable oil spray.

In a large bowl, mash potatoes.

Stir in remaining ingredients until well mixed.

Bake, uncovered, for 25 minutes, or until heated through.

Cook's Tip on Sweet Potatoes and Yams: Although sweet potatoes and yams are similar, they come from different plants. Yams are common in Central and South America, but almost all "yams" sold in the United States are really sweet potatoes.

Calories 153	Total Fat 2 g	Fiber 2 g
Protein 2 g	Saturated 0 g	Sodium 16 mg
Carbohydrates 31 g	Polyunsaturated 1 g	Potassium 263 mg
Cholesterol 0 mg	Monounsaturated 0 g	Calcium 30 mg

Asian Fried Rice with Peas

Serves 8 • ½ cup per serving

*On its own, this dish is an excellent accompaniment to almost any
Asian entrée. Add some chicken, shrimp, beef, or pork to transform it
into an entrée.*

1	tablespoon acceptable vegetable oil
4	to 5 green onions, thinly sliced (green and white parts)
4	cups cooked white rice, chilled or at room temperature (preferably long-grain)
2	tablespoons snipped fresh cilantro
1½	tablespoons rice vinegar
1	tablespoon light soy sauce
1	teaspoon ground cumin
½	teaspoon sugar
1	cup frozen peas
2	green onions, thinly sliced (optional)

In a large nonstick skillet or wok, heat oil over medium-high heat and
swirl to coat bottom. Cook 4 to 5 green onions for 1 minute, or until fragrant, stirring occasionally.

Stir in rice and cilantro; cook for 2 minutes, or until heated, stirring
constantly to separate grains.

Stir in rice vinegar, soy sauce, cumin, and sugar until well combined.

Add peas; cook for 2 to 3 minutes, or until mixture is hot and peas are
warmed, stirring occasionally. Transfer to a serving plate.

Garnish with remaining green onions.

ASIAN FRIED RICE WITH PEAS

Calories 139	Total Fat 2 g	Fiber 1 g
Protein 3 g	Saturated 0 g	Sodium 72 mg
Carbohydrates 26 g	Polyunsaturated 1 g	Potassium 87 mg
Cholesterol 0 mg	Monounsaturated 1 g	Calcium 20 mg

Rice and Vegetable Pilaf

Serves 6 • ½ cup per serving

Full of mushrooms and carrots, this dish tastes great with Herbed Fillet of Sole (page 79).

1	teaspoon olive oil
1	cup sliced fresh mushrooms (about 4 ounces)
1	cup shredded carrots (about 2 medium)
1	cup Chicken Broth (page 23) or commercial low-sodium broth
¼	teaspoon pepper
½	cup uncooked long-grain rice
½	cup snipped fresh parsley
¼	cup sliced green onions (green and white parts) (2 medium)

Heat a medium saucepan over medium-high heat. Add oil and swirl to coat bottom. Cook mushrooms and carrots for 2 to 3 minutes, or until mushrooms are tender, stirring occasionally.

Add broth and pepper; bring to a boil over high heat.

Add rice. Reduce heat and simmer, covered, for 20 minutes. Remove from heat.

Stir in remaining ingredients. Let stand for 5 minutes. Fluff with a fork before serving.

Calories 72	Total Fat 0 g	Fiber 1 g
Protein 2 g	Saturated 0 g	Sodium 16 mg
Carbohydrates 16 g	Polyunsaturated 0 g	Potassium 177 mg
Cholesterol 0 mg	Monounsaturated 0 g	Calcium 18 mg

Dilled Summer Squash

Serves 3 • ½ cup per serving

This squash is so tender and tasty, you'll double the recipe next time.

  ¼   cup water
  2   medium yellow summer squash, sliced (about 1⅔ cups)
  1½ teaspoons finely chopped onion
  1½ teaspoons snipped fresh dillweed or ½ teaspoon dried,
       crumbled
  ⅛   teaspoon pepper
  ¼   teaspoon light-sodium butter-flavor sprinkles

In a medium saucepan, bring water to a boil over high heat. Add remaining ingredients except butter-flavor sprinkles. Reduce heat to medium and cook, covered, for 10 minutes, or until squash is tender. Drain well.

Sprinkle with butter-flavor sprinkles.

Calories 28	Total Fat 0 g	Fiber 3 g
Protein 1 g	Saturated 0 g	Sodium 8 mg
Carbohydrates 6 g	Polyunsaturated 0 g	Potassium 351 mg
Cholesterol 0 mg	Monounsaturated 0 g	Calcium 28 mg

Baked Tomatoes

Serves 4 • ½ tomato per serving

*Baked tomatoes are a tasty way to get another vegetable into your
diet. Try serving them with Easy Roast Beef (page 130) and fresh corn.*

> *Vegetable oil spray*
> 2 *medium tomatoes, halved*
> 1 *teaspoon olive oil*
> 1 *tablespoon plus 1 teaspoon shredded or grated Parmesan
>   cheese*
> 1 *teaspoon snipped fresh parsley or ¼ teaspoon dried parsley,
>   crumbled*
> ¼ *teaspoon dried oregano, crumbled*
> ¼ *teaspoon dried basil, crumbled*

Preheat oven to 350° F. Lightly spray a 9-inch square baking dish
with vegetable oil spray.

Place tomato halves with cut side up in baking dish. Drizzle with oil.
Sprinkle with remaining ingredients.

Bake for 20 to 25 minutes, or until tomatoes are heated through.

Calories 39	Total Fat 2 g	Fiber 1 g
Protein 2 g	Saturated 1 g	Sodium 47 mg
Carbohydrates 4 g	Polyunsaturated 0 g	Potassium 211 mg
Cholesterol 1 mg	Monounsaturated 1 g	Calcium 37 mg

Sauces, Condiments, & Seasonings

white sauce
white sauce with parmesan cheese
white sauce with dijon mustard

gourmet mushroom sauce

yogurt dill sauce

spaghetti sauce

creamy lime and mustard sauce

chocolate sauce

strawberry orange sauce
cinnamon blueberry sauce

ketchup

chili sauce

barbecue sauce

roasted tomato chipotle salsa

hot mustard

horseradish

easy dill pickles

sweet bread-and-butter pickles
sweet pickle relish

herb seasoning

lemon herb seasoning

savory herb blend

chili powder

creole seasoning

White Sauce

Serves 8 • ¼ cup per serving

Whenever you need a basic white sauce for creamed vegetables or pasta, this recipe does the trick. It's also a useful low-sodium substitute when a casserole recipe calls for a can of condensed creamy soup.

> 2 tablespoons light stick margarine
> 3 tablespoons all-purpose flour
> 2 cups fat-free milk
> 1 teaspoon fresh lemon juice
> ¼ teaspoon pepper, or to taste

In a medium saucepan, melt margarine over medium-low heat. Whisk in flour; cook for 1 to 2 minutes, whisking occasionally. Gradually whisk in milk. Whisk in lemon juice and pepper. Increase heat to medium-high and bring to a simmer, 4 to 5 minutes, whisking constantly. Remove from heat or continue cooking until sauce has thickened to desired consistency.

White Sauce with Parmesan Cheese

Add ¼ cup shredded or grated Parmesan cheese with the lemon juice and pepper for a great sauce to serve over pasta.

White Sauce with Dijon Mustard

For a different flavor to go with chicken or fish, add 2 tablespoons Dijon mustard with the lemon juice and pepper.

WHITE SAUCE		
Calories 45	Total Fat 2 g	Fiber 0 g
Protein 2 g	Saturated 0 g	Sodium 50 mg
Carbohydrates 5 g	Polyunsaturated 0 g	Potassium 108 mg
Cholesterol 1 mg	Monounsaturated 0 g	Calcium 76 mg

WHITE SAUCE WITH PARMESAN CHEESE

Calories 59	Total Fat 3 g	Fiber 0 g
Protein 4 g	Saturated 1 g	Sodium 109 mg
Carbohydrates 6 g	Polyunsaturated 0 g	Potassium 111 mg
Cholesterol 4 mg	Monounsaturated 1 g	Calcium 119 mg

WHITE SAUCE WITH DIJON MUSTARD

Calories 49	Total Fat 2 g	Fiber 0 g
Protein 2 g	Saturated 0 g	Sodium 140 mg
Carbohydrates 6 g	Polyunsaturated 0 g	Potassium 115 mg
Cholesterol 1 mg	Monounsaturated 0 g	Calcium 81 mg

Gourmet Mushroom Sauce

Serves 8 • ¼ cup per serving

Dress up any main dish, such as a plain broiled steak, pork chop, or chicken breast, with this sauce. Even leftover Meat Loaf (page 136) can be served in a new light with this sauce.

  2   tablespoons light stick margarine
  8   ounces fresh button or exotic mushrooms, such as shiitake, golden Italian, oyster, or chanterelle, or a combination, sliced (about 2½ cups)
  2   medium shallots, finely chopped
  3   tablespoons all-purpose flour
  2   cups fat-free milk
  ⅛   teaspoon pepper
  ⅛   teaspoon garlic powder
  1   tablespoon dry white wine (regular or nonalcoholic) or 1 to 2 teaspoons lemon juice

In a large nonstick skillet, melt margarine over medium heat. Cook mushrooms and shallots for 4 to 5 minutes, or until mushrooms are tender, stirring occasionally.

Sprinkle flour over mushrooms, stirring to combine. Gradually add milk, stirring constantly. Stir in pepper and garlic powder. Cook over medium-high heat for 4 to 5 minutes, or until mixture is thickened, stirring occasionally. Stir in wine.

Calories 56	Total Fat 2 g	Fiber 1 g
Protein 3 g	Saturated 0 g	Sodium 52 mg
Carbohydrates 7 g	Polyunsaturated 0 g	Potassium 226 mg
Cholesterol 1 mg	Monounsaturated 0 g	Calcium 79 mg

Yogurt Dill Sauce

Serves 9 • 2 tablespoons per serving

Serve this easy sauce over fish or use it as a dip for raw vegetables. It's also great as a dressing for sliced cucumbers.

> 1 cup fat-free or low-fat plain yogurt
> 2 tablespoons snipped fresh dillweed or 2 teaspoons dried, crumbled
> 2 tablespoons nonfat or light sour cream
> 1 teaspoon Dijon mustard
> ½ teaspoon sugar
> ½ teaspoon fresh lemon juice
> ¼ teaspoon pepper

In a small bowl, whisk together all ingredients. Cover and refrigerate for at least 1 hour before serving.

Calories 21	Total Fat 0 g	Fiber 0 g
Protein 2 g	Saturated 0 g	Sodium 38 mg
Carbohydrates 3 g	Polyunsaturated 0 g	Potassium 80 mg
Cholesterol 1 mg	Monounsaturated 0 g	Calcium 60 mg

Spaghetti Sauce

Serves 6 • ½ cup per serving

Make a batch of this wonderful sauce ahead of time for the best blending of flavors. It will keep in the refrigerator for up to a week, or freeze it for longer storage. You can adjust the herbs and spices to suit your own taste without affecting the sodium level.

2	6-ounce cans no-salt-added tomato paste
2	cups water
¼	cup finely chopped onion
2	medium cloves garlic, minced, or 1 teaspoon bottled minced garlic
1	teaspoon dried basil, crumbled
1	teaspoon dried oregano, crumbled
½	teaspoon dried thyme, crumbled
½	teaspoon sugar
¼	teaspoon baking soda
⅛	teaspoon pepper
⅛	teaspoon crushed red pepper flakes (optional)

Put tomato paste in a medium saucepan. Whisk in water, 1 cup at a time. Whisk in remaining ingredients. Bring to a boil over medium-high heat. Reduce heat and simmer, covered, for 30 minutes, or until flavors are blended, stirring occasionally.

Calories 54	Total Fat 0 g	Fiber 3 g
Protein 2 g	Saturated 0 g	Sodium 105 mg
Carbohydrates 13 g	Polyunsaturated 0 g	Potassium 560 mg
Cholesterol 0 mg	Monounsaturated 0 g	Calcium 35 mg

Creamy Lime and Mustard Sauce

Serves 8 • 2 tablespoons per serving

The distinctive combination of capers and Chinese hot mustard makes this sauce a standout. Tasting it over Grilled Salmon Fillet (page 87) will hook you.

6	tablespoons fat-free, cholesterol-free or low-fat mayonnaise dressing
6	tablespoons fat-free or low-fat sour cream
1½	to 2 tablespoons fresh lime juice
1	tablespoon finely chopped green onions (green part only)
1	tablespoon finely chopped capers packed in balsamic vinegar, rinsed and drained
1	teaspoon Chinese hot mustard powder, or to taste
⅛	to ¼ teaspoon sugar, or to taste

In a medium glass bowl, whisk together all ingredients. Cover and refrigerate until ready to serve.

Calories 25	Total Fat 0 g	Fiber 0 g
Protein 1 g	Saturated 0 g	Sodium 118 mg
Carbohydrates 4 g	Polyunsaturated 0 g	Potassium 39 mg
Cholesterol 1 mg	Monounsaturated 0 g	Calcium 17 mg

Chocolate Sauce

Serves 8 • 2 tablespoons per serving

*Try this chocolate-lover's dream over fresh fruit, such as bananas,
raspberries, or strawberries.*

> $\frac{1}{2}$ cup sugar
> 3 tablespoons unsweetened cocoa powder
> 1 tablespoon light tub margarine
> $\frac{1}{3}$ cup fat-free milk
> 1 teaspoon vanilla extract

In a small bowl, combine sugar and cocoa.

In a medium skillet, melt margarine over medium-high heat. Whisk
in milk and cook for 2 to 3 minutes (no stirring necessary). Gently
whisk in sugar mixture. Bring to a boil, whisking constantly. Remove
from heat and whisk in vanilla. Mixture will thicken as it cools.

Calories 64	Total Fat 1 g	Fiber 1 g
Protein 1 g	Saturated 0 g	Sodium 15 mg
Carbohydrates 14 g	Polyunsaturated 0 g	Potassium 49 mg
Cholesterol 0 mg	Monounsaturated 0 g	Calcium 15 mg

Strawberry Orange Sauce

Serves 9 • ¼ cup per serving

Easy to make, this topping turns fat-free vanilla yogurt, vanilla ice milk, or Angel Food Cake (page 255) into a dazzling dessert.

1	quart fresh strawberries (about 3½ cups)
1	tablespoon orange-flavored liqueur (optional)
1	tablespoon orange juice (2 tablespoons if not using liqueur)
1	tablespoon sugar

Remove stems from strawberries and slice lengthwise.

In a small saucepan, heat liqueur and orange juice over medium heat. Add half the strawberries; cook for 2 to 3 minutes, stirring frequently. Stir in sugar and cook for 2 minutes, or until berries soften. Remove from heat and stir in remaining strawberries. Serve hot or cover and refrigerate until ready to serve.

Cinnamon Blueberry Sauce

Substitute fresh blueberries for the strawberries and ½ teaspoon ground cinnamon for the liqueur; use 2 tablespoons of orange juice.

STRAWBERRY ORANGE SAUCE

Calories 29	Total Fat 0 g	Fiber 1 g
Protein 0 g	Saturated 0 g	Sodium 8 mg
Carbohydrates 6 g	Polyunsaturated 0 g	Potassium 97 mg
Cholesterol 0 mg	Monounsaturated 0 g	Calcium 1 mg

CINNAMON BLUEBERRY SAUCE

Calories 38	Total Fat 0 g	Fiber 2 g
Protein 0 g	Saturated 0 g	Sodium 3 mg
Carbohydrates 10 g	Polyunsaturated 0 g	Potassium 54 mg
Cholesterol 0 mg	Monounsaturated 0 g	Calcium 5 mg

Ketchup

Makes 4 cups • 2 tablespoons per serving

It can be difficult to find low-sodium ketchup, so here's a simple recipe to make yourself. The ingredients list is long, but the preparation is almost effortless.

4	cups water
3	6-ounce cans no-salt-added tomato paste
½	cup chopped onion
½	cup chopped celery
½	cup cider vinegar
½	cup sugar
2	tablespoons light tub or light stick margarine
1	tablespoon light brown sugar
1	teaspoon light molasses
⅛	teaspoon ground cloves
⅛	teaspoon ground cinnamon
⅛	teaspoon dried basil, crumbled
⅛	teaspoon dried tarragon, crumbled
⅛	teaspoon pepper
⅛	teaspoon onion powder
⅛	teaspoon garlic powder

In a food processor or blender, process water, tomato paste, onion, celery, and vinegar until smooth. Transfer to a medium saucepan; stir in remaining ingredients. Simmer, uncovered, for 1 hour 30 minutes, or until ketchup is reduced to about 1 quart, one-half original volume, stirring occasionally. Refrigerate in a jar with a tight-fitting lid for up to one month. For longer storage, freeze it in small quantities.

Calories 32	Total Fat 0 g	Fiber 1 g
Protein 1 g	Saturated 0 g	Sodium 21 mg
Carbohydrates 7 g	Polyunsaturated 0 g	Potassium 167 mg
Cholesterol 0 mg	Monounsaturated 0 g	Calcium 9 mg

Chili Sauce

Makes 3 cups • 2 tablespoons per serving

Add some zing to your food, but without the sodium usually found in chili sauce. Drizzle this chili sauce on Spicy Baked Fish (page 69) or shrimp cocktail.

2	16-ounce cans no-salt-added tomato sauce
½	cup sugar
½	cup chopped onion
½	cup chopped celery
½	cup chopped green bell pepper
½	cup cider vinegar
2	tablespoons light tub or light stick margarine
1	tablespoon fresh lemon juice
1	teaspoon light brown sugar
1	teaspoon light molasses
¼	teaspoon red hot-pepper sauce
⅛	teaspoon ground cloves
⅛	teaspoon ground cinnamon
⅛	teaspoon pepper
⅛	teaspoon dried basil, crumbled
⅛	teaspoon dried tarragon, crumbled

In a large saucepan, whisk together all ingredients. Bring to a boil over high heat, whisking frequently. Reduce heat and simmer, uncovered, for 1 hour 30 minutes, or until reduced to about 3 cups, one-half original volume, whisking occasionally. Refrigerate in a jar with a tight-fitting lid for up to one month. For longer storage, freeze in small quantities; use an ice cube tray with 1 tablespoon sauce per compartment.

Calories 36	Total Fat 0 g	Fiber 1 g
Protein 1 g	Saturated 0 g	Sodium 13 mg
Carbohydrates 8 g	Polyunsaturated 0 g	Potassium 169 mg
Cholesterol 0 mg	Monounsaturated 0 g	Calcium 9 mg

Barbecue Sauce

Makes 4 cups • 2 tablespoons per serving

*After trying our healthful version of barbecue sauce, you'll wonder
why you ever bought the bottled kind.*

    2   cups water
    2   6-ounce cans no-salt-added tomato paste
    ½   cup Ketchup (page 212) or commercial no-salt-added ketchup
    ¼   cup firmly packed dark brown sugar
    ¼   cup chopped onion
    2   tablespoons Chili Powder (page 225) or commercial no-salt-
        added chili powder
    2   tablespoons fresh lemon juice
    2   tablespoons cider vinegar
    2   tablespoons acceptable vegetable oil
    1   tablespoon snipped fresh parsley
    1   teaspoon dry mustard
    1   teaspoon paprika
    1   medium clove garlic, minced, or ½ teaspoon bottled minced
        garlic
    ⅛   teaspoon pepper
        Dash of red hot-pepper sauce (optional)

In a large saucepan, whisk together all ingredients. Bring to a boil
over high heat. Reduce heat to low and simmer, uncovered, for 20 minutes, or until flavors have blended, whisking occasionally. Refrigerate
in a jar with a tight-fitting lid for up to one month. For longer storage,
freeze it in small quantities.

Calories 30	Total Fat 1 g	Fiber 1 g
Protein 1 g	Saturated 0 g	Sodium 14 mg
Carbohydrates 5 g	Polyunsaturated 0 g	Potassium 144 mg
Cholesterol 0 mg	Monounsaturated 1 g	Calcium 9 mg

Roasted Tomato Chipotle Salsa

Serves 6 • 2 tablespoons per serving

Chipotle pepper lends its smoky flavor to this roasted salsa. Regulate the heat from mild to spicy by the amount of chipotle you add. Spice up lean grilled hamburgers, chicken breasts, or pork tenderloin with this wonderful salsa.

	Vegetable oil spray
1	*large tomato*
1	*large shallot or 1½-inch-thick slice red onion, quartered*
2	*medium cloves garlic, unpeeled*
1	*tablespoon whole cilantro leaves*
1	*to 2 teaspoons lime juice*
½	*to 2 teaspoons chopped canned chipotle pepper in adobo sauce (see Cook's Tip on Chipotle Peppers, page 15) or 1 teaspoon chopped fresh jalapeño*

Preheat oven to 400° F. Spray a large baking sheet with vegetable oil spray.

Cut tomato in half horizontally. If desired, squeeze out tomato seeds. Cut each half in half and put on baking sheet with shallot and garlic cloves (they will be easier to peel after roasting).

Bake for 20 minutes, or until garlic is a light, golden brown.

Peel tomato and garlic, discarding peels. In a food processor or blender, process all ingredients for 10 to 15 seconds, or until desired consistency. Cover and refrigerate for up to four days.

Calories 11	Total Fat 0 g	Fiber 0 g
Protein 0 g	Saturated 0 g	Sodium 15 mg
Carbohydrates 2 g	Polyunsaturated 0 g	Potassium 84 mg
Cholesterol 0 mg	Monounsaturated 0 g	Calcium 5 mg

Hot Mustard

Use this zesty mustard on your favorite sandwich or in our tasty Red-Potato Salad (page 54).

- ¼ cup all-purpose flour
- 2 tablespoons sugar
- 2 tablespoons dry mustard
- ¼ teaspoon onion powder
- ¼ teaspoon turmeric
- 2 tablespoons fresh lemon juice
- 2 tablespoons water

In a small bowl, whisk together flour, sugar, mustard, onion powder, and turmeric. Whisk in lemon juice and water. Put in a jar with a tight-fitting lid and refrigerate.

Calories 40	Total Fat 1 g	Fiber 0 g
Protein 1 g	Saturated 0 g	Sodium 0 mg
Carbohydrates 7 g	Polyunsaturated 0 g	Potassium 27 mg
Cholesterol 0 mg	Monounsaturated 0 g	Calcium 6 mg

Horseradish

Makes 1½ cups • 1 tablespoon per serving

This great-tasting, low-sodium condiment livens up a wide variety of foods, from sour cream sauce on lean roast beef to any spread for sandwiches.

½   **medium horseradish root, peeled and cubed (12 ounces)**
½   **cup vinegar**

In a food processor or blender, process horseradish and vinegar to desired consistency. Refrigerate for up to one week in a jar with a tight-fitting lid.

Cook's Tip: If you don't want to use a food processor or blender, finely grate horseradish into a medium bowl and mix it with the vinegar.

Calories 14	Total Fat 0 g	Fiber 1 g
Protein 1 g	Saturated 0 g	Sodium 4 mg
Carbohydrates 3 g	Polyunsaturated 0 g	Potassium 81 mg
Cholesterol 0 mg	Monounsaturated 0 g	Calcium 15 mg

Easy Dill Pickles

Serves 16 • ¹⁄₄ cup per serving

If you've never made pickles before, don't worry. These are so easy! Just let the cucumbers simmer in a flavorful liquid, then cool and refrigerate them. The flavor of these pickles really brightens lean grilled burgers or your favorite potato salad or tuna salad recipe.

> 4   pickling, or Kirby, cucumbers, unpeeled (about 1 pound)
> 1   cup water
> ³⁄₄ cup cider vinegar
> 1   tablespoon dill seeds
> 1   tablespoon whole pickling spices
> 1   tablespoon sugar
> 2   medium cloves garlic, peeled, or 1 teaspoon bottled minced garlic
> 4   to 5 sprigs fresh dillweed (optional)

With a sharp knife or crinkle cutter, cut cucumbers crosswise into ¼-inch slices. You should have 4 cups. Line a colander with two or three paper towels; put cucumbers in colander, cover with a paper towel, and set a plate on top to slightly weigh the cucumbers down (this will help remove any excess moisture). Let stand for 5 to 10 minutes.

In a large saucepan, bring remaining ingredients to a boil over high heat. Reduce heat to medium, add cucumbers, and cook, uncovered, for 3 minutes, or until tender-crisp, stirring occasionally. Remove from heat and let cool for 15 minutes. Transfer to an airtight container large enough to hold the cucumbers and liquid (a clean large pickle jar works well) and refrigerate for at least 4 hours before serving. Pickles will keep in refrigerator for up to two weeks.

Cook's Tip on Pickling, or Kirby, Cucumbers: As its name tells you, this small cucumber variety is primarily used for pickles. It's also used as a garnish in many Asian dishes and can be used in place of the more common cucumber. Pickling cucumbers have thin skin, are crisp, and have very small seeds. Many groceries carry them regularly, or you can look for them at a local farmers' market or Asian grocery store. A great alternative is the English, or hothouse, cucumber, which is 8 to 12 inches long and usually tightly wrapped in plastic. Its skin is very thin, and its seeds, if it has any, are tiny. You can also pickle the common cucumber.

Cook's Tip on Crinkle Cutter: For a wavy cut on your pickle slices, look for a crinkle cutter at a gourmet shop or at the supermarket in the utensils section.

Cook's Tip on Pickling Spices: You'll find pickling spices in the spice section of the grocery. Commercial brands of this aromatic mix of spices vary but can include allspice, cinnamon, mustard seeds, coriander seeds, ginger, bay leaves, chiles, black pepper, cloves, cardamom, and mace. Use 1 teaspoon to 1 tablespoon of the mixture in marinades, water for cooking shrimp, or soups and stews. Use kitchen twine to tie the spices in a small piece of cheesecloth so you can remove them easily.

Calories 11	Total Fat 0 g	Fiber 1 g
Protein 1 g	Saturated 0 g	Sodium 3 mg
Carbohydrates 2 g	Polyunsaturated 0 g	Potassium 65 mg
Cholesterol 0 mg	Monounsaturated 0 g	Calcium 18 mg

Sweet Bread-and-Butter Pickles

Serves 16 • ¼ cup per serving

Sure to be a hit with your family, these quick-fix pickles have a traditional sweet bread-and-butter pickle taste. Great for a picnic or your next cookout.

> 4 pickling, or Kirby, cucumbers, unpeeled (about 1 pound) (see
>   Cook's Tip on Pickling, or Kirby, Cucumbers, page 218)
> 1 medium onion, sliced
> 1 cup water
> ¾ cup cider vinegar
> ½ cup sugar
> 1 teaspoon pink peppercorns (optional)
> ½ teaspoon mustard seeds
> ¼ teaspoon turmeric

With a sharp knife or crinkle cutter (see Cook's Tip on Crinkle Cutter, page 219), cut cucumbers crosswise into ¼-inch slices. You should have 4 cups. Line a colander with two or three paper towels; put cucumbers and onion in colander, cover with a paper towel, and set a plate on top to slightly weigh the cucumber mixture down (this will help remove any excess moisture). Let stand for 5 to 10 minutes.

In a large saucepan, bring remaining ingredients to a boil over high heat. Reduce heat to medium, add cucumbers and onion, and cook, uncovered, for 3 minutes, or until tender-crisp, stirring occasionally. Remove from heat and let mixture cool for 15 minutes. Transfer to an airtight container large enough to hold the cucumbers and liquid (a clean large pickle jar works well) and refrigerate for at least 4 hours before serving. Pickles will keep in refrigerator for up to two weeks.

Sweet Pickle Relish

Finely chop the cucumbers and onion, and add one finely chopped medium green or red bell pepper. Bring all ingredients to a simmer over medium-high heat, then reduce heat and simmer for 10 to 15 minutes, or until relish is thickened, stirring occasionally. Store as directed above.

Cook's Tip on Pink Peppercorns: These dried berries from the Baies rose plant are not true peppercorns, but are peppery in taste and beautiful in color. Find them in gourmet shops or upscale grocery stores.

SWEET BREAD-AND-BUTTER PICKLES

Calories 33	Total Fat 0 g	Fiber 1 g
Protein 1 g	Saturated 0 g	Sodium 3 mg
Carbohydrates 8 g	Polyunsaturated 0 g	Potassium 72 mg
Cholesterol 0 mg	Monounsaturated 0 g	Calcium 10 mg

SWEET PICKLE RELISH

Calories 35	Total Fat 0 g	Fiber 1 g
Protein 1 g	Saturated 0 g	Sodium 3 mg
Carbohydrates 9 g	Polyunsaturated 0 g	Potassium 85 mg
Cholesterol 0 mg	Monounsaturated 0 g	Calcium 10 mg

Herb Seasoning

Makes ¼ cup • ½ teaspoon per serving

*An all-purpose replacement for the salt shaker, this flavorful
seasoning is perfect for keeping on the table and on the kitchen
counter. The mixture is good on vegetables and meats and in
casseroles and stews.*

1	tablespoon garlic powder
1	teaspoon dried basil, crumbled
1	teaspoon dried marjoram, crumbled
1	teaspoon dried thyme, crumbled
1	teaspoon dried parsley, crumbled
1	teaspoon dried savory, crumbled
1	teaspoon ground mace or nutmeg
1	teaspoon onion powder
1	teaspoon pepper
1	teaspoon sage, rubbed or crumbled
½	teaspoon cayenne (optional)

In a small bowl, stir together all ingredients until well blended. Store
in a jar with a tight-fitting lid in a cool, dry, dark place for up to six
months.

Calories 2	Total Fat 0 g	Fiber 0 g
Protein 0 g	Saturated 0 g	Sodium 0 mg
Carbohydrates 0 g	Polyunsaturated 0 g	Potassium 9 mg
Cholesterol 0 mg	Monounsaturated 0 g	Calcium 4 mg

Lemon Herb Seasoning

Makes ¹/₂ cup plus 1 tablespoon • ¹/₂ teaspoon per serving

Use a sprinkle of this seasoning to bring out the flavor of seafood, poultry, or green salads.

¹/₄	cup plus 1 tablespoon dried basil, crumbled
¹/₄	cup dried oregano, crumbled
1¹/₂	tablespoons pepper
1¹/₂	tablespoons dried onion flakes, crumbled
1¹/₂	tablespoons whole celery seeds
¹/₂	teaspoon garlic powder
¹/₂	teaspoon dried grated lemon zest

In a small bowl, stir all ingredients until well blended. Store in a jar with a tight-fitting lid in a cool, dry, dark place for up to six months.

Calories 3	Total Fat 0 g	Fiber 0 g
Protein 0 g	Saturated 0 g	Sodium 0 mg
Carbohydrates 1 g	Polyunsaturated 0 g	Potassium 20 mg
Cholesterol 0 mg	Monounsaturated 0 g	Calcium 13 mg

Savory Herb Blend

Makes 1 cup • ½ teaspoon per serving

The herbs in this blend will make you want to discover salad all over again.

¼	cup dried parsley, crumbled
¼	cup dried marjoram, crumbled
2½	tablespoons dried basil, crumbled
1½	tablespoons sesame seeds
1½	tablespoons crushed red pepper flakes
1½	tablespoons dried rosemary, crushed
1¼	tablespoons celery seeds, crushed
2½	teaspoons dried savory, crumbled
2½	teaspoons dried sage, rubbed or crumbled
2¼	teaspoons dried thyme, crumbled
2	teaspoons dried onion flakes, crumbled
2	teaspoons dried dillweed, crumbled
1¼	teaspoons pepper
¾	teaspoon garlic powder

In a small bowl, stir together all ingredients until well blended. Store in a jar with a tight-fitting lid in a cool, dry, dark place for up to six months.

Calories 3	Total Fat 0 g	Fiber 0 g
Protein 0 g	Saturated 0 g	Sodium 1 mg
Carbohydrates 0 g	Polyunsaturated 0 g	Potassium 12 mg
Cholesterol 0 mg	Monounsaturated 0 g	Calcium 9 mg

Chili Powder

Makes ¼ cup • 1 teaspoon per serving

Try this in your own favorite chili recipe, our Chili (page 143), or Eggplant Mexicana (page 189).

    3   tablespoons paprika
    2   teaspoons dried oregano, crumbled
    1   teaspoon ground cumin
    1   teaspoon turmeric
    1   teaspoon garlic powder
    ¼   teaspoon cayenne

In a small bowl, stir together all ingredients until well blended. Store in a jar with a tight-fitting lid in a cool, dark, dry place for up to six months.

Calories 8	Total Fat 0 g	Fiber 1 g
Protein 0 g	Saturated 0 g	Sodium 1 mg
Carbohydrates 2 g	Polyunsaturated 0 g	Potassium 56 mg
Cholesterol 0 mg	Monounsaturated 0 g	Calcium 9 mg

Creole Seasoning

Makes 2 tablespoons • ½ teaspoon per serving

Use this spicy mix in Creole Tuna Steak Sandwich with Caper Tartar Sauce (page 82) or in Zesty Oven-Fried Potatoes (page 197).

1	*teaspoon Chili Powder (page 225) or commercial no-salt-added chili powder*
1	*teaspoon paprika*
1	*teaspoon ground cumin*
1	*teaspoon dried thyme, crumbled*
½	*teaspoon garlic powder*
½	*teaspoon onion powder*
½	*teaspoon pepper*

In a small bowl, combine all ingredients. Store in an airtight container for up to four months.

Calories 6	Total Fat 0 g	Fiber 0 g
Protein 0 g	Saturated 0 g	Sodium 1 mg
Carbohydrates 1 g	Polyunsaturated 0 g	Potassium 32 mg
Cholesterol 0 mg	Monounsaturated 0 g	Calcium 9 mg

Breads

whole-wheat bread

rosemary rye bread

basic white bread

bread machine cinnamon rolls

dinner rolls

oatmeal banana breakfast bread

chocolate chip banana bread

french toast

corn muffins

corn bread

mexican corn muffins

blueberry muffins

oat bran and yogurt muffins

biscuits

herb-seasoned biscuits

drop biscuits

herbed soft pretzels with peppercorn mustard

pancakes

blueberry pancakes

cheese blintzes

Whole-Wheat Bread

Serves 32 • 1 slice per serving

What could be more basic and nourishing than whole-wheat bread? Get back to basics, and take pleasure in baking your own bread.

	1-pound machine (12 servings)	1½-pound machine (18 servings)	2-pound machine (24 servings)
Fat-free milk	⅔ cup	¾ cup + 2 tablespoons	1¼ cups + 1 tablespoon
Water	2 tablespoons	3 tablespoons	¼ cup
Acceptable vegetable oil	2¼ teaspoons	1 tablespoon	1½ tablespoons
All-purpose flour	1 cup	1½ cups	2 cups
Whole-wheat flour	1 cup	1½ cups	2 cups
Gluten flour	1 tablespoon	1½ tablespoons	2 tablespoons
Molasses	1 tablespoon	1½ tablespoons	2 tablespoons
Active dry yeast	2 teaspoons	2½ teaspoons	1 tablespoon

Put all ingredients in bread machine container in order given or use manufacturer's directions. When adding yeast, use a small spoon to make a well in dry ingredients. Put yeast in well unless your machine has a yeast dispenser. Select whole-grain cycle or basic/white bread cycle. Proceed as directed. When bread is done, let cool on cooling rack.

WHOLE-WHEAT BREAD (1-POUND MACHINE)

Calories 93	Total Fat 1 g	Fiber 2 g
Protein 4 g	Saturated 0 g	Sodium 9 mg
Carbohydrates 18 g	Polyunsaturated 0 g	Potassium 113 mg
Cholesterol 0 mg	Monounsaturated 1 g	Calcium 26 mg

WHOLE-WHEAT BREAD (1½-POUND MACHINE)

Calories 92	Total Fat 1 g	Fiber 2 g
Protein 3 g	Saturated 0 g	Sodium 8 mg
Carbohydrates 18 g	Polyunsaturated 0 g	Potassium 108 mg
Cholesterol 0 mg	Monounsaturated 1 g	Calcium 24 mg

WHOLE-WHEAT BREAD (2-POUND MACHINE)

Calories 93	Total Fat 1 g	Fiber 2 g
Protein 3 g	Saturated 0 g	Sodium 9 mg
Carbohydrates 18 g	Polyunsaturated 0 g	Potassium 109 mg
Cholesterol 0 mg	Monounsaturated 1 g	Calcium 26 mg

Rosemary Rye Bread

Serves 16 • 1 slice per serving

It won't take you long to do the actual preparation for this aromatic bread. During its resting and baking times, you can take a walk, fix dinner, or just relax.

	Olive oil spray
1¼	cups all-purpose flour
¾	cup rye flour
1	tablespoon gluten flour
1	tablespoon fresh rosemary, chopped, or 1 teaspoon dried, crushed
1	tablespoon caraway seeds
1	tablespoon olive oil
2	teaspoons fast-rising yeast
½	teaspoon salt
1¼	cups warm water (120° F to 130° F)
1	cup all-purpose flour (plus more as needed)

Spray a baking sheet with olive oil spray. Set aside.

In a large bowl, combine 1¼ cups all-purpose flour, rye flour, gluten flour, rosemary, caraway seeds, olive oil, yeast, and salt.

Add water, stirring with a sturdy spoon for about 30 seconds.

Gradually add some of the remaining 1 cup all-purpose flour, beating with a sturdy spoon after each addition, until dough starts to pull away from side of bowl. Add more flour if necessary to make dough smooth enough to handle.

Lightly flour a flat surface; turn out dough. Gradually knead in enough of remaining flour until dough is smooth and elastic, 6 to 7 minutes. Dough shouldn't be dry or stick to surface. You may not need all the flour, or you may need up to ½ cup more if dough is too sticky. Leave dough on work surface. Cover dough with a damp dish towel and let rest for 10 minutes.

Shape dough into a 9 × 5-inch oval loaf. Put loaf on baking sheet and flatten slightly with your hands. Using a serrated knife, cut a few horizontal slashes about 3 inches long and ½ inch deep in top of loaf.

Cover loaf with a dry dish towel and let rise for 30 to 45 minutes, or until doubled in bulk. Near end of rising cycle, preheat oven to 375° F.

Bake for 35 to 40 minutes, or until bread registers 190° F on an instant-read thermometer or sounds hollow when rapped with knuckles. Invert bread onto cooling rack. Let cool for 15 minutes before slicing.

Bread Machine Instructions

Follow manufacturer's instructions for quick baking cycle. If you prefer, use quick dough cycle, shape loaf by hand when dough is ready, and bake bread in oven as directed above.

	1-pound machine (12 servings)	1½-pound machine (16 servings)	2-pound machine (24 servings)
Water (tap)	¾ cup	1¼ cups	1½ cups
Olive oil	1 tablespoon	1½ tablespoons	2 tablespoons
All-purpose flour	1½ cups	2¼ cups	3 cups
Rye flour	½ cup	¾ cup	1 cup
Gluten flour	2 teaspoons	1 tablespoon	1 tablespoon + 1 teaspoon
Fresh rosemary, chopped	2 teaspoons	1 tablespoon	1 tablespoon + 1 teaspoon
(or dried rosemary, crushed)	½ teaspoon	1 teaspoon	½ tablespoon
Caraway seeds	2 teaspoons	1 tablespoon	1 tablespoon + 1 teaspoon
Salt	¼ teaspoon	½ teaspoon	½ teaspoon
Fast-rising yeast	1 teaspoon	1½ teaspoons	2 teaspoons

(continued on following page)

ROSEMARY RYE BREAD

Calories 93	Total Fat 1 g	Fiber 2 g
Protein 3 g	Saturated 0 g	Sodium 74 mg
Carbohydrates 18 g	Polyunsaturated 0 g	Potassium 52 mg
Cholesterol 0 mg	Monounsaturated 1 g	Calcium 8 mg

ROSEMARY RYE BREAD (1-POUND MACHINE)

Calories 86	Total Fat 1 g	Fiber 1 g
Protein 2 g	Saturated 0 g	Sodium 50 mg
Carbohydrates 16 g	Polyunsaturated 0 g	Potassium 44 mg
Cholesterol 0 mg	Monounsaturated 1 g	Calcium 7 mg

ROSEMARY RYE BREAD (1½-POUND MACHINE)

Calories 97	Total Fat 2 g	Fiber 1 g
Protein 3 g	Saturated 0 g	Sodium 74 mg
Carbohydrates 18 g	Polyunsaturated 0 g	Potassium 49 mg
Cholesterol 0 mg	Monounsaturated 1 g	Calcium 8 mg

ROSEMARY RYE BREAD (2-POUND MACHINE)

Calories 86	Total Fat 1 g	Fiber 1 g
Protein 2 g	Saturated 0 g	Sodium 50 mg
Carbohydrates 16 g	Polyunsaturated 0 g	Potassium 44 mg
Cholesterol 0 mg	Monounsaturated 1 g	Calcium 7 mg

Basic White Bread

Serves 32 • 1 slice per serving

The alluring aroma and superior taste are only two of the rewards of baking your own bread. Another is that you control the sodium content.

¼	cup lukewarm water (105° F to 115° F)
2	¼-ounce packages active dry yeast
1¾	cups fat-free milk
3	tablespoons sugar
2	tablespoons acceptable vegetable oil
6	cups all-purpose flour, divided use (plus more as needed)
	Vegetable oil spray

Pour water into a large bowl. Add yeast and stir to dissolve. Let stand for 5 minutes until mixture bubbles.

Stir milk, sugar, and oil into yeast mixture.

Gradually stir 4 cups flour into yeast mixture. Beat with a sturdy spoon for about 30 seconds, or until smooth.

Gradually add up to 1½ cups flour, about ¼ cup at a time, stirring after each addition, until dough starts to pull away from side of bowl.

Lightly flour a flat surface; turn dough out onto floured surface. Gradually knead in remaining flour for 6 to 8 minutes, or until dough is smooth and elastic. (Dough shouldn't be dry or stick to surface. You may not need all the flour, or you may need up to ½ cup more if dough is too sticky.)

Lightly spray a large bowl with vegetable oil spray. Put dough in bowl and turn to coat all sides. Cover bowl with a damp dish towel and let dough rise in a warm, draft-free place (about 85° F) until doubled in bulk, about 1 hour.

Punch down dough. Divide in half and shape into loaves. Lightly spray two 10 × 5 × 3-inch loaf pans with vegetable oil spray. Put dough into loaf pans.

Cover each with a damp dish towel and let dough rise in a warm, draft-free place (about 85° F) until doubled in bulk, about 30 minutes.

Preheat oven to 425° F.

Bake loaves for 25 to 30 minutes, or until bread registers 190° F on an instant-read thermometer or sounds hollow when rapped with knuckles.

(continued on following page)

Invert bread on cooling racks. Let cool for 15 to 20 minutes before cutting.

BREAD MACHINE VARIATION

	1-pound machine (12 servings)	1½-pound machine (18 servings)	2-pound machine (24 servings)
Fat-free milk	⅔ cup	¾ cup + 2 tablespoons	1¼ cups + 1 tablespoon
Water	2 tablespoons	3 tablespoons	¼ cup
Acceptable vegetable oil	2¼ teaspoons	1 tablespoon	1½ tablespoons
All-purpose flour	2 cups	3 cups	4 cups
Sugar	1 tablespoon	1½ tablespoons	2 tablespoons
Active dry yeast	2 teaspoons	2½ teaspoons	1 tablespoon

Put all ingredients in bread machine container in order given or use manufacturer's directions. When adding yeast, use a small spoon to make a well in dry ingredients. Put yeast in well unless your machine has a yeast dispenser. Select basic/white bread cycle. Proceed as directed. When bread is done, let cool on cooling rack.

Cook's Tip on Bread Making: Practice makes perfect when you're trying to develop a feel for when dough has the proper consistency. You can wind up with a heavy loaf if you knead in too much flour or overknead the dough, making it feel dry and stiff. If you use too little flour or don't knead the dough enough, your loaf may lose its shape during baking.

For basic kneading, fold the dough toward you. Using the heels of one or both hands, push the dough forward and slightly down in a rocking motion. Don't knead the dough completely flat against your counter or board. This can cause your dough to become sticky. Rotate the dough a quarter-turn and repeat until the dough is smooth and elastic. Add small amounts of flour to the dough when it starts to stick to the counter or board.

BASIC WHITE BREAD

Calories 103	Total Fat 1 g	Fiber 1 g
Protein 3 g	Saturated 0 g	Sodium 8 mg
Carbohydrates 20 g	Polyunsaturated 0 g	Potassium 56 mg
Cholesterol 0 mg	Monounsaturated 1 g	Calcium 20 mg

BASIC WHITE BREAD (1-POUND MACHINE)

Calories 94	Total Fat 1 g	Fiber 1 g
Protein 3 g	Saturated 0 g	Sodium 8 mg
Carbohydrates 18 g	Polyunsaturated 0 g	Potassium 58 mg
Cholesterol 0 mg	Monounsaturated 1 g	Calcium 20 mg

BASIC WHITE BREAD (1½-POUND MACHINE)

Calories 92	Total Fat 1 g	Fiber 1 g
Protein 3 g	Saturated 0 g	Sodium 7 mg
Carbohydrates 18 g	Polyunsaturated 0 g	Potassium 53 mg
Cholesterol 0 mg	Monounsaturated 1 g	Calcium 18 mg

BASIC WHITE BREAD (2-POUND MACHINE)

Calories 94	Total Fat 1 g	Fiber 1 g
Protein 3 g	Saturated 0 g	Sodium 8 mg
Carbohydrates 18 g	Polyunsaturated 0 g	Potassium 55 mg
Cholesterol 0 mg	Monounsaturated 1 g	Calcium 20 mg

Bread Machine Cinnamon Rolls

Serves 32 • 1 roll per serving

When these come out of the oven, stand back! Even the neighbors may drop by for a sample.

> 1   recipe Basic White Bread (page 233)
>   Vegetable oil spray
>   Flavoring (see chart, below)   •
>   Glaze (see chart, below)

Prepare white bread dough using bread machine variation for your size machine (select dough cycle).

Lightly spray a large baking sheet with vegetable oil spray.

On a lightly floured flat surface, roll dough into a rectangle (refer to chart for size of rectangle and for ingredient measurements). Brush melted margarine over dough. Sprinkle cinnamon, brown sugar, and pecans evenly over dough. Roll dough jelly-roll style into a cylinder and cut in 1-inch slices (refer to chart for number of rolls).

Place with cut side up ½ inch apart on prepared baking sheet. Cover with a dry dish towel and allow to rise until almost doubled in size, 30 to 35 minutes.

Preheat oven to 375° F.

Bake for 15 to 20 minutes, or until golden brown. Let rolls partially cool on a cooling rack. Meanwhile, for glaze, whisk together confectioners' sugar, vanilla, and water in a small bowl. Drizzle over warm rolls.

	1-pound machine (12 rolls)	1½-pound machine (18 rolls)	2-pound machine (24 rolls)
Size of rectangle	8 × 12 inches	12 × 18 inches	12 × 24 inches
Light stick margarine, melted	1½ tablespoons	2 tablespoons	3 tablespoons
Cinnamon	1 teaspoon	1½ teaspoons	2 teaspoons
Brown sugar	⅓ cup, firmly packed	½ cup, firmly packed	⅔ cup, firmly packed
Chopped pecans	3 tablespoons	¼ cup	⅓ cup
Glaze (mix separately)			
Confectioners' sugar	⅓ cup	½ cup	⅔ cup
Vanilla extract	¼ teaspoon	½ teaspoon	¾ teaspoon
Water	1 to 2 teaspoons	1½ teaspoons to 1 tablespoon	1½ to 2 tablespoons

CINNAMON ROLLS (1-POUND MACHINE)

Calories 150	Total Fat 3 g	Fiber 1 g
Protein 3 g	Saturated 0 g	Sodium 20 mg
Carbohydrates 28 g	Polyunsaturated 1 g	Potassium 88 mg
Cholesterol 0 mg	Monounsaturated 2 g	Calcium 29 mg

CINNAMON ROLLS (1½-POUND MACHINE)

Calories 146	Total Fat 3 g	Fiber 1 g
Protein 3 g	Saturated 0 g	Sodium 18 mg
Carbohydrates 28 g	Polyunsaturated 1 g	Potassium 83 mg
Cholesterol 0 mg	Monounsaturated 1 g	Calcium 26 mg

CINNAMON ROLLS (2-POUND MACHINE)

Calories 148	Total Fat 3 g	Fiber 1 g
Protein 3 g	Saturated 0 g	Sodium 20 mg
Carbohydrates 28 g	Polyunsaturated 1 g	Potassium 84 mg
Cholesterol 0 mg	Monounsaturated 1 g	Calcium 28 mg

Dinner Rolls

Serves 32 • 1 roll per serving

This recipe is just the thing to provide that crowning touch to a festive evening meal.

> *Vegetable oil spray*
> 1   *recipe Basic White Bread (page 233)*

Preheat oven to 375° F. Lightly spray a large baking sheet with vegetable oil spray. Make dough as for white bread through first rise.

Punch down dough. Divide dough into 32 pieces; shape each into a ball. Place on baking sheet with sides touching for soft rolls or 1½ inches apart for crusty rolls. Cover rolls with a dry dish towel and let rise until almost doubled in size, about 30 minutes.

Bake for 15 to 20 minutes, or until light golden brown. Remove from baking sheet and let cool on a cooling rack.

Bread Machine Variation

Use the ingredients listed for your size bread machine, and select the dough cycle. When the dough cycle has finished, shape the rolls as directed (the number of rolls will correspond to the number of servings listed in the table), let them rise, and bake as directed.

Calories 103	Total Fat 1 g	Fiber 1 g
Protein 3 g	Saturated 0 g	Sodium 8 mg
Carbohydrates 20 g	Polyunsaturated 0 g	Potassium 56 mg
Cholesterol 0 mg	Monounsaturated 1 g	Calcium 20 mg

Oatmeal Banana Breakfast Bread

Serves 16 • 1 slice per serving

Banana, cranberries, and orange zest give this bread a lively flavor that will get your day off to just the right start.

	Vegetable oil spray
¾	cup fat-free milk
½	cup quick-cooking oatmeal
½	cup firmly packed light brown sugar
1	medium banana, mashed (about ½ cup)
½	cup dried cranberries, raisins, or dried mixed fruit bits (optional)
	Egg substitute equivalent to 1 egg, or 1 large egg
2	tablespoons acceptable vegetable oil
1½	teaspoons grated orange zest or ½ teaspoon dried orange peel
1½	cups all-purpose flour
½	cup oat bran
2	teaspoons baking powder
1	teaspoon ground cinnamon
¼	teaspoon baking soda
1	tablespoon quick-cooking oatmeal (optional)

Preheat oven to 350° F. Spray an 8½ × 4½ × 2½-inch loaf pan with vegetable oil spray.

In a medium bowl, stir together milk, ½ cup oatmeal, brown sugar, banana, dried cranberries, egg substitute, oil, and orange zest.

In another medium bowl, stir together remaining ingredients except 1 tablespoon oatmeal. Add to milk mixture, stirring just until moistened. Don't overmix. Pour batter into loaf pan. Sprinkle with remaining oatmeal.

Bake for 45 to 50 minutes, or until a toothpick or thin, sharp knife inserted in center comes out clean. Invert bread onto a cooling rack. Let cool for at least 10 minutes before slicing.

Calories 113	Total Fat 2 g	Fiber 1 g
Protein 3 g	Saturated 0 g	Sodium 98 mg
Carbohydrates 22 g	Polyunsaturated 1 g	Potassium 115 mg
Cholesterol 0 mg	Monounsaturated 1 g	Calcium 62 mg

Chocolate Chip Banana Bread

Serves 16 • 1 slice per serving

Warm slices of this bread, with its moist banana flavor, surprise chocolate chips in the center, and crunchy vanilla wafer topping, are particularly inviting on a chilly winter evening.

	Vegetable oil spray
1¾	cups all-purpose flour
⅔	cup sugar
⅓	cup reduced-fat semisweet chocolate chips
2	teaspoons baking powder
¼	teaspoon ground cinnamon
⅛	teaspoon ground nutmeg
1	cup mashed ripe banana (1 to 2 medium)
⅓	cup unsweetened applesauce
	Egg substitute equivalent to 1 egg, or 1 large egg
1	tablespoon acceptable vegetable oil
6	reduced-fat vanilla wafer cookies, crushed (about ¼ cup)

Preheat oven to 350° F. Lightly spray an 8½ × 4½ × 2½-inch loaf pan with vegetable oil spray.

In a large bowl, stir together flour, sugar, chocolate chips, baking powder, cinnamon, and nutmeg. Make a well in center. Add remaining ingredients except cookie crumbs; stir until just moistened. Don't overmix. Batter should be lumpy. Pour into loaf pan and sprinkle with cookie crumbs.

Bake for 55 minutes, or until a toothpick or thin, sharp knife inserted in center comes out clean. Invert bread onto a cooling rack and let cool.

Calories 133	Total Fat 2 g	Fiber 1 g
Protein 2 g	Saturated 1 g	Sodium 74 mg
Carbohydrates 28 g	Polyunsaturated 0 g	Potassium 81 mg
Cholesterol 0 mg	Monounsaturated 1 g	Calcium 40 mg

French Toast

Serves 4 • 2 slices per serving

Search for the bread with the lowest sodium or make your own (pages 228–229 or 233–235). Dip slices in a cinnamon-flavored milk mixture, then enjoy the aroma as they cook. Serve with fresh fruit, syrup, all-fruit spread, or honey.

$\frac{3}{4}$ cup fat-free milk
        Egg substitute equivalent to 2 eggs
$\frac{1}{2}$ teaspoon vanilla extract
$\frac{1}{4}$ teaspoon ground cinnamon
        Vegetable oil spray
  8   slices day-old light bread

In a shallow medium bowl, whisk together milk, egg substitute, vanilla, and cinnamon.

Heat a nonstick griddle over medium heat. Remove from heat and spray with vegetable oil spray (being careful not to spray near a gas flame). Test griddle by sprinkling a few drops of water on it. If water evaporates quickly, the griddle is ready.

Using a fork, dip a piece of bread into milk mixture; quickly turn to coat. Put bread slice on griddle. Repeat with three pieces of bread. Cook for 2 to 3 minutes, or until golden brown on bottom. Using a spatula, turn bread over and cook for 2 to 3 minutes, or until golden brown. Transfer to a plate and cover with aluminum foil to keep warm. Repeat procedure with remaining bread.

Calories 120	Total Fat 1 g	Fiber 3 g
Protein 9 g	Saturated 0 g	Sodium 280 mg
Carbohydrates 22 g	Polyunsaturated 0 g	Potassium 170 mg
Cholesterol 1 mg	Monounsaturated 0 g	Calcium 95 mg

Corn Muffins

Serves 12 • 1 muffin per serving

Homemade corn muffins make mealtime special. Any leftovers are super for a quick snack on the go, or crumble a muffin into a bowl and spoon over it some beef filling from the Southwestern Beef Pita-Tacos recipe (page 142). Top the beef with chopped bell peppers, onions, tomatoes, and shredded lettuce for a "taco in a bowl."

>   Vegetable oil spray
> 1   cup all-purpose flour
> ¾   cup yellow or white cornmeal
> 1   tablespoon sugar (optional)
> 2   teaspoons baking powder
> 1   cup fat-free milk
>   Egg substitute equivalent to 1 egg, or 1 large egg
> 1   tablespoon acceptable vegetable oil
> 1   tablespoon light stick margarine, melted

Preheat oven to 425° F. Lightly spray a 12-cup muffin tin with vegetable oil spray.

In a large bowl, stir together flour, cornmeal, sugar, and baking powder.

In a small bowl, whisk together remaining ingredients. Pour all at once into dry ingredients, stirring just until moistened. Don't overmix. Batter should be slightly lumpy.

Fill each muffin cup with about ¼ cup batter.

Bake for 15 to 20 minutes, or until a toothpick inserted in center of muffins comes out clean. Invert muffins onto a cooling rack. Let cool for at least 2 minutes.

Corn Bread

Pour batter into an 8-inch square baking pan that has been sprayed lightly with vegetable oil spray. Bake for 20 to 25 minutes, or until a toothpick or cake tester inserted in center comes out clean. Invert onto a cooling rack. Cut into 12 squares; 1 square per serving.

Mexican Corn Muffins

Add 1 cup no-salt-added canned or frozen whole-kernel corn, thawed; ½ cup fat-free shredded Cheddar cheese; 2 tablespoons canned mild green chiles, rinsed and drained; and 1 teaspoon Chili Powder (page 225) or commercial no-salt-added chili powder to milk mixture. Continue with recipe as directed on page 242. Makes 12 muffins; 1 muffin per serving.

CORN MUFFINS

Calories 94	Total Fat 2 g	Fiber 1 g
Protein 3 g	Saturated 0 g	Sodium 109 mg
Carbohydrates 16 g	Polyunsaturated 1 g	Potassium 67 mg
Cholesterol 0 mg	Monounsaturated 1 g	Calcium 74 mg

CORN BREAD

Calories 94	Total Fat 2 g	Fiber 1 g
Protein 3 g	Saturated 0 g	Sodium 109 mg
Carbohydrates 16 g	Polyunsaturated 1 g	Potassium 67 mg
Cholesterol 1 mg	Monounsaturated 1 g	Calcium 74 mg

MEXICAN CORN MUFFINS

Calories 114	Total Fat 2 g	Fiber 1 g
Protein 5 g	Saturated 0 g	Sodium 152 mg
Carbohydrates 19 g	Polyunsaturated 1 g	Potassium 103 mg
Cholesterol 1 mg	Monounsaturated 1 g	Calcium 120 mg

Blueberry Muffins

Serves 12 • 1 muffin per serving

*Plump blueberries in a lemon-scented muffin really hit the spot for
an early breakfast or an afternoon tea break.*

	Vegetable oil spray (optional)
1¾	*cups all-purpose flour*
⅓	*cup sugar*
2½	*teaspoons baking powder*
½	*cup fat-free milk*
	Egg substitute equivalent to 1 egg, or whites of 2 large eggs
¼	*cup unsweetened applesauce*
1	*teaspoon grated lemon zest*
1	*tablespoon acceptable vegetable oil*
1	*cup unsweetened blueberries, fresh or frozen*
1	*teaspoon sugar*

Preheat oven to 400° F. Lightly spray a 12-cup muffin tin with vegetable oil spray or line with foil or paper muffin cups.

In a large bowl, stir together flour, ⅓ cup sugar, and baking powder.

In a small bowl, whisk together milk, egg substitute, applesauce, lemon zest, and oil. Pour into flour mixture and stir just until moistened. Don't overmix. Batter should be lumpy. With a rubber scraper, carefully fold in blueberries.

Pour about ¼ cup batter into each muffin cup. Sprinkle with remaining sugar.

Bake for 20 to 22 minutes, or until toothpick inserted in center of muffin comes out clean.

Cook's Tip on Paper Muffin Cups: Let the muffins cool completely before removing paper muffin cups. This will keep the paper from sticking and pulling off part of the muffin.

Calories 115	Total Fat 1 g	Fiber 1 g
Protein 3 g	Saturated 0 g	Sodium 119 mg
Carbohydrates 23 g	Polyunsaturated 0 g	Potassium 59 mg
Cholesterol 0 mg	Monounsaturated 1 g	Calcium 74 mg

Oat Bran and Yogurt Muffins

Serves 12 • 1 muffin per serving

*These muffins boast more nutrition than a high-calorie snack bar.
Pack two in your lunchbox, and share your heart-healthy treat with a
friend.*

	Vegetable oil spray
¾	*cup all-purpose flour*
½	*cup whole-wheat flour*
½	*cup oat bran*
½	*cup raisins*
⅓	*cup sugar*
2	*teaspoons baking powder*
¼	*teaspoon baking soda*
1	*cup fat-free or low-fat plain yogurt*
	Egg substitute equivalent to 1 egg, or 1 large egg
1	*tablespoon acceptable vegetable oil*

Preheat oven to 425° F. Lightly spray a 12-cup muffin tin with vegetable oil spray or line with foil or paper muffin cups (see Cook's Tip on
Paper Muffin Cups, page 244).

In a large bowl, stir together flours, oat bran, raisins, sugar, baking
powder, and baking soda.

In a small bowl, whisk together remaining ingredients. Pour into
flour mixture and stir just until moistened. Don't overmix. Batter
should be lumpy. Pour about ¼ cup batter into each muffin cup.

Bake for 16 to 18 minutes, or until a toothpick inserted in center of
muffin comes out clean.

Cook's Tip: Make an extra batch of these muffins for future snacks-on-the-go.
Put each cooled muffin into a small airtight freezer bag and freeze them for up to one
month. On your way out the door, grab a muffin and a piece of fruit or can of juice to take
with you for a quick, heart-healthy snack.   •

Calories 121	Total Fat 2 g	Fiber 2 g
Protein 4 g	Saturated 0 g	Sodium 136 mg
Carbohydrates 25 g	Polyunsaturated 1 g	Potassium 167 mg
Cholesterol 0 mg	Monounsaturated 1 g	Calcium 95 mg

Biscuits

Serves 14 • 1 biscuit per serving

Split open one of these steaming, fluffy biscuits and spoon some all-fruit peach preserves on top. Or make your own sausage biscuits with Turkey Sausage Patties (page 125). Good for breakfast any time of day!

> Vegetable oil spray
> 2   cups all-purpose flour
> 2   teaspoons baking powder
> ¼   cup light stick margarine
> ¾   cup fat-free milk
> Flour for rolling out dough

Preheat oven to 450° F. Lightly spray a baking sheet with vegetable oil spray.

In a medium bowl, stir together 2 cups flour and baking powder. Using a pastry blender, a fork, or two knives, cut margarine in until margarine pieces are about pea-size. Add milk to mixture and stir with a fork until dough clings together.

Lightly flour a flat surface. Turn dough out and knead lightly four or five times. Pat dough out until it is about ½ inch thick. Dip edge of a 2-inch round cutter (or drinking glass) into flour to keep dough from sticking. Reflouring cutter as necessary, cut out biscuits and place on baking sheet with edges of biscuits touching.

Bake for 12 to 15 minutes, or until golden brown.

Herb-Seasoned Biscuits

Add one or more of the following to the flour mixture: 1 teaspoon garlic powder; 1 teaspoon onion powder; 2 teaspoons dried parsley, crumbled; 2 teaspoons dried dillweed, crumbled; or ½ teaspoon rubbed or crumbled sage.

Drop Biscuits

Increase milk by 2 tablespoons. Stir dough until well mixed. Make 14 biscuits, dropping dough by heaping tablespoonfuls onto baking sheet.

BISCUITS

Calories 84	Total Fat 2 g	Fiber 1 g
Protein 2 g	Saturated 0 g	Sodium 98 mg
Carbohydrates 15 g	Polyunsaturated 1 g	Potassium 43 mg
Cholesterol 0 mg	Monounsaturated 1 g	Calcium 57 mg

HERB-SEASONED BISCUITS

Calories 86	Total Fat 2 g	Fiber 1 g
Protein 2 g	Saturated 0 g	Sodium 99 mg
Carbohydrates 15 g	Polyunsaturated 1 g	Potassium 54 mg
Cholesterol 0 mg	Monounsaturated 1 g	Calcium 62 mg

DROP BISCUITS

Calories 85	Total Fat 2 g	Fiber 1 g
Protein 2 g	Saturated 0 g	Sodium 99 mg
Carbohydrates 15 g	Polyunsaturated 1 g	Potassium 46 mg
Cholesterol 0 mg	Monounsaturated 1 g	Calcium 60 mg

Herbed Soft Pretzels
with Peppercorn Mustard

Preparing these pretzels is great fun, and the results are chewy and delicious. Fast-rising yeast speeds up the cooking process, so you can enjoy them sooner!

Pretzels

1	cup lukewarm water (105° F to 115° F)
	¼-ounce package fast-rising yeast
½	teaspoon sugar
2	cups all-purpose flour
	Egg substitute equivalent to 1 egg, or 1 large egg
2	tablespoons light stick margarine
1	tablespoon sugar
1¼	to 1¾ cups all-purpose flour, plus more for rolling out dough

Topping

2	tablespoons egg substitute or white of 1 large egg
1	tablespoon water
1	tablespoon plus 1 teaspoon Savory Herb Blend (page 248) or commercial no-salt-added herb seasoning

Peppercorn Mustard

⅓	cup Hot Mustard (page 216) or commercial honey mustard
½	teaspoon pepper
	Vegetable oil spray

For pretzels, pour water into a large bowl. Add yeast and ½ teaspoon sugar, stirring to dissolve. Let stand for 5 minutes.

Stir in 2 cups flour, egg substitute, margarine, and 1 tablespoon sugar. Stir rapidly with a sturdy spoon for about 30 seconds. Gradually add the remaining 1¼ to 1¾ cups flour about ¼ cup at a time, beating with a spoon after each addition, until dough starts to pull away from side of bowl. Add more flour if necessary to make dough stiff enough to handle.

Lightly flour a flat surface; turn out dough. Gradually knead in remaining flour until dough is smooth and elastic, 3 to 4 minutes. (Dough shouldn't be dry or stick to surface. You may not need all the flour, or you may need up to ½ cup more if dough is too sticky.)

Sprinkle a small amount of flour in bowl to keep dough from sticking. Put dough back in bowl and cover with a damp dish towel. Let dough rise for 30 minutes, or until about doubled in bulk.

Meanwhile, in a small bowl, combine topping ingredients.

For peppercorn mustard, combine ingredients in another small bowl. (Mustard can be covered and refrigerated for up to one week.)

Preheat oven to 400° F. Lightly spray two baking sheets with vegetable oil spray.

Punch down dough and divide into 16 pieces. Roll each piece into an 18-inch-long cylinder. Place eight pretzels on each baking sheet. To form pretzel, press each end of cylinder to center; press down ends.

Brush tops of pretzels with topping, and sprinkle each with herb blend.

Bake one sheet of pretzels for 15 to 20 minutes, or until golden brown. Transfer pretzels to a cooling rack. Repeat with second sheet of pretzels.

To serve, spread about 1 teaspoon of mustard on each pretzel and enjoy warm or cooled.

Cook's Tip: These pretzels will keep in an airtight container for up to four days, or freeze them in an airtight, rigid container for up to one month. If you are storing them, spread them with the mustard mixture just before serving.

Calories 128	Total Fat 1 g	Fiber 1 g
Protein 4 g	Saturated 0 g	Sodium 23 mg
Carbohydrates 25 g	Polyunsaturated 0 g	Potassium 61 mg
Cholesterol 0 mg	Monounsaturated 0 g	Calcium 11 mg

Pancakes

Serves 4 • 2 4-inch pancakes per serving

Making pancakes is a great way to start a healthy lifestyle. Easy to prepare, they will help you become familiar with heart-healthy ingredients, such as fat-free milk and egg substitute. Whether you serve these pancakes for breakfast, lunch, or dinner, they'll soon be a family favorite.

    1   *cup all-purpose flour*
    2   *tablespoons sugar*
    2   *teaspoons baking powder*
   ⅛   *teaspoon ground cinnamon*
   ¾   *cup plus 2 tablespoons fat-free milk*
       Egg substitute equivalent to 1 egg, or 1 large egg
    2   *teaspoons acceptable vegetable oil*
   ¼   *teaspoon vanilla extract*
       Vegetable oil spray

In a medium bowl, stir together flour, sugar, baking powder, and cinnamon.

In a small bowl, whisk together remaining ingredients except vegetable oil spray. Pour into flour mixture and gently whisk until just moistened. Don't overmix. Batter should be lumpy.

Heat a nonstick griddle over medium heat. Test griddle by sprinkling a few drops of water on it. If water evaporates quickly, griddle is ready. Remove from heat and lightly spray with vegetable oil spray (being careful not to spray near a gas flame). Spoon ¼ cup batter onto griddle for each pancake. Cook for 2 to 3 minutes, or until bubbles appear all over surface. Flip pancakes; cook for another 2 minutes, or until bottom is golden brown. Repeat with remaining batter.

Blueberry Pancakes
Add ½ cup fresh or frozen blueberries to batter after combining all ingredients.

PANCAKES

Calories 186	Total Fat 3 g	Fiber 1 g
Protein 7 g	Saturated 0 g	Sodium 303 mg
Carbohydrates 34 g	Polyunsaturated 1 g	Potassium 145 mg
Cholesterol 1 mg	Monounsaturated 1 g	Calcium 212 mg

BLUEBERRY PANCAKES

Calories 196	Total Fat 3 g	Fiber 1 g
Protein 7 g	Saturated 0 g	Sodium 305 mg
Carbohydrates 36 g	Polyunsaturated 1 g	Potassium 161 mg
Cholesterol 1 mg	Monounsaturated 1 g	Calcium 213 mg

Cheese Blintzes

Serves 11 • 2 blintzes per serving

Blintzes are a real breakfast treat. Top them with cinnamon-sugar, warm applesauce and cinnamon, all-fruit spread, or nonfat sour cream. Keep in mind that they also make a delightful dessert when served with sliced strawberries or mandarin oranges and a dollop of fat-free whipped topping.

Filling

2	cups fat-free or low-fat cottage cheese
	White of 1 large egg
1/4	cup sugar
1/2	teaspoon grated lemon zest
2	tablespoons fresh lemon juice
1	recipe Crepes (page 278), prepared with 2 tablespoons margarine instead of 1/4 cup margarine
	Butter-flavor vegetable oil spray

Line a colander with paper towels and set inside a bowl deep enough so colander will not touch drained liquid. Pour cottage cheese into colander. Cover with plastic wrap and refrigerate for 10 to 15 minutes to allow excess liquid to drain.

For filling, in a medium bowl, combine cottage cheese with remaining ingredients. Place 1 tablespoon filling in center of each crepe; fold in half lengthwise, then fold in half crosswise. Blintzes may be refrigerated for up to 5 hours before heating.

Heat a large nonstick skillet over medium heat. Remove from heat and spray lightly with vegetable oil spray (being careful not to spray near a gas flame). Add blintzes in batches, cooking on each side for 5 minutes, or until heated thoroughly. Spray pan lightly with vegetable oil spray between batches.

Calories 128	Total Fat 1 g	Fiber 0 g
Protein 9 g	Saturated 0 g	Sodium 151 mg
Carbohydrates 20 g	Polyunsaturated 0 g	Potassium 89 mg
Cholesterol 4 mg	Monounsaturated 0 g	Calcium 48 mg

Desserts

angel food cake
chocolate cake
denver chocolate pudding cake
carrot cake
gingerbread
quick lemon frosting
quick chocolate frosting
apple pie with raisins
apple and cranberry pie
cherry pie
deep-dish cherry pie
deep-dish blueberry pie
raspberry and chocolate swirl pie
pumpkin pie
piecrust
matzo crumb piecrust
brownies
peanut butter cookies
date rounds
oatmeal cookies
praline cookies
gingerbread cookie cutouts
fudge
peanut butter fudge

(continued on following page)

warm chocolate soufflés with fruited custard sauce
crepes
banana crepes
strawberry crepes with ice cream
apple-filled crepes
flan caramel
spiced fruit
spiced fruit with frozen yogurt
raspberry sorbet

Angel Food Cake

Serves 12 • 1 slice per serving

Strawberry Orange Sauce (page 211) makes a heavenly topping for this light-as-a feather cake.

1	cup sifted cake flour
½	cup sugar
1¼	cups egg whites, at room temperature (whites of about 10 large eggs)
1	teaspoon cream of tartar
½	teaspoon vanilla extract
½	teaspoon almond extract
¾	cup sugar

Preheat oven to 350° F.

Alternating between two medium bowls, sift together flour and ½ cup sugar three times.

In a large copper, stainless steel, or glass mixing bowl, beat egg whites until foamy with an electric mixer on medium-low. Add cream of tartar and vanilla and almond extracts. Gradually increasing speed, continue beating until soft, moist, glossy peaks form. Gradually add remaining ¾ cup sugar, beating at high speed until volume increases and stiff peaks form. By hand, gently fold in flour mixture only until all flour has been moistened.

Pour batter into a 9-inch tube pan. Cut through batter carefully with a thin spatula to break up large air pockets.

Bake for 40 to 45 minutes, or until a toothpick inserted in center comes out clean. Invert pan and let cool for 1 hour 30 minutes, or until thoroughly cooled. (If pan doesn't have feet, invert it over a soda bottle.) Remove cake from pan before storing.

Cook's Tip on Egg Whites: Even a single drop of egg yolk will prevent egg whites from forming peaks when beaten, so separate eggs very carefully. Separate each white into a small bowl. Then pour it into the mixing bowl.

Calories 124	Total Fat 0 g	Fiber 0 g
Protein 3 g	Saturated 0 g	Sodium 42 mg
Carbohydrates 28 g	Polyunsaturated 0 g	Potassium 87 mg
Cholesterol 0 mg	Monounsaturated 0 g	Calcium 3 mg

Chocolate Cake

Serves 24 • 1 slice per serving

A wonderfully moist cake, this is good with Quick Chocolate Frosting (page 260) or without.

	Vegetable oil spray
2½	cups all-purpose flour
⅓	cup unsweetened cocoa powder (Dutch process preferred)
1	tablespoon plus ½ teaspoon baking powder
¾	cup water
⅔	cup fat-free milk
	4-ounce jar baby-food prunes (about ½ cup)
¼	cup acceptable vegetable oil
1	teaspoon vanilla extract
	Whites of 4 large eggs
¼	teaspoon cream of tartar
1¾	cups sugar

Preheat oven to 375° F. Lightly spray a 13 × 9 × 2-inch cake pan or two 8-inch square or 9-inch square cake pans with vegetable oil spray. Line pan with wax paper cut to fit bottom.

In a large mixing bowl, sift together flour, cocoa powder, and baking powder. Make a well in center.

In a small bowl, whisk together water, milk, prunes, oil, and vanilla. Pour into well in flour mixture, stirring until well combined. Batter will resemble a thick paste.

In a medium mixing bowl, beat egg whites with an electric mixer until foamy. Add cream of tartar. Gradually add sugar, beating after each addition until egg whites form soft peaks. Gently fold egg whites into batter. Pour into prepared pan.

Bake for 35 to 40 minutes, or until toothpick inserted in center comes out clean. Set on cooling rack for 5 minutes. Remove cake from pan; peel off wax paper. Serve cake warm or at room temperature.

Calories 139	Total Fat 3 g	Fiber 1 g
Protein 3 g	Saturated 0 g	Sodium 85 mg
Carbohydrates 27 g	Polyunsaturated 1 g	Potassium 114 mg
Cholesterol 0 mg	Monounsaturated 1 g	Calcium 53 mg

Denver Chocolate Pudding Cake

Serves 9 • 3-inch square per serving

This cake is so easy, you don't even have to make any frosting. Just bake the cake and voilà, the topping magically appears.

	Vegetable oil spray
1	cup all-purpose flour
¾	cup sugar
3	tablespoons unsweetened cocoa powder (Dutch process preferred)
2	teaspoons baking powder
½	cup fat-free milk
3	tablespoons light stick margarine, melted
½	teaspoon vanilla extract
½	cup firmly packed light brown sugar
½	cup sugar
¼	cup unsweetened cocoa powder (Dutch process preferred)
1½	cups cold water or cold coffee

Preheat oven to 350° F. Lightly spray a 9-inch square baking pan with vegetable oil spray.

In a large bowl, sift together flour, ¾ cup sugar, 3 tablespoons cocoa, and baking powder.

Whisk in milk, margarine, and vanilla. Pour batter into pan and sprinkle with brown sugar, then ½ cup sugar, then ¼ cup cocoa powder; don't mix. Pour water over top; don't mix.

Bake for 40 minutes, or until top of cake looks dry and is firm to the touch.

To serve, cut cake into 9 pieces. Invert each piece onto a dessert plate so sauce is on top.

Calories 243	Total Fat 2 g	Fiber 2 g
Protein 3 g	Saturated 1 g	Sodium 149 mg
Carbohydrates 54 g	Polyunsaturated 1 g	Potassium 295 mg
Cholesterol 0 mg	Monounsaturated 1 g	Calcium 97 mg

Carrot Cake

Serves 16 • 2 × 3-inch piece per serving

This hefty snack cake gives you a scrumptious double dose of carrots.

Vegetable oil spray

Cake

1	cup honey
2	tablespoons acceptable vegetable oil
	4-ounce jar baby-food carrots (about ½ cup)
	Egg substitute equivalent to 1 egg, or whites of 2 large eggs
1	teaspoon vanilla extract
2	cups shredded carrots (3 to 4 medium)
1	cup all-purpose flour
1	cup whole-wheat flour
¼	cup nonfat dry milk
2	teaspoons baking powder
1	teaspoon ground cinnamon
⅛	teaspoon ground nutmeg

Topping

2	cups frozen fat-free or light whipped topping, thawed (optional)
½	teaspoon ground nutmeg or cinnamon (optional)

Preheat oven to 350° F. Lightly spray a 13 × 9 × 2-inch baking pan with vegetable oil spray.

For cake, in a medium bowl, stir together honey and oil until smooth. Stir in baby-food carrots, egg substitute, and vanilla. Stir in shredded carrots.

In a large mixing bowl, stir together remaining cake ingredients. Stir in carrot mixture. Mix well. Pour into baking pan.

Bake for 25 minutes, or until toothpick inserted in center comes out clean. Remove from oven and let cool in pan. Cut into 16 slices.

For topping, in a small bowl, stir together whipped topping and nutmeg. Dollop about 2 tablespoons onto each piece of cake.

Calories 150	Total Fat 2 g	Fiber 2 g
Protein 3 g	Saturated 0 g	Sodium 91 mg
Carbohydrates 32 g	Polyunsaturated 1 g	Potassium 129 mg
Cholesterol 0 mg	Monounsaturated 1 g	Calcium 63 mg

Gingerbread

Adding fruit gives this gingerbread a deep sweetness.

	5-ounce can fat-free evaporated milk
2	teaspoons cider vinegar
	Vegetable oil spray
1	cup all-purpose flour
1	cup whole-wheat flour
1	teaspoon ground ginger
½	teaspoon baking soda
½	teaspoon ground cinnamon
¾	cup honey
	6-ounce jar baby-food sweet potatoes
2	tablespoons egg substitute, or white of 1 large egg
1	tablespoon plus 2 teaspoons acceptable vegetable oil
½	cup raisins, dried cherries, dried cranberries, or chopped peeled apple

In a medium bowl, combine milk and vinegar. Let stand for 10 minutes. Preheat oven to 350° F. Lightly spray a 9-inch square baking pan with vegetable oil spray.

In another medium bowl, combine flours, ginger, baking soda, and cinnamon.

To milk mixture, add remaining ingredients except raisins. Beat with an electric mixer on medium until blended. Gradually add flour mixture, stirring well after each addition. Fold in raisins. Pour into pan.

Bake for 30 minutes, or until toothpick inserted in center comes out clean. Set on cooling rack for at least 10 minutes before slicing.

Calories 291	Total Fat 3 g	Fiber 3 g
Protein 6 g	Saturated 0 g	Sodium 117 mg
Carbohydrates 63 g	Polyunsaturated 1 g	Potassium 304 mg
Cholesterol 1 mg	Monounsaturated 2 g	Calcium 79 mg

Quick Lemon Frosting

Frosts 13 × 9 × 2-inch or two-layer cake • Serves 16 • 2 tablespoons per serving

Need some frosting in a hurry? This easy-to-do recipe is your answer. Try it on Carrot Cake (page 258).

1	cup confectioners' sugar
2	tablespoons fat-free milk
½	teaspoon lemon zest
1½	tablespoons fresh lemon juice
1	teaspoon vanilla extract
2	cups frozen fat-free or light whipped topping, thawed

In a medium bowl, using a rubber scraper, stir together all ingredients except whipped topping. Gently fold in whipped topping.

Quick Chocolate Frosting

Add ¼ cup unsweetened cocoa powder, 1 tablespoon fat-free milk, and substitute ¼ teaspoon mint or vanilla extract for the lemon zest and juice.

QUICK LEMON FROSTING

Calories 46	Total Fat 0 g	Fiber 0 g
Protein 0 g	Saturated 0 g	Sodium 6 mg
Carbohydrates 11 g	Polyunsaturated 0 g	Potassium 6 mg
Cholesterol 0 mg	Monounsaturated 0 g	Calcium 3 mg

QUICK CHOCOLATE FROSTING

Calories 49	Total Fat 0 g	Fiber 0 g
Protein 0 g	Saturated 0 g	Sodium 7 mg
Carbohydrates 11 g	Polyunsaturated 0 g	Potassium 26 mg
Cholesterol 0 mg	Monounsaturated 0 g	Calcium 5 mg

Apple Pie with Raisins

This recipe combines the ingredients of apple strudel to give you the same taste without as much work.

	Vegetable oil spray
⅔	*cup sugar*
1	*teaspoon ground cinnamon*
2½	*pounds tart, firm apples, peeled, cored, and sliced (about 8 medium)*
½	*cup raisins*
1	*recipe Piecrust (page 267), unbaked*

Preheat oven to 425° F. Lightly spray a 9-inch pie pan with vegetable oil spray.

In a large bowl, stir together sugar and cinnamon. Add apples and raisins, stirring thoroughly.

Pour apple mixture into pie pan, and top with crust. Cut off excess crust and crimp around edges to create a ruffle. Make four to six slits in crust about ½ inch deep.

Bake for 35 to 45 minutes, or until crust is lightly browned.

Calories 248	Total Fat 3 g	Fiber 3 g
Protein 2 g	Saturated 1 g	Sodium 38 mg
Carbohydrates 56 g	Polyunsaturated 1 g	Potassium 241 mg
Cholesterol 0 mg	Monounsaturated 1 g	Calcium 18 mg

Apple and Cranberry Pie

Serves 8 • 1 slice per person

Apples and cranberries are the perfect pie duo. For a pretty presentation, top this pie with an array of star shapes.

Vegetable oil spray

Piecrust

2	cups all-purpose flour
¾	cup firmly packed light brown sugar
½	cup regular oats (not quick-cooking)
1	teaspoon ground cinnamon
½	teaspoon ground ginger
½	cup unsweetened applesauce
	White of 1 large egg
½	tablespoon acceptable vegetable oil
	Flour for rolling out dough

Filling

4	large Rome apples
	Juice of ½ medium lemon
2	cups fresh or frozen cranberries
¾	cup firmly packed light brown sugar
¼	cup granulated sugar
⅓	cup all-purpose flour, plus more for dusting surface
1	teaspoon ground cinnamon

Topping (optional)

½	cup frozen fat-free or light whipped topping, thawed
	Ground cinnamon

For piecrust, lightly spray a 9-inch pie pan with vegetable oil spray.

In a large bowl, stir together flour, brown sugar, oats, cinnamon, and ginger; mix with a fork to break up any lumps of sugar.

In a separate small bowl, whisk together applesauce, egg white, and oil. Stir into flour mixture with a fork until a dough forms. Remove dough to a lightly floured board (if dough is sticky, add a sprinkle more flour); knead until soft. Shape the dough into two rounds, one larger than the other (the larger round should use about two-thirds of the dough).

Roll out larger round of dough to ¼-inch thickness; fit dough into pie pan. Roll out remaining dough to ⅛ inch thick. Use different sizes of star cookie cutters to cut shapes out of the smaller round of dough.

Place oven rack in lowest position. Preheat oven to 425° F.

For filling, peel, core, and slice apples about ¼ inch thick. You should have 4 cups. Put apples in a large bowl, sprinkle with lemon juice, and stir gently to coat. Stir in cranberries.

In a small bowl, stir together both sugars, flour, and cinnamon. Gently stir into apple mixture. Mound apple mixture inside crust. Top with star-shaped dough pieces; put pie on a baking sheet.

Bake for 15 minutes. Reduce heat to 350° F and bake for 55 to 60 minutes, or until crust is lightly golden and apples are tender. Cut into eight slices and top each with a dollop of whipped topping and a dusting of cinnamon.

Cherry Pie

Substitute 10 cups frozen sour cherries for the apples and cranberries. Increase sugar to ½ cup. If that's not sweet enough for you, also increase the brown sugar to 1 cup.

Cook's Tip: If dough is too sticky, add a bit more flour. If dough seems dry, add a bit more applesauce. Use a metal pastry scraper to lift dough if it is hard to remove from surface. While this dough is pliable, it's best not to patch dough if it tears—just re-roll.

APPLE AND CRANBERRY PIE		
Calories 424	Total Fat 2 g	Fiber 5 g
Protein 5 g	Saturated 0 g	Sodium 25 mg
Carbohydrates 99 g	Polyunsaturated 1 g	Potassium 366 mg
Cholesterol 0 mg	Monounsaturated 1 g	Calcium 57 mg

CHERRY PIE		
Calories 463	Total Fat 3 g	Fiber 5 g
Protein 7 g	Saturated 0 g	Sodium 26 mg
Carbohydrates 108 g	Polyunsaturated 1 g	Potassium 465 mg
Cholesterol 0 mg	Monounsaturated 1 g	Calcium 76 mg

Deep-Dish Cherry Pie

Serves 8 • 1 slice per serving

This pie is so wonderful, you'll want to eat it straight from the oven.

	Vegetable oil spray
1	cup sugar
½	cup all-purpose flour
½	teaspoon ground cinnamon
2	16-ounce cans sour cherries, drained
⅛	teaspoon almond extract
1	recipe Piecrust (page 267), unbaked

Preheat oven to 425° F. Spray a 9-inch deep-dish glass pie pan with vegetable oil spray.

In a medium bowl, stir together sugar, flour, and cinnamon.

In another medium bowl, stir together cherries and almond extract. Stir into sugar mixture. Pour into pie pan. Top with crust. Cut off excess crust and crimp around edges to create a ruffle. Make four to six slits in crust about ½ inch deep. Cover rim of pie with aluminum foil to prevent overbrowning.

Bake for 25 minutes. Remove foil and bake for 20 minutes, or until crust is golden. Set on cooling rack.

Deep-Dish Blueberry Pie

Substitute 4 cups fresh or frozen unsweetened blueberries for cherries and reduce sugar to ¾ cup.

DEEP-DISH CHERRY PIE

Calories 250	Total Fat 3 g	Fiber 2 g
Protein 3 g	Saturated 1 g	Sodium 43 mg
Carbohydrates 54 g	Polyunsaturated 1 g	Potassium 139 mg
Cholesterol 0 mg	Monounsaturated 1 g	Calcium 22 mg

DEEP-DISH BLUEBERRY PIE

Calories 226	Total Fat 3 g	Fiber 3 g
Protein 3 g	Saturated 1 g	Sodium 40 mg
Carbohydrates 48 g	Polyunsaturated 1 g	Potassium 92 mg
Cholesterol 0 mg	Monounsaturated 1 g	Calcium 14 mg

Raspberry and Chocolate Swirl Pie

Serves 8 • 1 slice per serving

The refreshing taste of raspberry sorbet blends well with the down-home goodness of vanilla and chocolate swirl frozen yogurt.

Crust
  1¼   cups low-fat graham cracker crumbs (about 20 squares)
  3   tablespoons light stick margarine, melted

Filling
  1   pint raspberry sorbet
  2   pints fat-free or low-fat vanilla and chocolate swirl frozen yogurt or ice cream

Topping
  ½   cup frozen fat-free or light whipped topping, thawed
  2   tablespoons fat-free chocolate syrup

Preheat oven to 375° F.

For crust, in a medium bowl, stir together ingredients. Press on bottom and up sides of a 9-inch pie pan.

Bake for 6 minutes. Let cool completely on a cooling rack.

For filling, remove sorbet and frozen yogurt from freezer to soften to spreading consistency, about 20 minutes. Drop heaping tablespoons of sorbet onto the prepared crust. Drop heaping tablespoons of frozen yogurt between mounds of sorbet. Gently swirl sorbet into the frozen yogurt, being careful not to overmix. Smooth top of pie.

Mound whipped topping on the pie; using a knife, create decorative swirls. Drizzle chocolate syrup in swirls on top. Gently cover pie with plastic wrap and return to freezer for 1 hour, or until firm.

Cook's Tip: If preparing ahead, make the crust and filling as directed. Cover with plastic wrap and freeze. About 1 hour before serving, spoon on the whipped topping and drizzle with the syrup. Return the pie to the freezer until ready to serve.

Calories 263	Total Fat 3 g	Fiber 2 g
Protein 6 g	Saturated 1 g	Sodium 172 mg
Carbohydrates 53 g	Polyunsaturated 1 g	Potassium 269 mg
Cholesterol 2 mg	Monounsaturated 1 g	Calcium 172 mg

Pumpkin Pie

Serves 8 • 1 slice per serving

Our version of this old-time favorite is so tasty you'll want to have it year-round.

	Vegetable oil spray
	16-ounce can solid-pack pumpkin (1½ cups)
⅔	cup firmly packed light brown sugar
1	teaspoon ground cinnamon
½	teaspoon ground ginger
¼	teaspoon ground cloves or allspice
	13-ounce can fat-free evaporated milk
	Whites of 3 large eggs, beaten until foamy
1	recipe Piecrust (page 267), unbaked
1	cup frozen fat-free or light whipped topping, thawed (optional)

Preheat oven to 400° F. Spray a 9-inch deep-dish glass pie pan with vegetable oil spray.

In a large mixing bowl, stir together pumpkin, brown sugar, cinnamon, ginger, and cloves. Add milk and egg whites. With an electric mixer, beat on medium until thoroughly combined.

Line pan with pie dough and fill with pumpkin mixture. Cover rim of pie with aluminum foil to prevent overbrowning.

Bake for 25 minutes. Remove foil from pie and bake for 20 minutes, or until knife inserted near center of pie comes out clean. Remove from oven and spray lightly with vegetable oil spray. Set on cooling rack.

Serve each slice with 2 tablespoons whipped topping.

Cook's Tip: Lightly spraying the pie with vegetable oil spray provides a sheen to the pie filling.

Calories 228	Total Fat 3 g	Fiber 2 g
Protein 7 g	Saturated 1 g	Sodium 125 mg
Carbohydrates 44 g	Polyunsaturated 1 g	Potassium 357 mg
Cholesterol 2 mg	Monounsaturated 1 g	Calcium 178 mg

Piecrust

Makes 1 9-inch pie • Serves 8 • 1/8 crust per serving

Remember your grandmother's homemade piecrust? This "grandmother-style" crust has all the same goodness but little of the fat.

2/3	cup all-purpose flour
3	tablespoons sugar
2	tablespoons acceptable stick margarine, diced
1 1/2	tablespoons fat-free milk
1	teaspoon all-purpose flour

Put all ingredients except 1 teaspoon flour in a food processor. Process until dough begins to stick together. Form pie dough into a disk about 4 inches in diameter. Cover with plastic wrap and refrigerate for 15 minutes.

Place a sheet of plastic wrap on a flat surface and sprinkle with 1 teaspoon flour. Put dough on floured surface, press lightly, and turn dough over (this allows some flour to stick to both sides of dough). Cover dough with another sheet of plastic wrap. Roll out dough to a 10-inch-diameter circle. Remove top sheet of plastic wrap. Use crust according to recipe directions.

Cook's Tip on Baking Unfilled Pie Crust: When baking an unfilled crust, or "baking blind," use the weight of dried beans, dried rice, or metal or ceramic pie weights to prevent the crust from puffing up and slipping down the sides of the pan. If you don't have any of these, you can nestle a pie pan of equal size into the pan with the uncooked crust, then bake it.

Calories 83	Total Fat 3 g	Fiber 0 g
Protein 1 g	Saturated 1 g	Sodium 35 mg
Carbohydrates 13 g	Polyunsaturated 1 g	Potassium 18 mg
Cholesterol 0 mg	Monounsaturated 1 g	Calcium 6 mg

Matzo Crumb Piecrust

Makes 1 9-inch piecrust • Serves 8 • ⅛ crust per serving

This crust is particularly suited to a pudding or cream pie filling. It turns fat-free pudding made from a mix into a special sweet treat.

1	cup unsalted matzo meal
¼	cup sugar
¼	teaspoon ground cinnamon (optional)
3	tablespoons light stick margarine, melted

Preheat oven to 350° F.

In a small bowl, stir together matzo meal and sugar. Stir in cinnamon and margarine. Press firmly into a 9-inch pie pan.

Bake for 20 minutes, or until lightly browned.

Calories 108	Total Fat 2 g	Fiber 0 g
Protein 2 g	Saturated 0 g	Sodium 28 mg
Carbohydrates 20 g	Polyunsaturated 1 g	Potassium 27 mg
Cholesterol 0 mg	Monounsaturated 1 g	Calcium 0 mg

Brownies

For that melt-in-your-mouth flavor, serve these brownies as soon as they're cool.

	Vegetable oil spray
1	cup sugar
¾	cup all-purpose flour
½	cup unsweetened cocoa powder
½	teaspoon baking powder
	4-ounce jar baby-food prunes (about ½ cup)
	Whites of 3 large eggs
3	tablespoons acceptable stick margarine, melted
1	teaspoon vanilla extract
2	tablespoons confectioners' sugar

Preheat oven to 350° F. Lightly spray an 8-inch square baking pan with vegetable oil spray.

In a medium bowl, sift together sugar, flour, cocoa, and baking powder. Stir in remaining ingredients except confectioners' sugar. Pour into baking pan.

Bake for 30 minutes, or until edges begin to pull away from sides of pan. Set on a cooling rack. Cut into 12 squares. Sift confectioners' sugar evenly over all before removing from pan.

Cook's Tip: You can make these brownies up to 48 hours in advance, but don't add the confectioners' sugar then. The sugar may dissolve into the brownie, giving it a mottled appearance. You can add the sugar up to 4 hours before serving, but a little of it will dissolve.

Calories 146	Total Fat 3 g	Fiber 2 g
Protein 3 g	Saturated 1 g	Sodium 69 mg
Carbohydrates 28 g	Polyunsaturated 1 g	Potassium 107 mg
Cholesterol 0 mg	Monounsaturated 2 g	Calcium 21 mg

Peanut Butter Cookies

Serves 48 • 2 cookies per serving

*You're sure to have a crowd gather when you set out a plate of these
freshly baked treats.*

	Vegetable oil spray
½	cup acceptable stick margarine
½	cup granulated sugar
½	cup firmly packed light brown sugar
	Egg substitute equivalent to 1 egg, or 1 large egg
1	cup unsalted peanut butter
½	teaspoon vanilla extract
1½	cups all-purpose flour
1¼	teaspoons baking powder

Preheat oven to 350° F. Lightly spray two baking sheets with vegetable oil spray.

In a large mixing bowl, cream margarine and sugars with an electric mixer. Beat in egg substitute. Add peanut butter and vanilla; beat until smooth.

In a medium bowl, sift together flour and baking powder. Gradually add to margarine mixture and beat on medium for 15 to 20 seconds.

Roll dough into ¾-inch balls and put 1½ to 2 inches apart on baking sheets. Flatten with a fork.

Bake for 15 minutes, or until a toothpick inserted in center comes out clean. Let cookies cool for 2 to 3 minutes on baking sheets before transferring cookies to cooling racks. Repeat with remaining dough.

Calories 80	Total Fat 5 g	Fiber 0 g
Protein 2 g	Saturated 1 g	Sodium 39 mg
Carbohydrates 8 g	Polyunsaturated 1 g	Potassium 51 mg
Cholesterol 0 mg	Monounsaturated 2 g	Calcium 13 mg

Date Rounds

Serves 30 • 1 cookie per serving

*Enjoy these rich-tasting cookies at your holiday parties, or bake a
batch as a gift to please a friend.*

½	cup acceptable stick margarine
⅓	cup sifted confectioners' sugar
1	tablespoon fat-free milk
1	teaspoon vanilla extract
1¼	cups sifted all-purpose flour
⅔	cup chopped dates
½	cup chopped walnuts
⅓	cup sifted confectioners' sugar

Preheat oven to 300° F.

In a large mixing bowl, beat margarine with ⅓ cup confectioners'
sugar until soft and smooth. Stir in milk and vanilla extract. Add flour
and stir well. Stir in dates and nuts.

Roll dough into 1-inch balls; place cookies 2 inches apart on ungreased baking sheets.

Bake for 20 to 25 minutes, or until lightly browned. Let sit on cooling
rack until cool enough to handle but still warm. Roll cookies in remaining ⅓ cup confectioners' sugar.

Cook's Tip on Dates: Because they are so sugary, dates may be stuck together. To separate them easily, microwave them on 50 percent power (medium) for
30 to 60 seconds; let them stand for about 1 minute before separating them. Another
way is to put a block of dates on a baking sheet and heat them in a 300° F oven for
about 5 minutes. Spray your kitchen scissors or food processor blade with vegetable
oil spray to make chopping dates easier.

Calories 79	Total Fat 4 g	Fiber 1 g
Protein 1 g	Saturated 1 g	Sodium 36 mg
Carbohydrates 10 g	Polyunsaturated 2 g	Potassium 44 mg
Cholesterol 0 mg	Monounsaturated 2 g	Calcium 6 mg

Oatmeal Cookies

Serves 16 • 2 cookies per serving

Moist, chewy, and delicious, these will become the new "traditional" oatmeal cookies in your household.

	Vegetable oil spray
6	*tablespoons light stick margarine*
1/2	*cup firmly packed light brown sugar*
1	*tablespoon light corn syrup*
1/2	*teaspoon vanilla extract*
1	*cup all-purpose flour*
1/4	*teaspoon baking soda*
1/4	*teaspoon ground cinnamon*
1	*cup uncooked quick-cooking oatmeal*
	Flour for rolling dough

Preheat oven to 375° F. Lightly spray two baking sheets with vegetable oil spray.

In a large mixing bowl, beat margarine and brown sugar with an electric mixer on medium until creamy, about 2 minutes. Stir in corn syrup and vanilla.

In a medium bowl, stir together 1 cup flour, baking soda, and cinnamon. Gradually add to margarine mixture, stirring after each addition until dough pulls away from side of bowl. Stir in oatmeal.

Lightly flour hands and roll dough into 1-inch balls. Place 2 inches apart on baking sheets.

Dip a fork in flour and slightly flatten each cookie to about 1/2 inch thick.

Bake for 8 to 9 minutes, or until lightly browned. Immediately transfer cookies from baking sheet to cooling racks. Cookies can be stored in an airtight container for up to one week.

Calories 95	Total Fat 3 g	Fiber 1 g
Protein 2 g	Saturated 1 g	Sodium 52 mg
Carbohydrates 17 g	Polyunsaturated 1 g	Potassium 52 mg
Cholesterol 0 mg	Monounsaturated 1 g	Calcium 10 mg

Praline Cookies

Serves 36 • 2 cookies per serving

Loaded with toasted pecans, these cookies look and taste like pralines. The batter will be creamy, not stiff.

    Vegetable oil spray
1/3 cup light stick margarine
1   cup firmly packed light brown sugar
    Egg substitute equivalent to 1 egg, or 1 large egg
1   tablespoon vanilla, butter, and nut flavoring or vanilla extract
1 1/2 cups sifted all-purpose flour
3/4 cup chopped toasted pecans (see Cook's Tip on Dry-Roasting
    Seeds or Nuts, page 106)

Preheat oven to 375° F. Lightly spray two baking sheets with vegetable oil spray.

In a large mixing bowl, beat margarine and brown sugar with an electric mixer on medium for 2 minutes, or until creamy. Beat in egg and flavoring. Stir in flour, blending well. Stir in pecans.

Drop dough by teaspoonfuls on baking sheet. Bake for 8 to 9 minutes, or until lightly browned. Transfer cookies from baking sheets to cooling racks.

Calories 66	Total Fat 3 g	Fiber 0 g
Protein 1 g	Saturated 0 g	Sodium 7 mg
Carbohydrates 10 g	Polyunsaturated 1 g	Potassium 40 mg
Cholesterol 0 mg	Monounsaturated 1 g	Calcium 17 mg

Gingerbread Cookie Cutouts

Serves 18 • 2 4-inch cookies per serving

You'll know the holidays have arrived when the spicy aroma of these traditional gingerbread cookies fills the house!

> Vegetable oil spray
> 3   cups all-purpose flour
> 1   teaspoon baking powder
> 1   teaspoon ground cinnamon
> 1   teaspoon ground ginger
> ½   teaspoon baking soda
> ½   teaspoon salt
> ½   teaspoon ground cloves
> ¾   cup firmly packed light brown sugar
> ½   cup molasses
> ¼   cup acceptable vegetable oil
>   Egg substitute equivalent to 1 egg, or 1 large egg
> 2   tablespoons granulated sugar

In a medium bowl, stir together flour, baking powder, cinnamon, ginger, baking soda, salt, and cloves.

In a large bowl, combine remaining ingredients. Gradually add flour mixture to brown sugar mixture, stirring to form a soft dough. Return dough to medium bowl, cover tightly with plastic wrap, and refrigerate for 2 hours or overnight.

Preheat oven to 375° F. Spray two baking sheets with vegetable oil spray.

On a floured board or pastry cloth, roll half the cookie dough to ⅛-inch thickness. Dip edges of cookie cutters in flour, shaking off excess. Cut out cookies, continuing to dip cookie cutters in flour as needed to keep dough from sticking. Place cookies on cookie sheets.

Bake for 5 to 6 minutes, or until cookies are slightly firm to the touch (cookies shouldn't brown). Let cookies cool slightly, then transfer from baking sheet to a cooling rack.

Calories 169	Total Fat 3 g	Fiber 1 g
Protein 3 g	Saturated 0 g	Sodium 141 mg
Carbohydrates 33 g	Polyunsaturated 1 g	Potassium 195 mg
Cholesterol 0 mg	Monounsaturated 2 g	Calcium 48 mg

Fudge

Serves 25 • 1 piece per serving

This delightful chocolate treat is easy, easy, easy.

   Vegetable oil spray
1 cup firmly packed light brown sugar
1 cup granulated sugar
2/3 cup fat-free milk
1/3 cup unsweetened cocoa powder
2 tablespoons light tub margarine
1 teaspoon vanilla extract

Lightly spray an 8-inch square baking pan with vegetable oil spray.

In a medium saucepan, whisk together sugars, milk, and cocoa powder. Cook over medium-high heat until mixture reaches 236° F on a candy thermometer, or until a small amount of syrup dropped into cold water forms a soft ball. Remove from heat. Add margarine but don't stir. Let cool until bottom of pan is lukewarm to the touch.

Add vanilla and beat with an electric mixer on medium speed for 5 to 10 minutes, or until fudge is thick and no longer glossy. Spread in baking pan. Let cool until firm. Cut into 25 pieces.

Peanut Butter Fudge

After beating fudge, stir in 1/2 cup reduced-fat peanut butter just until combined.

FUDGE		
Calories 43	Total Fat 1g	Fiber 0 g
Protein 0 g	Saturated 0 g	Sodium 12 mg
Carbohydrates 9 g	Polyunsaturated 0 g	Potassium 31 mg
Cholesterol 0 mg	Monounsaturated 0 g	Calcium 9 mg

PEANUT BUTTER FUDGE		
Calories 56	Total Fat 2 g	Fiber 0 g
Protein 1 g	Saturated 0 g	Sodium 27 mg
Carbohydrates 10 g	Polyunsaturated 1 g	Potassium 50 mg
Cholesterol 0 mg	Monounsaturated 1 g	Calcium 10 mg

Warm Chocolate Soufflés with Fruited Custard Sauce

Serves 8 • 1 soufflé and 2 tablespoons sauce per serving

Indulge yourself without regret! These chocolate soufflés are covered with creamy custard and fresh raspberries to bring out the raspberry flavor in the cocoa.

Vegetable oil spray

Soufflés

⅓	cup plus 2 tablespoons sugar
¼	cup raspberry-flavored cocoa or unsweetened cocoa powder
2	tablespoons all-purpose flour
¾	cup fat-free evaporated milk
	Yolk of 1 large egg
	Whites of 5 large eggs
½	teaspoon cream of tartar

Custard Sauce

3½	tablespoons sugar
1	tablespoon powdered egg substitute
1½	teaspoons cornstarch
¾	cup fat-free milk
1	teaspoon vanilla extract
¼	cup hot water
6	ounces fresh raspberries, divided use (about 1 cup)

Lightly spray eight 3-ounce ramekins or custard cups with vegetable oil spray. Set aside.

For soufflés, in a large heavy saucepan, combine sugar, cocoa, and flour. Slowly whisk in evaporated milk. Cook over medium heat, whisking constantly, until mixture is thick and bubbling, 5 to 6 minutes. Remove pan from heat.

In a small bowl, whisk egg yolk until pale yellow and thick, about 3 minutes. Slowly whisk in about one-fourth chocolate mixture. Whisk yolk mixture into remaining chocolate mixture.

Preheat oven to 375° F.

In a large mixing bowl, using an electric mixer on medium to medium-high, beat egg whites and cream of tartar until stiff peaks form. With a rubber scraper, gently fold about one-fourth egg whites into chocolate mixture. Gently fold chocolate mixture into remaining egg whites. Spoon into ramekins, filling three-quarters full. Place filled ramekins on a baking sheet.

Bake for 18 minutes, or until soufflés rise.

Meanwhile, for custard sauce, combine sugar, powdered egg substitute, and cornstarch in a small saucepan. Slowly whisk in milk. Cook over medium-high heat until mixture is thick and bubbling, about 4 minutes, whisking constantly. Remove from heat and whisk in vanilla. Slowly pour in hot water, whisking to keep custard smooth.

Set aside eight of the prettiest raspberries for garnish; gently stir remaining raspberries into custard sauce.

To serve, spoon warm custard sauce over soufflés as soon as they are taken from the oven, garnishing each serving with a fresh raspberry.

Variations

Try other flavored cocoas, extracts, or liquid nonfat nondairy creamers and fruit that is similar or complementary, such as either orange-flavor cocoa or chocolate extract with mandarin orange sections.

Instead of custard sauce, serve the soufflés with pureed fruit.

Replace the custard sauce with fat-free or light whipped topping sprinkled with cinnamon or shaved chocolate.

Calories 140	Total Fat 1 g	Fiber 2 g
Protein 6 g	Saturated 1 g	Sodium 80 mg
Carbohydrates 27 g	Polyunsaturated 0 g	Potassium 261 mg
Cholesterol 31 mg	Monounsaturated 0 g	Calcium 112 mg

Crepes

Makes 22 crepes • 2 6-inch crepes per serving

For a flavorful, yet simple dessert, spray rolled crepes with butter spray, warm them in the oven, and serve topped with maple syrup, sifted confectioners' sugar, or cinnamon sugar. For a more elegant dessert, see the recipes for Banana Crepes, Strawberry Crepes with Ice Cream, or Apple-Filled Crepes (pages 280, 281, and 282).

1½   cups sifted all-purpose flour
¾   cup fat-free milk
¾   cup cold water
       Egg substitute equivalent to 1 egg, or whites of 2 large eggs
       (see Cook's Tip on Egg Whites, page 255)
¼   cup light stick margarine, melted
2   tablespoons rum or orange-flavored liqueur (optional)
1   tablespoon sugar
       Vegetable oil spray
2   to 3 tablespoons water, as needed

In a large mixing bowl, combine all ingredients except 2 to 3 tablespoons water. Beat with an electric mixer on high for about 1 minute, or until smooth. Cover tightly with plastic wrap and refrigerate for 2 to 24 hours. Batter will be thin.

Heat a small nonstick skillet over medium heat. Remove from heat and lightly spray with vegetable oil spray (being careful not to spray near a gas flame). Pour 2 tablespoons batter into center of skillet. Tilt pan until batter covers bottom of pan or forms a circle 6 inches in diameter. Return to heat for 2 to 3 minutes, or until lightly browned. Lightly grasping edge of crepe with your fingers, turn crepe over. Lightly brown other side, about 1 minute. Place crepe on wax paper to cool. If first crepe is too thick, whisk 2 to 3 tablespoons water into remaining batter. Spray skillet lightly with vegetable oil spray. Repeat process with remaining batter.

To store crepes, stack with wax paper between layers and place in airtight plastic bags. Refrigerate overnight or freeze. For ease in rolling when filled, crepes should be at room temperature when used.

Cook's Tip on Crepes: Test the crepe pan's readiness just as you test a pancake griddle's. Sprinkle a few drops of water on the hot surface; if they dance, your pan is hot enough. Properly cooked crepes taste delicate but actually are fairly sturdy. If one tears, it probably needed a few more seconds of cooking time.

Calories 88	Total Fat 2 g	Fiber 0 g
Protein 3 g	Saturated 0 g	Sodium 48 mg
Carbohydrates 14 g	Polyunsaturated 1 g	Potassium 54 mg
Cholesterol 0 mg	Monounsaturated 1 g	Calcium 25 mg

Banana Crepes

Serves 10 • 1 crepe per serving

To make these luscious crepes even more interesting, top them with a dollop of nonfat plain yogurt and a sprinkling of nutmeg.

    2   tablespoons light stick margarine
    1/2 cup all-fruit orange marmalade
    2   tablespoons granulated sugar
    1   tablespoon cornstarch
    3   large bananas, sliced (about 3 1/4 cups)
    10 6-inch crepes (1/2 recipe for Crepes, page 278)
    1/4 cup confectioners' sugar (optional)

In a medium saucepan, heat margarine and marmalade over medium heat until margarine melts, stirring constantly.

In a small bowl, stir together sugar and cornstarch. Slowly stir into marmalade mixture. Cook over medium heat for about 3 minutes, or until mixture is smooth and bubbly, stirring constantly. Remove from heat. Fold in bananas.

Wrap crepes in plastic wrap and microwave on 100 percent power (high) for 10 seconds, or until just heated through.

Spoon banana mixture into center of warm crepes. Roll crepes jelly-roll style around filling. Top each crepe with about 1 teaspoon confectioners' sugar.

Calories 141	Total Fat 3 g	Fiber 2 g
Protein 2 g	Saturated 1 g	Sodium 42 mg
Carbohydrates 29 g	Polyunsaturated 1 g	Potassium 192 mg
Cholesterol 0 mg	Monounsaturated 1 g	Calcium 64 mg

Strawberry Crepes with Ice Cream

Serves 10 • 1 crepe per serving

Add a French flair to your meal by finishing with these flavorful strawberry-filled crepes.

3	tablespoons dark brown sugar
2	tablespoons orange juice
1/4	teaspoon ground cinnamon
2 1/2	cups sliced strawberries
10	6-inch crepes (1/2 recipe for Crepes, page 278)
2 1/2	cups fat-free or low-fat vanilla ice cream or frozen yogurt

In a large bowl, stir together brown sugar, orange juice, and cinnamon. Stir in strawberries.

Wrap crepes in plastic wrap and microwave on 100 percent power (high) for 10 seconds, or until just heated through.

Spoon about 1/4 cup strawberry mixture into center of each warm crepe. Roll crepes jelly-roll style around filling. Spoon 1/4 cup ice cream over each crepe and serve immediately.

Calories 256	Total Fat 3 g	Fiber 2 g
Protein 8 g	Saturated 0 g	Sodium 122 mg
Carbohydrates 53 g	Polyunsaturated 1 g	Potassium 269 mg
Cholesterol 0 mg	Monounsaturated 1 g	Calcium 63 mg

Apple-Filled Crepes

Serves 10 • 1 crepe per serving

For dessert, sprinkle these crepes with confectioners' sugar just before serving. They're also terrific for brunch with Turkey Sausage Patties (page 125).

Vegetable oil spray

Filling

2	tablespoons light stick margarine
5	large apples, peeled and sliced (Golden Delicious preferred) (about 2½ pounds)
¼	cup sugar
1	teaspoon grated lemon zest
1	tablespoon fresh lemon juice
⅛	teaspoon ground nutmeg

10 6-inch crepes (½ recipe for Crepes, page 278)

Preheat oven to 325° F. Lightly spray a 9-inch square casserole dish with vegetable oil spray.

In a large nonstick skillet, melt margarine over medium-high heat. Add remaining filling ingredients and cook for 5 minutes, or until apples are tender, stirring occasionally. Remove from heat.

Spoon ⅓ cup apple mixture into center of each crepe. Roll jelly-roll style and place with seam side down in casserole dish. Spoon remaining apple mixture over crepes.

Bake, covered, for 25 minutes, or until hot.

Cook's Tip: Substitute two 20-ounce cans of apple pie filling for apples and sugar. Cook for 3 minutes, or until heated through.

Calories 115	Total Fat 3 g	Fiber 2 g
Protein 2 g	Saturated 1 g	Sodium 42 mg
Carbohydrates 23 g	Polyunsaturated 1 g	Potassium 106 mg
Cholesterol 0 mg	Monounsaturated 1 g	Calcium 17 mg

Flan Caramel

Serves 6 • $\frac{1}{2}$ cup per serving

You can make this flan up to 24 hours ahead of time. For a special treat, serve sliced peaches or nectarines on the caramel topping.

	Vegetable oil spray
2½	cups fat-free milk
	Egg substitute equivalent to 2 eggs, or whites of 4 large eggs
¼	cup sugar
1	tablespoon dry or sweet sherry
1	teaspoon vanilla extract
	Dash of nutmeg
¼	cup plus 2 tablespoons fat-free caramel ice cream topping

Preheat oven to 325° F. Lightly spray six custard cups with vegetable oil spray.

In a large mixing bowl, whisk together remaining ingredients except caramel topping. Pour about ½ cup batter into each custard cup. Place custard cups in a large pan with a rim, place in oven, and pour about 1 inch of hot water into large pan.

Bake for 50 minutes, or until toothpick or knife inserted near center of custard comes out clean. Remove from pan and let cool completely on cooling rack. Cover with plastic wrap and refrigerate until serving time. Run knife around edge of custard, place dessert plate on top, and flip to remove custard.

In a microwave-safe bowl, microwave caramel topping on 100 percent power (high) for 10 seconds. Spoon 1 tablespoon topping over each serving. Serve immediately.

Cook's Tip on Egg Whites: If you're using egg whites in a light-colored recipe, such as this one, you can add several drops of yellow food coloring to make it look as though you used whole eggs.

Calories 147	Total Fat 0 g	Fiber 0 g
Protein 6 g	Saturated 0 g	Sodium 150 mg
Carbohydrates 29 g	Polyunsaturated 0 g	Potassium 201 mg
Cholesterol 2 mg	Monounsaturated 0 g	Calcium 133 mg

Spiced Fruit

Serves 8 • ³/₄ cup per serving

This is so good on its own, it's hard to believe it's even better served over half a cup of nonfat vanilla frozen yogurt.

1	cup firmly packed light brown sugar
½	cup sauterne, dry white wine (regular or nonalcoholic), or apple juice
¼	cup cider vinegar
15	whole cloves
2	sticks cinnamon (each about 3 inches long)
⅛	teaspoon curry powder
	15-ounce can sliced peaches in fruit juice, drained
	15-ounce can sliced pears in fruit juice, drained
16	to 20 honeydew melon balls, fresh or frozen, or 4 medium kiwifruit, peeled and sliced
8	fresh pineapple spears or 20-ounce can pineapple chunks in their own juice, drained
2	to 4 plums, sliced

In a medium saucepan, combine brown sugar, wine, vinegar, cloves, cinnamon, and curry powder. Cook over medium heat for 3 to 5 minutes, or until thoroughly heated, stirring frequently.

Meanwhile, combine remaining ingredients in a large bowl. Pour hot syrup over fruit; stir well. Let cool at room temperature for 30 minutes. Cover and refrigerate for 8 to 24 hours. Before serving, remove cloves and cinnamon sticks.

Spiced Fruit with Frozen Yogurt

Serves 12 • 1 cup per serving

Spoon ½ cup vanilla nonfat frozen yogurt into each of 12 dessert bowls. Top each with ½ cup spiced fruit.

SPICED FRUIT

Calories 216	Total Fat 1 g	Fiber 2 g
Protein 1 g	Saturated 0 g	Sodium 19 mg
Carbohydrates 52 g	Polyunsaturated 0 g	Potassium 395 mg
Cholesterol 0 mg	Monounsaturated 0 g	Calcium 38 mg

SPICED FRUIT WITH FROZEN YOGURT

Calories 239	Total Fat 1 g	Fiber 2 g
Protein 6 g	Saturated 0 g	Sodium 77 mg
Carbohydrates 53 g	Polyunsaturated 0 g	Potassium 478 mg
Cholesterol 2 mg	Monounsaturated 0 g	Calcium 193 mg

Raspberry Sorbet

Serves 4 • ½ cup per serving

*One taste of this vibrant dessert and you'll be transported to
raspberry paradise.*

1¾   cups water
1   cup sugar
3   cups fresh raspberries (about 2 pints)
2   tablespoons fresh lemon juice

In a medium saucepan, bring water and sugar to a boil over medium-high heat, stirring constantly. Boil until sugar has completely dissolved. Remove from heat and allow to cool.

In a food processor, process all ingredients until smooth.

Pour mixture into a 9-inch square pan and freeze until firm.

Cook's Tip: For a smoother consistency, press pureed mixture through a sieve before freezing.

Calories 241	Total Fat 1 g	Fiber 6 g
Protein 1 g	Saturated 0 g	Sodium 4 mg
Carbohydrates 61 g	Polyunsaturated 0 g	Potassium 151 mg
Cholesterol 0 mg	Monounsaturated 0 g	Calcium 23 mg

Appendix A

How to Protect Your Heart and Your Brain

Certain risk factors increase the chance that you may develop cardiovascular disease, especially heart disease and stroke. You have no control over some of these factors, such as age, sex, family history, and race. However, you can control or treat other risk factors, such as high blood pressure, high blood cholesterol, physical inactivity, obesity, diabetes, and exposure to tobacco smoke. No matter what your history, you may still be able to reduce your personal risk of disease by making healthful choices in the foods you eat, by deciding not to smoke, by maintaining a desirable body weight, and by staying active.

High Blood Pressure

Blood pressure is a measurement of two pressures—the pressure that blood exerts against the inside of the artery wall when the heart beats and the pressure when the heart is at rest. Any blood pressure device measures pressure in millimeters of mercury (mm Hg). The measurement is written as systolic blood pressure (taken while the heart is beating) over diastolic blood pressure (taken between heartbeats). An example is 120/80 (read as "one-twenty over eighty"). Blood pressure is considered high when systolic blood pressure is

140 mm Hg or greater and/or diastolic blood pressure is 90 mm Hg or greater.

About 50 million Americans over the age of 6 have high blood pressure, sometimes called hypertension. That translates to about one in four adults. Although many people with high blood pressure follow medical treatment recommended by their doctors, only about 27 percent have their condition under control. Meanwhile, concern over the potential danger of lifelong drug therapy for people with high blood pressure has grown. Shouldn't there be ways to reduce high blood pressure in some cases without relying entirely on drugs?

The answer is yes. Nonmedical treatments for high blood pressure include some of the recommendations the American Heart Association makes for avoiding heart attack, stroke, and other forms of cardiovascular disease. These treatments call for reducing the amount of sodium in your diet, controlling weight, being physically active, and limiting your consumption of alcohol.

The cause of more than 90 percent of all high blood pressure is unknown. All the same, it has been found that too much salty food may contribute to high blood pressure in certain "salt-sensitive" people. A diet high in sodium can also limit how well certain blood pressure medications work. Unfortunately, no test exists that can determine who is salt-sensitive.

Even though it's impossible to know how effective a sodium-restricted diet would be for *all* people with high blood pressure, it does appear that a large group could benefit greatly. Some people can control their high blood pressure just by reducing the amount of sodium in their diet. For example, someone could move from mild (Stage 1) high blood pressure to high normal blood pressure. (See Blood

Pressure Levels, this page.) Other people may need medicine as well.

Occasionally, high blood pressure is caused by another medical problem or a condition such as pregnancy and will disappear once the problem is treated or the condition changes.

BLOOD PRESSURE LEVELS

Blood Pressure Level*	Systolic (mm Hg)		Diastolic (mm Hg)
Optimal	less than 120	and	less than 80
Normal	less than 130	and	less than 85
High normal	130 to 139	or	85 to 89
High			
Stage 1	140 to 159	or	90 to 99
Stage 2	160 to 179	or	100 to 109
Stage 3	180 or higher	or	110 or higher

*Based on the average of at least two readings on a given visit. These levels apply only to people who are not taking medication for high blood pressure. Individuals with diabetes, heart failure, or kidney disease should keep their blood pressure below 130/86 mm Hg.

Does a Cure Exist?

Unfortunately, for the people with high blood pressure for which there is no known cause, there is also no cure. However, you can do many things to help bring your blood pressure under control. You can keep your weight at a normal level, get regular exercise, limit your alcohol consumption—men who drink should consume no more than two drinks per day and women, no more than one—and use this cookbook to help reduce your sodium intake.

Both high blood pressure and high blood cholesterol are risk factors for heart attack, and high blood pressure is the greatest risk factor for stroke. This cookbook will show you how to help reduce these risks by limiting your intake of sodium, saturated fat, and cholesterol.

Too much sodium in your system holds water in your body and puts an extra burden on your heart and blood vessels. If you can get rid of the extra sodium, you can also lose the fluid. This is the reason a low-sodium diet can often help treat high blood pressure. For the same reason, a low-sodium diet is also one of the treatments for congestive heart failure. (See Congestive Heart Failure, page 301.)

Changing Your Diet to Lower Blood Pressure

The three major ways you can reduce blood pressure through diet are

- Cutting sodium intake
- Controlling weight
- Restricting alcohol intake

In addition, experts now believe that eating more foods that contain potassium or calcium, such as fruits, vegetables, and nonfat dairy products, may help lower blood pressure. The National Heart, Lung, and Blood Institute recommends such a diet, along with whole grains, for people with high blood pressure. This plan is called the DASH (Dietary Approaches to Stop Hypertension) Diet.

To help you add potassium and calcium to your diet, we've included the content of these important minerals in the nutrient analyses in this book. (Also see Potassium Sources on page 293.) Your doctor can recommend a specific number of milligrams you should consume daily.

Also, be sure to read Changing Your Diet to Lower Blood Cholesterol (page 297).

SODIUM

Salt is the most common source of the mineral sodium. Salt, or sodium chloride, is 40 percent sodium and 60 percent chloride. Americans typically consume from 4,000 to 5,800 milligrams of sodium per day, about ten times more than is needed for good health.

The amount of sodium contained in one teaspoon of salt is very close to the American Heart Association's recommendation of a maximum of 2,400 milligrams per day for healthy people. For people with high blood pressure or heart disease, their physicians may recommend a lower level.

Where does the national average of 4,000 to 5,800 milligrams come from? Each of the following sources provides a portion of the sodium found in the typical American diet:

- Sodium added to food during preparation or at the table (about 18 percent)
- Sodium added to food during processing (about 67 percent)
- Sodium occurring naturally in food and water (about 15 percent)

Everyone needs some sodium, but this need can easily be met without adding even a pinch of salt to food. Sodium occurs naturally in meat, seafood, poultry, dairy products, grain products, fruits, and vegetables. If you eat a balanced diet consisting of these foods without adding salt, you would get plenty of sodium to meet your body's needs.

The water supply is another source of sodium. Most adults use 2 to 2½ quarts (8 to 10 glasses) of water each day in beverages and in cooking. The source of the water determines its sodium content, which varies from 1 to 1,500 milligrams per quart. Ten glasses of water containing 1,500 milligrams of sodium per quart would total about 3,750 milligrams.

Chemicals used in the "softening" process of most water softeners increase the sodium content of water. You can get information from your local water department about the sodium content of your water. If it contains more than 80 parts per million (approximately 200 milligrams of sodium in 10 glasses of water), and you are trying to cut down to less than 2,400 milligrams per day, you should use bottled water without sodium for drinking and cooking. Another way to reduce the sodium in your drinking water is to buy a water filtration system, such as a pitcher with a filter or a filter—not a softener—for your kitchen tap.

ALCOHOL

Research shows that people who drink too much alcohol tend to have high blood pressure. To help control blood pressure, it's best to drink only in moderation or not at all. The American Heart Association recommends that men who drink should consume no more than two drinks per day, and women no more than one. The size of one drink of beer, wine, and spirits is listed below. Remember that alcohol is also a major source of calories and can contribute to obesity.

ALCOHOLIC BEVERAGES, PORTION SIZE

Beer	12 fluid ounces
Wine, red or white	4 fluid ounces
80-proof spirits (bourbon, gin, rum, Scotch, tequila, vodka, whiskey)	1½ fluid ounces

POTASSIUM

Healthy adults need at least 2,000 milligrams of potassium daily. People with high blood pressure are often advised to take in extra potassium. Some major sources of potassium are listed below.

POTASSIUM SOURCES

Potassium	Foods
400 mg or more	Banana, 1 medium
	Cantaloupe, 1 cup, cubed
	Honeydew melon, 1 cup, cubed
	Milk, fat free, 1 cup
	Nectarine, 1 large
	Orange juice, 1 cup
	Potato, 1 medium
	Prunes, 10 medium
	Prune juice, ¾ cup
	Red beans, cooked, ½ cup
	Tomato juice, no salt added, 1 cup
200 to 399 mg	Apple juice, 1 cup
	Beef, lean, cooked, 3 ounces
	Beets, cooked, ½ cup
	Blackberries, 1 cup

(continued on following page)

Potassium	Foods
200 to 399 mg (con't.)	Brussels sprouts, fresh, ½ cup
	Carrot, raw, 1 large
	Celery, 3 ribs
	Cherries, raw, 15
	Chicken, cooked, 3 ounces
	Flounder, cooked, 3 ounces
	Grapefruit, ½ medium
	Grapefruit juice, 1 cup
	Lentils, cooked, ½ cup
	Lima beans, green, ½ cup
	Orange, 1 medium
	Pork, fresh, lean, cooked, 3 ounces
	Salmon, pink, unsalted, canned, 3 ounces
	Spinach, cooked, ½ cup
	Strawberries, sliced, 1 cup
	Tomatoes, canned, no salt added, ½ cup
	Tuna, canned, packed in distilled water, ½ cup
	Turkey, unprocessed, 3 ounces
	Watermelon, 2 cups, cubed

CALCIUM

A vital nutrient for healthy bones, calcium may also be important in lowering high blood pressure. Adolescents, adults under the age of 25, and pregnant or lactating women need at least 1,200 milligrams of calcium a day. Other adults need at least 800 milligrams a day. However, your doctor may advise that you need more. For the best sources of calcium, choose fat-free or low-fat dairy products.

WEIGHT CONTROL

Losing weight can help lower both blood pressure and blood cholesterol. The key to losing weight is to consume fewer calories and increase your physical activity. If you are over what your normal weight should be, losing the excess is one of the smartest health moves you can make.

One way to lose weight is to cut down on calories by reducing the amount of fat you eat. To make weight loss easier, we recommend eating no more than 30 percent of calories as fat. Since fat (saturated and unsaturated) is the most concentrated source of calories in your diet, eating less of it automatically decreases your caloric total. Fat has more than twice the calories of the same weight of protein and carbohydrate. Protein and carbohydrate each have about 4 calories per gram; alcohol has 7 calories per gram; and all fats have 9 calories per gram.

To maintain your ideal weight, eat no more calories than your body needs. As a guideline, typical calorie levels for men are 2,000 to 2,500 calories a day to maintain weight and 1,600 to 2,000 calories to lose weight. For women, typical calorie levels are 1,600 to 2,000 calories a day to maintain weight and 1,200 to 1,600 calories to lose weight.

TIPS TO HELP YOU PREVENT OVEREATING

- Eat foods that are low in fat and added sugar instead of higher-calorie foods.
- Eat slowly. Give yourself time to feel full.
- Take small portions. Most serving sizes are at least double what you should be eating.
- Avoid second helpings.
- Avoid all-you-can-eat restaurants.
- Check before you eat; are you really hungry? Avoid eating because you're bored, need comfort, or because "it's time to eat." Let the hunger be your guide.

For most people who decide to lose weight, a steady loss of 1 to 2 pounds a week is safe until they reach their goal weight. At the beginning of a weight-loss program, much of the weight lost is water. Long-term success depends on two things: physical activity and an eating plan sufficiently low in calories to maintain the desirable lower weight. Such lifestyle changes help people who have lost weight keep it off. Check with your doctor before beginning any weight loss plan.

High Blood Cholesterol

A high level of cholesterol in the blood (hypercholesterolemia) is a risk factor for heart disease. High blood cholesterol contributes to a disease process called atherosclerosis. In atherosclerosis, cholesterol and other elements in blood are deposited along the smooth inner linings of arteries to form plaque. Over time, plaque builds up and narrows the inside of the arteries. If the plaque ruptures, a blood clot will form, and a narrowed artery can become entirely blocked. Then blood cannot reach the body's cells with life-sustaining oxygen. If the blocked artery is in the heart itself—a coronary artery—the result is a heart attack. If the blocked artery is in the neck or the head, the result is a stroke.

The following chart shows what category your blood cholesterol falls into.

BLOOD CHOLESTEROL CATEGORIES FOR PEOPLE 20 YEARS OF AGE OR OLDER

Desirable	Borderline-High	High
Less than 200 mg/dl*	200 to 239 mg/dl*	240 mg/dl and above*

*Milligrams of cholesterol per deciliter of blood (mg/dl).

Changing Your Diet to Lower Blood Cholesterol

Research shows that lowering elevated blood cholesterol levels helps reduce the risk of heart disease. A diet lower in saturated fat and cholesterol will help lower blood cholesterol. The American Heart Association recommends that over the course of a week, healthy people should take in less than 10 percent of their total calories as saturated fat. Also, they should consume less than 300 milligrams per day of cholesterol. Another recommendation for people attempting to control blood cholesterol is to achieve and maintain their ideal body weight. Eating soluble fiber also may help lower blood cholesterol.

For people with heart disease or high cholesterol, we recommend eating less than 7 percent of calories as saturated fat and less than 200 milligrams of cholesterol each day.

FAT

Fat in food is mostly made up of two types: saturated and unsaturated. Unsaturated fat may be either polyunsaturated or monounsaturated. All fats are a mixture of saturated, polyunsaturated, and monounsaturated fat. However, some fats are a concentrated source of saturated fat, and others are high in polyunsaturated or monounsaturated fat.

• *Saturated and trans fat.* Eating foods high in saturated fat or trans fat raises your blood cholesterol level. Saturated fat is found in animal products and in some plant products. Animal fats high in saturated fat include butterfat (in butter, cheese, whole milk, cream, and ice cream); fat in and around beef, pork, and lamb; fat in and under poultry skin; and lard.

Plant sources of saturated fat are coconuts, cocoa butter, and coconut, palm kernel, and palm oils. Some recent research even suggests that a high intake of saturated fat may increase your risk of developing insulin resistance, which may in turn increase your risk of diabetes.

Trans fat is a special case. It's unsaturated, but in the body, it acts like saturated fat. Watch out for products made with hydrogenated oil or fat, because they contain trans fat. Manufacturers use hydrogenation to change oils from their liquid form to a solid or semisolid form. This process makes the oils more saturated. As a by-product, hydrogenation also produces trans fat, which raises total blood cholesterol levels, although not as much as saturated fat does. Trans fat also raises LDL ("bad") cholesterol and lowers HDL ("good") cholesterol.

Since hydrogenation is used in manufacturing margarines and shortenings, these products may be partially or almost completely hydrogenated. To limit your intake of trans fat, look for products that are lower in saturated fat. Liquid and tub or soft margarines have very little trans fat. French fries, doughnuts, and commercial baked goods, such as cookies, crackers, and pie crusts are high in trans fat.

• *Unsaturated fat.* You can use unsaturated fat to replace some of the saturated fat in your diet. The two types of unsaturated fat are polyunsaturated and monounsaturated. Both types help lower blood cholesterol when consumed in a diet low in saturated fat. Safflower oil is the most polyunsaturated vegetable oil, followed by sunflower oil, corn oil, and soybean oil. Foods high in monounsaturated fat include canola oil, olive oil, peanut oil, avocados, olives, and some nuts.

Fish is also a source of polyunsaturated fat. Some fish, including cold-water fish such as salmon, mackerel, and herring, are rich in fat (fish oil) containing omega-3 fatty acids. The effects of these fats on the body are complicated. They are still being studied for potential benefits related to blood cholesterol levels, high blood pressure, and heart disease.

Fish from warm waters, such as red snapper and flounder, are generally low in total fat. Because the fat in high- and low-fat fish is low in saturated fat, the American Heart Association recommends eating fish two or three times a week. However, the association does not recommend the use of fish oil supplements unless prescribed by a physician.

The unsaturated fat content of selected foods is listed in the chart below. Foods with the highest level of polyunsaturated fat are listed first.

UNSATURATED FAT CONTENT OF SELECTED FOODS (LISTED IN ORDER OF POLYUNSATURATION)

1 Tablespoon	Polyunsaturated Fat (Grams)	Monounsaturated Fat (Grams)	Saturated Fat (Grams)
POLYUNSATURATED OILS			
Safflower oil	10.1	1.6	1.2
Sunflower oil	8.9	2.7	1.4
Corn oil	8.0	3.3	1.7
Soybean oil	7.9	3.2	2.0
MONOUNSATURATED OILS			
Peanut oil	4.3	6.2	2.3
Canola oil	4.1	8.2	1.0
Olive oil	1.1	9.9	1.8
MARGARINES, UNSALTED			
Safflower oil margarine (tub)	6.3	3.3	1.3
Corn oil margarine (tub)	4.4	4.5	2.0

(continued on following page)

1 Tablespoon	Polyunsaturated Fat (Grams)	Monounsaturated Fat (Grams)	Saturated Fat (Grams)
MARGARINES, UNSALTED (CON'T)			
Soybean oil margarine (tub)	3.8	5.1	1.9
Soybean oil margarine (stick)	3.7	5.3	1.8
Corn oil margarine (stick)	3.4	5.4	2.0
SHORTENING			
Soybean and cottonseed oil	3.2	5.7	3.3
NUTS, UNSALTED			
Walnuts, black	2.9	1.0	0.3
Brazil nuts	2.1	2.0	1.4
Peanuts	1.4	2.2	0.6
Pecans	1.1	3.0	0.4
Almonds	1.0	3.0	0.4
Cashews	0.7	2.3	0.8
Pistachios	0.6	2.6	0.5
Macadamias	0.1	4.9	0.9
SEEDS, UNSALTED			
Sunflower seeds	2.9	0.9	0.5
Sesame seeds	1.9	1.7	0.6
Pumpkin/squash seeds	1.8	1.2	0.7

DIETARY CHOLESTEROL

Dietary cholesterol is found only in foods of animal origin, including meat, poultry, seafood, egg yolks, and dairy products. Egg yolks and organ meats are very high in cholesterol. Fruits, vegetables, grains, cereals, nuts, and seeds do not contain cholesterol.

FIBER

Fiber is the indigestible part of food. The two types of fiber are soluble and insoluble. Some research shows that large amounts of soluble fiber can help lower blood cholesterol levels by an additional 2 percent when combined with a diet low in saturated fat and cholesterol. Good sources of soluble fiber include oatmeal, oat bran, and beans. Many so-called oat bran products (muffins, chips, waffles), however, actually contain very little oat bran and are high in sodium and saturated fat. Read the nutrition label carefully.

Insoluble fiber, such as wheat bran, adds bulk to stools and helps with normal bowel function. Large amounts of insoluble fiber may interfere with the body's ability to absorb certain nutrients, such as calcium. Insoluble fiber does not appear to lower blood cholesterol.

WEIGHT CONTROL

Losing weight can also help you lower high blood pressure. Details on weight control are on pages 295–296.

Congestive Heart Failure

Having congestive heart failure doesn't mean that your heart is about to stop. Heart failure means that your heart isn't pumping as well as it should. Congestive means that fluid is building up in your body. This disease can be a long-term effect of living with other forms of heart disease. In a way, congestive heart failure can be a product of earlier lifesaving treatment, such as bypass surgery or angioplasty. This is why more people are now diagnosed with congestive heart failure—they have survived a disease or condition such as coronary heart disease, a congenital heart defect, or cardiomyopathy, a disease of the heart muscle itself.

Treatment for congestive heart failure involves taking

medication and reducing salt intake to reduce your heart's workload. Since salt makes you retain fluid, reducing your salt intake will decrease the amount of fluid that the heart has to pump against. This also helps the body maintain the right balance of potassium and magnesium, minerals that are important to the heart's function.

Appendix B

Shopping

Now that many familiar items are available in no-salt-added or low-salt varieties, shopping for a low-sodium menu is easier than you might think. Your local grocery store probably stocks most of the recipe ingredients called for in this cookbook. If the items you want are not in stock, ask your grocer to order them for you.

With a little effort, you can learn to cut the sodium, change the kind of fat, and reduce the amount of saturated fat and cholesterol in your food. As part of that effort, you'll need to read the product labels on prepared foods to make sure they're low in sodium, saturated fat, and cholesterol.

What to Shop For

First make your shopping list. The key to a healthful diet is to make sure you eat a variety of foods. Your daily food choices should include:

- No more than 6 ounces (cooked weight) of lean meat, seafood, or poultry; 3 ounces is about the size of a deck of cards.
- Five or more servings of fruit and vegetables (include 1 serving of citrus fruit or a vegetable high in vitamin C and 1 serving of a dark green, leafy or deep yellow vegetable).

- Six or more servings of whole-grain or enriched bread or low-sodium cereal products.
- Two or more servings of fat-free milk or low-sodium, low-fat milk products for adults; 3 to 4 servings for children or adolescents.
- Five to 8 teaspoons of polyunsaturated and monounsaturated fats and oils in the form of unsalted margarine, cooking oil, and unsalted salad dressing. (If you need to lose weight, use 5 teaspoons. If you need more calories, use 8.)

In addition, substitute dried beans, peas, lentils, or tofu for meat a few times a week.

Meats and Poultry

A balanced diet requires some protein every day. With meats, keep your sodium intake to a minimum by buying only unsalted fresh or frozen lean meat. Because meats contain saturated fat and cholesterol, you'll want to emphasize vegetables and limit yourself to a total of 6 ounces (cooked weight) of meat, poultry, and seafood per day.

The best meats for you are trimmed lean cuts with less fat around the outside and less marbled fat throughout. Some of the leanest cuts are round steak, sirloin tip, tenderloin, and extra-lean ground beef. Look for lean pork, such as fresh center-cut ham, tenderloin, and loin chops. All cuts of veal are lean except cutlets. Leg of lamb is the leanest cut of lamb.

Fresh poultry cooked without skin is an excellent protein choice. However, when using whole chickens and turkeys, roast them with the skin on. This will help prevent the meat from drying out. Remove the skin before eating the poultry. Stay away from self-basting turkeys because commercial basting fats are highly saturated. Even when the turkey is basted in broth, the broth is usually high in sodium. It's better to baste your own turkey with an unsalted broth or cook it in an oven-cooking bag, which produces a more healthful "self-basted" turkey.

In general, avoid the following meats, which contain large amounts of one or more of the things you're trying to limit (sodium, saturated fat, and cholesterol): luncheon meats; frankfurters; sausage; spareribs; corned beef; salt pork; liver and other organ meats; smoked, cured, or dried meats, such as ham and bacon; and canned meat or poultry, unless packed without salt.

Seafood

A versatile low-sodium favorite, seafood contains a smaller percentage of saturated fat than meat and poultry. Although not free of cholesterol, fish generally contains less cholesterol than red meat. These features give fish a slight edge over poultry and lean red meat and a definite edge over fatty red meat in a cholesterol-lowering diet.

Fish itself can be either fat or lean, but a high percentage of fish fat—oil—is polyunsaturated. This fat, omega-3 fatty acids, is currently being studied for potential lipid (blood fat)-lowering benefits. Some fish high in omega-3 fatty acids are Atlantic and coho salmon, albacore tuna, mackerel, carp, lake whitefish, sweet smelt, and lake and brook trout.

Shrimp, lobster, crab, crayfish, and most other shellfish are very low in saturated fat. However, ounce for ounce, some varieties contain more sodium and cholesterol than poultry, meat, or fish. Even these, however, can be eaten occasionally within the recommended guideline of less than 300 milligrams of cholesterol per day.

The American Heart Association recommends at least two servings of fish per week.

Fruits and Vegetables

Fresh foods in these categories have no cholesterol, tend to be low in sodium and saturated fat, and, in many cases, are high in fiber and vitamins.

The exceptions include coconut, avocados, and olives. Coconut is high in saturated fat. Both avocados and olives are high in fat, although the fat is largely monounsaturated. Green olives are high in sodium (800 milligrams in 10 small), and black olives are moderately high in sodium (250 milligrams in 5 extra-large).

Stay away from vegetables packed in brine, such as pickles and sauerkraut, because they're loaded with sodium. It's simple and fun to make your own no-salt-added pickles, such as Easy Dill Pickles or Sweet Bread-and-Butter Pickles (pages 218 and 220).

Always read the labels on frozen and processed foods. Many of them contain added salt, butter, or sauces. Also note that fresh fruits or those canned in water are lower in calories than fruits canned in juice or in syrup.

Breads, Grains, and Pasta

Whole-grain or enriched breads, grains, and pastas are an important part of a balanced diet. They provide plenty of nutrients and relatively few calories. (But steer clear of the high-fat or salty sauces and condiments that often accompany them.)

Go ahead and experiment with different kinds of bread, such as whole or cracked wheat, rye, and pumpernickel. They do contain some sodium and a small amount of fat, but not enough to outweigh their natural goodness for you.

Check the labels on crackers for sodium, fats, and oils. There is so much variation, and sometimes low-sodium products are higher in fat than regular products. Look for low-sodium crackers and pretzels if you want something crunchy. Scandinavian-style rye crackers and other whole-grain crackers are often made without fats or oils and with little or no salt. Also look for unsalted matzo and melba toast.

Be wary of commercially baked goods such as muffins, biscuits, sweet rolls, cakes, cookies, and pastries. Also, shop carefully for mixes for these products. They usually contain significant amounts of sodium, saturated fat, and cholesterol. It's much better to bake your own. Just use the recipes in this book or adjust your own favorites by omitting the salt and using the Ingredient Substitutions listed on pages 330–332.

Whole-grain cereals are great for anyone on a low-sodium, low-fat diet. Most cereals don't contain saturated fat or cholesterol. (One notable exception is granola.) Most do, however, contain sodium. Be sure to read the labels and choose those that are low in sodium and saturated fat.

Hot cereals, rice, and pastas contain almost no sodium.

Just remember to leave the salt out of the cooking water when you prepare these foods.

Dairy Products

Include two or more servings of fat-free or low-fat milk or milk products every day. With the exception of buttermilk and cheese, most milk and milk products do not contain added salt, but watch out for the saturated fat and cholesterol found in whole milk and whole-milk products. Try to make your dairy selections from the wide variety of fat-free and low-fat dairy products on the market instead.

As an example of how much saturated fat and cholesterol you can eliminate from your diet by using fat-free or low-fat milk products, look at regular sour cream: It has 3 grams of saturated fat and 19 milligrams of cholesterol per ounce (2 tablespoons), compared with low-fat sour cream with just 1 gram of saturated fat and 6 milligrams of cholesterol per ounce. Nonfat sour cream has no saturated fat and no cholesterol.

Here are some products you can use to replace whole-milk products:

- Fat-free milk, fat-free evaporated milk, nonfat dry milk
- Dry-curd cottage cheese that has no salt added
- Cheese made from fat-free or part-skim milk (no more than 5 grams of fat per ounce)
- Nonfat or low-fat yogurt or fat-free or low-fat frozen yogurt, low-fat ice cream, and sherbets
- Polyunsaturated nondairy creamers or whiteners

Eggs

One large egg yolk contains two-thirds of the entire daily allowance for cholesterol, about 213 milligrams, so it's a good idea to limit your egg yolk consumption.

On the other hand, egg whites contain no cholesterol and are an excellent source of protein. You can often use egg whites in place of whole eggs. In fact, in most recipes, two egg whites will substitute nicely for a whole egg.

Be sure to eat only cooked eggs and egg whites; raw eggs can carry salmonella, which causes food poisoning.

Nuts and Seeds

Nuts and seeds are tasty snacks, and most kinds are available in their natural state—unsalted. Just remember that although the fat in nuts and seeds is mostly unsaturated, there's lots of it, so the calorie count is higher than most people realize. Also, some nuts, such as Brazil nuts and macadamia nuts, are quite high in saturated fat. Nuts and seeds are good sources of incomplete proteins and can replace other high-protein foods to some degree—especially when eaten with beans, peas, or grains, which also contain incomplete proteins. Together, they provide complete protein. That is, they contain all the essential amino acids the body needs to build protein.

Fats and Oils

Polyunsaturated and monounsaturated fats and oils are the kinds of fat you'll want to include in your daily diet. In fact,

5 to 8 teaspoons of these fats and oils daily is a reasonable amount.

You can use them in the form of unsalted salad dressing, margarine, or cooking oil. Oils are cholesterol-free and do not contain sodium. Mayonnaise and most margarines, on the other hand, do contain some salt, but they're still okay to use occasionally. Most commercial salad dressings contain large amounts of salt and should be avoided. It's easy to make your own low-salt dressings using our recipes on pages 59–66.

When reading the labels on packaged goods, pay particular attention to the kinds of fat and oil listed.

Saturated and Trans Fat

Both saturated and trans fat raise blood cholesterol levels. Fats and oils high in saturated fat tend to become hard at room temperature. Butter, lard, and tallow from animals and coconut, palm, and palm kernel oils from plants are common examples. These saturated fats should be avoided.

Trans fat is found in products with hydrogenated oil or fat, usually highly processed foods, such as margarines, shortenings, crackers, and other snack foods. Choose liquid or tub margarines or stick margarines that have a liquid oil listed as the first ingredient.

Remember, you should try to keep your weekly saturated fat intake to no more than 10 percent of the calories in your total diet, and use the following lists to help you identify recommended fats and oils.

FATS AND OILS

Recommended	Not recommended (saturated)
Safflower oil	Butter
Sunflower oil	Vegetable shortening
Corn oil	Bacon, salt pork
Soybean oil	Suet, lard
Sesame seed oil	Chicken fat, meat fat
Canola oil	Coconut oil
Olive oil	Palm kernel oil
Polyunsaturated margarine	Palm oil
Unsalted oil-based salad dressing (using recommended oils)	

Monounsaturated and Polyunsaturated Fat

Oils that stay liquid at room temperature are high in unsaturated fats. They include corn, safflower, soybean, sunflower, olive, and canola oils. All are low in saturated fat and can be used to help lower blood cholesterol. They do not contain sodium.

Beverages

When you're thirsty, look for beverages low in sodium, saturated fat, and cholesterol. These include water, fat-free milk, fruit juices, fruit drinks, and low-sodium carbonated beverages. Some diet soft drinks and mineral waters are high in sodium. Be sure to read the label before selecting your beverage. Don't forget that the sodium content of tap water varies widely from one location to another. If your water supply is high in sodium, use low-sodium bottled water for drinking and for making drinks such as tea and coffee.

If you're trying to lose weight, avoid sugared carbonated beverages, fruit drinks, beer, wine, and other alcoholic drinks.

Apart from the effect of its calories on your weight, excess alcohol can raise your blood pressure. If you drink, it's smart to limit your alcohol intake to one or two drinks per day. For portion sizes of alcoholic drinks, see page 293.

Snacks

Many snack products, such as chips and rich crackers, are high in sodium and saturated fat. However, some chips are cooked in unsaturated oil. Choose only those labeled as having lower salt content and more polyunsaturated than saturated fat. Better yet, make your own crisp snack foods, cookies, and cakes without salt and with acceptable oils or margarines. See the Appetizers and Snacks and the Desserts chapters (pages 3–20 and 253–286).

Miscellaneous Foods and Flavorings

On a low-sodium eating plan, be careful of the many commonly used commercial seasonings and sauces containing large amounts of sodium or salt. These include soy sauce, Worcestershire sauce, steak sauce, ketchup, chili sauce, meat tenderizer, flavored seasoning salts, and bouillon cubes. Look for no-salt-added or low-sodium versions of these items, or use the recipes we've included in this cookbook to make your own. Also see Ingredient Substitutions, pages 330–332.

Seasoning mixes don't usually have a nutrition label to indicate the amount of sodium they contain. For these, check the ingredients label, and if any of the first three ingredients contains the word "salt" or "sodium," look for another product. Often monosodium glutamate, the flavor enhancer, is abbreviated MSG. Stay away from it—whatever it's called.

Instead, cook with spices, flavorings, freshly grated horseradish, hot peppers, garlic, herbs, and fruit juices.

Many commercial soups, green olives, relishes, and pickles contain lots of salt. Some of them are available commercially in no-salt-added varieties. Try the recipes in this cookbook for soups, sauces—and even pickles.

You'll want to substitute unsweetened cocoa powder for baking chocolate. Chocolate and cocoa butter contain lots of saturated fat, but most of the fat has been removed from cocoa powder.

COMMON FOODS HIGH IN SODIUM

Anchovies	Monosodium glutamate (MSG)
Bacon	Mustard
Barbecue sauce	Nuts, salted
Bologna	Olives, green
Bouillon cubes or granules	Pastrami
Buttermilk	Pepperoni
Celery salt	Pickles*
Cereal, dry*	Pizza
Cheese	Salami
Chips, potato* and corn	Salt

(continued on following page)

Crackers*	Sauerkraut
Cured meat	Sausage
Frankfurters	Seasoned salt
Frozen dinners and entrées	Seeds, salted
Garlic salt	Soup, canned
Ham, cured	Soy sauce
Ketchup*	Steak sauce
Kosher processed meat	Wieners—beef, pork, and turkey
Meat, canned or frozen in sauce	Worcestershire sauce

*Unsalted varieties are available.

Reading Food Labels

One of the greatest challenges of following a special eating plan is finding foods that fit your needs. You can obtain useful information by learning to read and compare food labels.

Nutrition Labels

Now that nutrition labels list sodium, fat, saturated fat, and cholesterol content, shopping for low-sodium, low-fat foods is much easier. The nutrition label also gives you the number of calories and the amount of carbohydrates, fiber, sugar, and protein per serving. In addition, the label tells you what percentage of the U.S. Recommended Daily Allowances (RDA) for vitamins A and C, calcium, and iron are in a serving. For example, if a serving contains 100 percent of the RDA for iron, you don't need to eat any other foods with iron that day.

Check for Sodium

Comparing nutrition labels can help you find the foods with the lowest sodium content. For example, the next time you go shopping, check the sodium in canned soups. Many of them are in the range of 800 to 900 milligrams per serving. That's one-third to one-half of your daily intake! Look for one that's low in sodium.

SORTING OUT SODIUM

Food labels use certain terms to describe sodium content. Each term has a meaning defined by the U.S. Food and Drug Administration. Knowing what each means can help you select low-sodium food.

FOOD LABEL TERMS THAT INDICATE A LOWER SALT CONTENT

Sodium Free	5 mg or less per serving
Very Low Sodium	35 mg or less per serving
Low Sodium	140 mg or less per serving
Reduced Sodium	Usual sodium level is reduced by 25%
Unsalted or No Salt Added	No salt added during processing

These terms refer only to sodium content. It's important to read labels carefully since some foods low in sodium are high in fat or saturated fat. The following sample of nutritional information shows how to compare labels to identify which product is lower in sodium, saturated fat, and cholesterol.

NUTRITIONAL INFORMATION: A COMPARISON OF LABELS

Nutrition Information Per Serving	Butter, Stick	Margarine, Tub	Unsalted Margarine, Tub	Liquid Margarine
Serving size	1 tablespoon	1 tablespoon	1 tablespoon	1 tablespoon
Calories	102	102	101	102
Protein (grams)	0	0	0	0
Carbohydrate (grams)	0	0	0	0
Fat (grams)	12	11	11	11
Polyunsaturated (grams)	0.4	5	4	5
Saturated (grams)	7	2	2	2
Cholesterol (milligrams)	31	0	0	0
Sodium (milligrams)	117	153	4	111

You can see that, as you would expect, unsalted margarine contains less sodium than regular margarine. Both types of margarine have less saturated fat and cholesterol than butter.

Here are some tips for shopping for lower-sodium products:

- Butter flavoring: Butter sprinkles are great for topping cooked vegetables, including baked potatoes, while they're hot. You can't use the sprinkles in cooking, however. Look for this nonfat, light-sodium product in the spice section.
- Capers: Capers are usually packed in brine. Look for capers packed in white balsamic vinegar for a low-sodium alternative.
- Chili powder: Check the labels on commercial chili powders. Most of them contain salt. Our homemade no-salt-

added variety (page 225) provides the flavor without the sodium. In a pinch, you can substitute two-thirds paprika and one-third ground cumin.

- Flour tortillas: Nonfat and low-fat tortillas can be high in sodium. Look for the one with the lowest sodium value.
- Ketchup: For the freshest-tasting ketchup, try our easy-to-make recipe on page 212. The bonus is that it's very low in sodium. At the supermarket, look for no-salt-added ketchup.
- Matzo meal: Look in the Jewish or kosher section of your supermarket for matzo meal. Made of ground matzo, a crackerlike mixture of flour and water, matzo meal is a good salt-free breading.
- Rice vinegar: If you prefer seasoned rice vinegar to the plain variety, check the label. Most seasoned rice vinegar has salt added.
- Salsa, teriyaki sauce, and Worcestershire sauce: All can be high in sodium. When shopping, select the products with the lowest sodium values.
- Soy sauce: Reading the nutrition labels is especially important when you select soy sauce. Some products labeled light are actually higher in sodium than some regular soy sauces.
- Tomato products (canned): Fortunately, many of these products are now available with no salt added. You'll need to read the nutrition labels when purchasing tomato paste, however: Some are very low in sodium but don't say so on the package label.
- Wine and sherry: Don't buy "cooking wine" or "cooking sherry." These products have salt added to make them unpalatable for drinking. Use regular or nonalcoholic wine and regular sherry instead.

To help consumers make food choices, the American Heart Association introduced its Food Certification Program in 1995. This program is designed to help consumers quickly and easily select grocery store foods that can be part of a balanced, heart-healthy eating plan. The heart-check mark on a food package means that the product meets American Heart Association food criteria for saturated fat and cholesterol for healthy people over age 2.

A few products with the heart-check may not be suitable for you if you are on a sodium-restricted diet. So always check the Nutrition Facts panel on food packages for the sodium content and follow the limits set by your physician or registered dietitian.

American Heart Association

Meets American Heart
Association food criteria
for saturated fat and
cholesterol for healthy
people over age 2.

Counting Calories

Many makers of fat-free and low-fat foods have replaced fats with sugars. Check the nutrition labels carefully for the number of calories—calories do count where your weight is concerned.

The term "low-calorie" means the product contains no more than 40 calories per serving. "Reduced-calorie" means the product has at least one-fourth fewer calories than the product for which this food is substituted. Check the serving size carefully; it's often less than you might think.

Appendix C

Cooking

Now you know what kinds of food are part of a low-salt, low-saturated fat, low-cholesterol eating plan. That's great, but it's just the beginning. It's not enough just to buy healthful foods. You also need to know how to prepare them so that they stay that way.

Seasonings

One source of sodium is salt added during food preparation (at home or in restaurants) and at the table. You weren't born with the taste for salt—you acquired it. You can decrease your taste for salt (and sodium) by using little or none in food preparation, by not adding it at the table, and by avoiding processed foods containing large amounts of sodium. It usually takes about a month of eating less salt and fewer high-sodium foods to reduce your desire to salt your food.

Replace salt with herbs and spices or some of the salt-free seasoning mixtures on the market. Prepare your own salt-free seasoning blends, using the recipes on pages 222–226. Add pepper, garlic, onion, and/or lemon to foods to give them a more distinct flavor and help replace the taste of salt. After a few weeks, many people who reduce the salt in their diet report that they are amazed at the good taste of different foods. Before, they were only noticing the salt!

Most salt substitutes are potassium chloride. Adding a small amount of salt substitute to food after cooking will make the food taste "salted." However, before using any salt substitute, you need to check with your doctor to see if it is all right for you. Products labeled "lite" salt are usually part sodium chloride (salt) and part potassium chloride. We don't recommend using "lite" salt because it adds sodium to food.

In fact, any seasoning that uses "salt" as part of the name is high in sodium. Examples are garlic salt, celery salt, and onion salt. However, plain garlic powder, celery powder, and onion powder are low in sodium and make an easy substitution possible if these are flavors you love.

Techniques

All cooking methods are not created equal. Some are better than others for retaining vitamins and minerals and for cutting cholesterol, saturated fat, and calories. Basically, stay away from cooking techniques, such as frying, that add fat or allow food to cook in its own fat.

Instead, look for cooking techniques that enhance flavor, preserve basic nutrients, and keep added fat and sodium to a minimum. To get you started, here are a few examples of cooking methods that will help you help your heart.

• *Roasting.* Always place a rack on the bottom of the roasting pan so the meat or poultry doesn't sit in its own fat drippings. Be sure to roast at a medium temperature, about 350°F, to avoid searing the meat or poultry and sealing in the fat. For basting, use low-sodium, fat-free liquids such as regular or nonalcoholic wine, no-salt-added tomato juice, or fresh lemon juice. (See Easy Roast Beef, page 130.)

• *Baking.* You can bake poultry, seafood, and meat in covered cookware with a little additional liquid. The moisture that the liquid adds makes this method particularly good for seafood or chicken breasts, which tend to be a little dry. (See Orange Roughy Roulade, page 72.)

• *Braising or Stewing.* This method uses a little more liquid than baking does. Try it in a covered container on top of the stove (using low heat) or in the oven (cook at 300° to 325°F). If you're braising or stewing meat or poultry, begin a day ahead of time and refrigerate the cooked dish overnight. The next day, when the chilled fat has congealed, you can remove it before reheating the dish. Braising is also an excellent way to cook vegetables. (See Beef Bourguignon, page 134.)

• *Poaching.* To poach chicken or seafood, immerse it in a pan of simmering liquid on top of the stove. This method works especially well when you serve the food with a sauce made of pureed vegetables and herbs. (See Poached Salmon, page 75.)

• *Grilling or Broiling.* Placing food on a rack and grilling or broiling allows the fat to drip away from meat or poultry. It's also a tasty way to cook fish steaks or whole fish. For extra flavor, try marinating food before putting it over the coals or under the broiler. Skewered vegetables also taste great browned over an open flame. (See Chicken with Yogurt-Cilantro Sauce, page 105.)

• *Sautéing.* Seafood, poultry, and vegetable dishes can be sautéed in an open skillet with little or no fat; the high temperature and motion keep food from sticking. Try sautéing with a tiny bit of unsaturated oil rubbed onto the pan with a paper towel. Better still, use vegetable oil spray or sauté in a small amount of low-sodium broth or table wine. (See Glazed Raspberry-Ginger Chicken, page 102.)

• *Steaming.* Cooking food in a basket over simmering water keeps the natural flavor, color, and nutritional value of vegetables intact. Try adding herbs to the steaming water or using low-sodium broth instead of water to add even more flavor to the finished dish.

• *Stir-frying.* Done in a wok or large skillet, stir-frying relies on the same principle as sautéing. The high temperature and the constant movement of the food keep it from sticking and burning. Try stir-frying vegetables and diced poultry or seafood with a tiny bit of peanut oil. Use the low-sodium version when your recipe calls for soy sauce. (See Stir-Fried Noodles with Tofu and Vegetables, page 170.)

Microwave Cooking

Microwaving is a fast, easy cooking method that requires no added fat. Foods don't tend to stick to the pan in the moist heat of microwave cooking. In fact, you can drain food of fat as it cooks by placing it in the microwave between two paper towels.

If you want to adapt a recipe for use in the microwave, try cutting the cooking time to one-fourth to one-third of the conventional time. If the food needs more cooking, increase it a little at a time. You might also look for a microwave recipe similar to the one you're trying to adapt. Keep the following in mind when microwave cooking:

• Choose foods that cook well in moist heat: chicken, seafood, ground meat, vegetables, sauces, and soups.

- Pieces that are about equal in size and shape will cook uniformly.
- You can reduce the liquid used in cooking beverages, soups, vegetables, fruits, and main dishes by about one-third because less evaporates in microwave cooking.
- Choose a microwave-safe container slightly larger than the dish required for cooking the recipe in a conventional oven.
- Use a high setting (100 percent power) for soups, beverages, fruits, vegetables, seafood, ground meat, and poultry. Use a medium-high setting (70 percent power) for simmering stews. Use a medium setting (50 percent power) for baking breads, cakes, and muffins and for cooking less-tender cuts of meat.
- To create a crusty look on baked items, grease pans with an acceptable vegetable oil and add ground nuts or crumbs. (Be sure to calculate the values for the saturated fat and/or sodium in these added nuts when deciding how these foods fit into your dietary plans.)
- Add low-fat cheese and other toppings near the end of cooking to keep them from becoming tough or soggy.
- Don't coat meat with flour if you will be adding liquid for cooking. The coating only becomes soggy.
- Use quick-cooking instead of long-grain rice.

Cooking Tips

- Use a nonstick skillet so that you can cook with a minimum of oil, or cook with vegetable oil spray, another good fat-cutting technique.
- Trim all visible fat before cooking meat.

- After you roast meat or poultry, chill the drippings in the refrigerator. Once they're cooled, the fat will rise to the top and harden; it can be removed easily and the broth saved to use in stews, sauces, and soups.
- Buy only the leanest ground beef and pork (no more than 10 percent fat). After browning it, put the ground meat into a strainer or colander. Rinse it under hot running water and let the fat drain. Wipe the skillet out with a paper towel. Return the browned meat to the skillet, add seasonings, and proceed with the recipe. This procedure reduces the fat by about 50 percent.
- When figuring serving sizes, remember that meat loses about 25 percent of its weight during cooking. (For example, 4 ounces of raw meat will be about 3 ounces cooked.)
- To make gravy without fat, blend a teaspoon of cornstarch with a cup of room-temperature, low-sodium broth by shaking the two together in a jar with a tight-fitting lid. Then heat the rest of the defatted broth in a saucepan and add the blended liquid. Simmer until thickened.
- Except when roasting whole chickens, make a habit of skinning chicken before cooking and remove all visible fat below the skin. Raw skin will be easier to remove if you use paper towels or a clean cloth to take hold of it. Be certain to scrub the cutting surface and utensils well with hot sudsy water after preparing poultry for cooking.
- Buy canned tuna and salmon packed in water, not in oil. Distilled water has less sodium than spring water.
- Use only one egg yolk per portion when preparing scrambled eggs or omelets. Add a few extra egg whites to the mixing bowl to make more generous servings.
- Seal natural juices into foods by wrapping the foods in aluminum foil before cooking. Another method is wrap-

ping foods in edible pouches made of large steamed lettuce or cabbage leaves and placing them seam side down in the baking dish before cooking.

- Cut down on cholesterol by using more vegetables and less poultry or meats in soups, stews, and casseroles. Finely chopped vegetables are great for stretching ground poultry or meat.
- Cut down on saturated fat in creamy salad dressing by mixing it with plain nonfat or low-fat yogurt.
- Sweeten plain nonfat or low-fat yogurt with pureed fruit or applesauce instead of buying prepared fruit yogurt.

Enhancing Flavors Without Using Salt

Spicing up low-salt cooking is easy when you know a few good tricks. The following ideas will help you enhance the flavor of a variety of foods without using salt. After trying a few of these techniques, you'll agree that the best things in life are salt free.

- Toast seeds, nuts, and whole spices to bring out their full flavor. Cook them in a dry skillet over moderate heat or on a baking sheet in a 350°F oven, stirring frequently to toast evenly and prevent burning.
- Roasting vegetables in a hot oven will caramelize their natural sugars.
- Grind garlic, chiles, and fresh herbs and spices with a mortar and pestle to release their flavors.
- Use citrus zest. The zest is the part of the peel without the bitter white pith; it holds the true flavor of the fruit. Grate it with either a food rasp or a flat, sheet-type grater or

remove the zest with a vegetable peeler and cut it into thin strips.

- Use fresh herbs instead of dried when possible. Chop and add them at the last minute for a fresher, more "alive" taste.

- Experiment with dried herbs such as thyme, rosemary, and marjoram for more pungent flavor, but start sparingly.

- Sprinkle vinegar or citrus juice on food for a wonderful flavor enhancer, but add it at the last minute. Vinegar is wonderful on vegetables such as greens; citrus, on fruits such as cantaloupe. Either is great on seafood.

- Use dry mustard or no-salt-added mustard. (See Hot Mustard, page 216.) You can also try bottled honey mustard, which is very low in sodium.

- For a little more "bite," add fresh hot peppers to your dishes. Remove the membrane and seeds before finely chopping the peppers. In the raw state, they have very little sodium and a lot more flavor than the pickled kind. A small amount can go a long way! (See Cook's Tip on Handling Hot Peppers, page 145.)

- Vegetables and fruits are easy to season without salt. Fill an herb shaker with a combination of fresh herbs and spices. Use that in place of a salt shaker. Try our favorites on pages 222–226.

- Some vegetables and fruits, such as mushrooms, tomatoes, chiles, cherries, cranberries, and currants, impart a more intense flavor when dried than when fresh. If they are soaked in water and reconstituted, you get as a bonus a natural "broth" to work with.

- Buy the best and the freshest whole spices and grind them in a spice grinder. You'll taste a big difference.

• If you buy spices already ground, buy them in small bottles and replace them more often so they'll be fresher.

Check nutrition labels periodically. New products appear all the time, and some are low in sodium without saying so on the front.

HERB, SPICE, AND SEASONING GUIDE

When preparing...	Try these for flavor...
BAKED GOODS	
Breads	Anise, caraway, cardamom, fennel, poppy seeds, sesame seeds
Desserts	Anise, caraway, cardamom, cinnamon, cloves, coriander, fennel, ginger, mace, mint, nutmeg, poppy seeds, sesame seeds
DIPS	Caraway, dill, garlic, oregano, parsley, black pepper
EGGS	Basil, chervil, chili powder, cumin, curry, fennel, marjoram, mustard, oregano, parsley, black pepper, poppy seeds, rosemary, saffron, savory, sesame seeds, tarragon, thyme, turmeric, watercress
FRUITS	Allspice, anise, basil, cardamom, cinnamon, cloves, cumin, curry, ginger, mint, nutmeg, poppy seeds, rosemary, watercress
MEAT, POULTRY, AND SEAFOOD	
Beef	Allspice, bay leaf,* cayenne, cumin, curry powder, garlic, green bell pepper, marjoram, fresh mushrooms, dry mustard, nutmeg, onion, black pepper, rosemary, sage, thyme, red wine
Game	Bay leaf,* garlic, fresh lemon juice, fresh mushrooms, onion, rosemary, sage, savory, tarragon, thyme, vinegar
Lamb	Curry powder, garlic, mint, mint jelly, onion, pineapple, rosemary, sage, savory, sesame seeds, red wine
Pork	Apple, applesauce, cinnamon, cloves, fennel, garlic, ginger, mint, onion, sage, savory, red wine

<u>When preparing…</u> <u>Try these for flavor…</u>

Veal	Apricot, bay leaf,* curry powder, ginger, fresh lemon juice, marjoram, mint, fresh mushrooms, oregano, saffron, sage, savory, tarragon, white wine
Poultry	Basil, bay leaf,* cinnamon, curry powder, garlic, green bell pepper, fresh lemon juice, mace, marjoram, fresh mushrooms, onion, paprika, fresh parsley, lemon pepper, poultry seasoning, rosemary, saffron, sage, savory, sesame seeds, thyme, tarragon, white wine
Seafood	Allspice, basil, bay leaf,* cayenne, curry powder, cumin, fennel, garlic, green bell pepper, fresh lemon juice, mace, marjoram, mint, fresh mushrooms, Dijon mustard, dry mustard, green onion, paprika, saffron, sage, sesame seeds, tarragon, thyme, turmeric, white wine
Various	Cayenne, chervil, chili powder, coriander, curry powder, dill, garlic, ginger, marjoram, onion, oregano, parsley, black pepper
SALADS	Basil, burnet, chervil, coriander, dill, fresh lemon juice, mint, fresh mushrooms, mustard, oregano, parsley, black pepper, rosemary, sage, savory, sesame seeds, turmeric, vinegar, watercress

SOUPS AND STEWS

Bean soup	Dry mustard
Chowders	Bay leaf,* peppercorns
Pea soup	Bay leaf,* coriander, parsley
Stews	Basil, bay leaf,* cayenne, chervil, chili powder, cinnamon, cumin, curry, fennel, garlic, ginger, marjoram, nutmeg, onion, parsley, saffron
Vegetable soup	Onion, vinegar
Various	Basil, bay leaf,* burnet, cayenne, chervil, chili powder, cloves, curry, dill, garlic, ginger, marjoram, mint, mustard, nutmeg, onion, oregano, parsley, black pepper, rosemary, sage, savory, sesame seeds, tarragon, thyme, watercress

(continued on following page)

When preparing . . .   Try these for flavor . . .

VEGETABLES

Asparagus	Garlic, fresh lemon juice, onion, vinegar
Beans	Caraway, cloves, cumin, mint, savory, tarragon, thyme
Beets	Anise, caraway, fennel, ginger, savory
Carrots	Anise, cinnamon, cloves, mint, sage, tarragon
Corn	Allspice, cumin, green bell pepper, pimiento, fresh tomato
Cucumbers	Chives, dill, garlic, vinegar
Green Beans	Dill, fresh lemon juice, marjoram, nutmeg, pimiento
Greens	Garlic, fresh lemon juice, onion, vinegar
Peas	Allspice, mint, fresh mushrooms, onions, fresh parsley
Potatoes	Chives, dill, green bell pepper, onion, pimiento, saffron
Squash	Allspice, brown sugar, cloves, fennel, ginger, nutmeg, onion
Tomatoes	Allspice, basil, garlic, marjoram, onion, oregano, sage, savory, tarragon, thyme
Various	Basil, burnet, cayenne, chervil, dill, marjoram, mint, fresh mushrooms, nutmeg, oregano, parsley, black pepper, poppy seeds, rosemary, sage, sesame seeds, sunflower seeds, tarragon, thyme, turmeric, watercress

---

* Always remove bay leaf from dish before serving.

Ingredient Substitutions

No need to toss out old family recipes and holiday treats because you're watching your salt intake. You can keep many of your favorite recipes if you're willing to make a few simple ingredient substitutions. Just by making these few changes, you will reduce enough of the sodium and fat to make almost any recipe fit right into your new eating plan.

Instead of	Use
Broth or bouillon	Chicken Broth (page 23); Beef Broth (page 22); Vegetable Broth (page 24); very low sodium bouillon granules or cubes, according to package directions; or commercially prepared low-sodium broth.
Tomato juice	No-salt-added tomato juice or 6-ounce can of no-salt-added tomato paste diluted with 3 cans of water.
Tomato sauce	6-ounce can of no-salt-added tomato paste diluted with 1 can of water.
Salt	Seasoning blends, pages 222–226.
Flavor salts, such as onion salt, garlic salt, and celery salt	Onion powder, garlic powder, celery seeds or flakes. Use about one-fourth of the amount of flavored salt indicated in the recipe.
Whipping cream	Fat-free evaporated milk (thoroughly chilled before whipping).
Unsweetened baking chocolate	Unsweetened cocoa powder blended with unsaturated oil or unsaturated, unsalted margarine (1-ounce square of chocolate = 3 tablespoons cocoa powder plus 1 tablespoon polyunsaturated oil or unsaturated, unsalted margarine).
Butter	Acceptable margarine or oil. When possible, use fat-free or light tub, light stick or fat-free spray margarine. However, if the type of fat is critical to the recipe, especially in baked goods, you may need to use an acceptable stick margarine (see page xvi).
Melted butter or shortening	Acceptable vegetable oil or melted acceptable margarine. When possible, use fat-free or light tub, light stick or fat-free spray margarine. However, if the type of fat is critical to the recipe, especially in baked goods, you may need to use an acceptable stick margarine (see page xvi).
Vegetable oil	Acceptable margarine. When possible, use fat-free or light tub, light stick or fat-free spray margarine. However, if the type of fat is critical to the recipe, especially in baked goods, you may need to use an acceptable stick margarine (see page xvi).

(continued on following page)

Instead of	Use
Eggs	Commercially produced, cholesterol-free egg substitutes, according to package directions. For 1 whole egg, substitute 2 egg whites.
Whole milk	Fat-free milk.
Cream	Polyunsaturated coffee creams; undiluted fat-free evaporated milk.
Evaporated milk	Fat-free evaporated milk.
Ice cream	Low-fat or light ice cream, sherbet, nonfat or low-fat frozen yogurt, or sorbet.

Appendix D

Dining Out

Dining out on a low-sodium diet is challenging but doable. You are more likely to find foods lower in sodium in restaurants that offer a wide variety of foods than in those that offer only a limited selection. Most restaurant food has salt and often monosodium glutamate (MSG) added to it. This is especially true if it is prepared ahead of time, frozen, and reheated before serving. When you choose a restaurant that prepares food as it is ordered, you can tell the waiter to leave salt and MSG out of your portion. Naturally, you'll want to avoid using salt at the table. Also remember to avoid high-sodium condiments, such as ketchup, mustard, soy sauce, steak sauce, and salad dressing. A single restaurant meal may have from 1,000 to 4,000 milligrams of sodium.

Choosing Restaurant Food

When dining at restaurants, following the tips below can help you avoid sodium—and fat—overload.

- Select a restaurant where food is cooked to order.
- Request that your food be prepared without added salt or fat.
- Avoid foods that have salt added during preparation, or select only one.
- Remove breading, topping, or sauce from your entrée.

- Avoid table salt and high-sodium condiments and garnishes, such as pickles and olives.
- Avoid salads and other foods containing cheese and cottage cheese.
- Squeeze lemon or use oil and vinegar (in separate bottles, not Italian dressing) on salad.
- Avoid soup and bread.
- Request that sauces and salad dressings be served on the side.
- Consider eating fruit as an appetizer, salad, or dessert.
- If fruit pie is served, eat only the filling.

Choose very low sodium foods, such as unsalted margarine, unsalted bread, and unsalted cereal, at home to compensate for high-sodium foods you eat at restaurants. If you eat out very often, you'll need to keep track of the sodium in restaurant food. This means adding up the milligrams of sodium in each food to be sure that your total does not go over 2,400 milligrams for the day—or whatever limit your physician has set for you. Approximate sodium values for some common restaurant foods are listed on pages 335–336.

If you don't eat away from home on a regular basis, you may be getting less sodium than the maximum amount your physician allows. If so, you may choose to use regular margarine instead of unsalted margarine at home. You may also be able to add other high-sodium foods, such as those listed on pages 313–314. Your physician can refer you to a registered dietitian, who can help you plan your meals.

SODIUM VALUES IN RESTAURANT AND OTHER COMMERCIAL FOODS

Foods	Approximate* Sodium (mg)
ENTRÉES, SALTED WHILE COOKING	
Chicken, breast or thigh and drumstick, grilled, skin removed after cooking** (1 medium)	250
Chicken, breast or thigh and drumstick, skin removed before cooking** (1 medium)	400
Chinese stir-fried entrées (2½ cups)	1,800
Fish, broiled or grilled (5 ounces)	600
Ham, lean (fat trimmed) (5 ounces)	1,700
Spaghetti with tomato and meat sauce (2½ cups)	1,050
Spaghetti with tomato sauce (2½ cups)	1,525
Steak, grilled (fat trimmed) (6 ounces)	650
Turkey, processed, from delicatessen (1 ounce)	120
Turkey, processed and commercially packaged (1 ounce)	400
SIDE DISHES, SEASONED WITH SALT AND MARGARINE	
Mashed potatoes (no gravy) (½ cup)	350
Rice, white (½ cup)	300
Sauerkraut (½ cup)	1,000
Vegetables, canned (½ cup)	400
Vegetables, frozen or fresh (½ cup)	250
SALADS	
Chicken salad (½ cup)	500
Coleslaw with vinaigrette (½ cup)	450
Cottage cheese (½ cup)	425
Pasta salad (½ cup)	400
Potato salad (½ cup)	600
Tuna salad (½ cup)	400
SALAD DRESSINGS, REGULAR OR LOW-CALORIE	
French dressing (1 tablespoon)	225

(continued on following page)

Foods	Approximate* Sodium (mg)
Italian dressing (1 tablespoon)	125
Ranch dressing (1 tablespoon)	125
Thousand Island dressing (1 tablespoon)	125
SOUPS	
Beef bouillon (1 cup)	650
Chicken with noodles (1 cup)	950
Split pea (1 cup)	1,000
CRACKERS	
Bread sticks (2 sticks, 4 × ½ inch)	120
Melba toast, rectangular (5)	250
Saltines, regular (6)	200
CEREALS	
Bran, bud type (⅛ cup)	175
Oatmeal, cooked in unsalted water (½ cup)	1
Oatmeal, instant or cooked in salted water, prepared (1 packet, or about ¾ cup cooked)	285
Ready-to-eat flake cereals, regular (1 individual serving box)	225
CONDIMENTS	
Cocktail sauce (1 tablespoon)	175
Ketchup (1 tablespoon)	175
Margarine (1 pat or 1 teaspoon)	35
Mayonnaise-type salad dressing (1 tablespoon)	100
Mustard (1 tablespoon)	200
Olives, green (10 small)	800
Olives, black (5 extra-large)	250
Pickles, dill (1 spear, 6 × ½ inch)	450
Soy sauce (1 tablespoon)	1,025
Steak sauce (1 tablespoon)	300
Taco sauce (1 tablespoon)	150

* Values rounded.

** In a restaurant, removing skin after cooking removes part of the salt used in cooking.

Choosing Fast Food

Fast food is a real challenge on a low-sodium diet. You also have to play a juggling game with the fat. Just do the best you can, and learn which restaurants you want to return to.

Some fast-food places have salad bars with good choices. In general, the less preparation that has gone into a food item, the less sodium it will contain. Choose fresh greens and other fresh vegetables. Avoid pickled items, such as olives and peppers, and the obviously salty items, such as ham, other cold cuts, cheese, and bacon. Use caution when choosing any "prepared" salads, such as potato salad and pasta salad, which frequently contain lots of mayonnaise and salt. Use a small amount of dressing or, better yet, plain oil and vinegar.

A plain baked potato is another good selection. Then add a tablespoon of sour cream—lower in fat and sodium than soft margarine—and as many chives as you want. Even if you must shake a *little* salt on the potato, you'll still be getting a lot less than if you added cheese, bacon, and margarine.

Most fast-food restaurants offer a green salad or a green salad with grilled chicken. Ask that the cheese be left off and get dressing on the side. Better yet, season your salad with lemon juice (usually available for tea) or vinegar.

For breakfast, try orange juice, fat-free milk, and an English muffin with jelly instead of margarine.

Most diet sodas are high in sodium. Choose water, tea, or limeade instead.

For dessert, a small nonfat frozen yogurt cone is better for you than a fried pie. A strawberry sundae is lower in fat and sodium than a hot fudge sundae.

If you're in the position of *having* to eat something that

is higher in fat and sodium than you would like, think
SMALL!

- Have one slice of mushroom or vegetarian pizza.
- Even though a chicken breast has less fat than an equal
  weight of dark meat, one drumstick has only half the fat
  and a lot less sodium than a prepared breast.
- Choose a small burger without cheese. Add lettuce, tomato, and onion. Ketchup, with less sodium than mustard
  and less fat than mayonnaise, is probably your best bet for
  a spread. Beware of "special sauces" unless you know
  what they contain.
- Split a small order of French fries.

These are general recommendations, so, when in doubt,
ask someone at the restaurant for nutrition information. National chains are required to have it available. Also request
exactly the products you want. If enough customers ask, the
restaurant should make them available.

Choosing Deli Food

- Request "fresh-cooked" turkey or lean roast beef. Most
  precooked deli meats have salt and sodium-containing
  preservatives added.
- Order lettuce, tomato, and onion for your sandwich.
- Use thinly sliced bread or one slice of regular bread for
  your sandwich to decrease the sodium.

Choose fruit, sherbet, or frozen yogurt for dessert.

Appendix E

American Heart Association National Center and Affiliates

Call 1-800-AHA-USA1 for more information about the American Heart Association, including Mended Hearts support groups, or visit www.americanheart.org. For stroke information, call 1-888-4STROKE, the American Stroke Association, a division of the American Heart Association. To subscribe to *Stroke Connection Magazine* (for stroke survivors and caregivers), call 1-800-553-6321.

National Center
American Heart Association
7272 Greenville Avenue
Dallas, TX 75231-4596
214/373-6300

Affiliates
Florida/Puerto Rico Affiliate
St. Petersburg, FL

Greater Midwest Affiliate
Illinois, Indiana, Michigan, Minnesota, North Dakota, South Dakota, Wisconsin,
Chicago, IL

Heartland Affiliate
Arkansas, Iowa, Kansas, Missouri, Nebraska, Oklahoma
Topeka, KS

Heritage Affiliate
Connecticut, Long Island, New Jersey, New York City
New York, NY

Mid-Atlantic Affiliate
District of Columbia, Maryland, North Carolina, South Carolina, Virginia
Glen Allen, VA

Northeast Affiliate

Maine, Massachusetts, New Hampshire, New
    York State (except New York City and
    Long Island), Rhode Island, Vermont
Framingham, MA

Ohio Valley Affiliate

Kentucky, Ohio, West Virginia
Columbus, OH

Pacific/Mountain Affiliate

Alaska, Arizona, Colorado, Hawaii, Idaho,
    Montana, New Mexico, Oregon,
    Washington, Wyoming
Seattle, WA

Pennsylvania/Delaware Affiliate

Delaware, Pennsylvania
Wormleysburg, PA

Southeast Affiliate

Alabama, Georgia, Louisiana, Mississippi,
    Tennessee
Marietta, GA

Texas Affiliate

Austin, TX

Western States Affiliate

California, Nevada, Utah
Los Angeles, CA

Index

The perennial bestseller—now fully updated and revised!

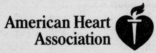

American Heart Association

Fighting Heart Disease and Stroke

THE NEW AMERICAN HEART ASSOCIATION COOKBOOK
SIXTH EDITION

"THE RECIPES WILL CONVINCE EVEN SKEPTICS THAT LOW-FAT FOODS CAN TASTE FANTASTIC. . . . Only you have the power to change your diet, reduce the amount of fat it contains and eat heathfully. . . . Get started without sacrificing taste, convenience, and pleasure."

—*Daily News* (New York)

Published by Ballantine Books
Available wherever books are sold